THE PARADOX OF BLACKNESS IN AFRICAN AMERICAN
VAMPIRE FICTION

NEW SUNS

RACE, GENDER, AND SEXUALITY IN THE SPECULATIVE

Susana M. Morris and Kinitra D. Brooks, Series Editors

# THE PARADOX OF BLACKNESS IN AFRICAN AMERICAN VAMPIRE FICTION

Jerry Rafiki Jenkins

THE OHIO STATE UNIVERSITY PRESS
COLUMBUS

Copyright © 2019 by The Ohio State University.
All rights reserved.
Library of Congress Cataloging-in-Publication Data
Names: Jenkins, Rafiki, 1967– author.
Title: The paradox of blackness in African American vampire fiction / Jerry Rafiki Jenkins.
Other titles: New suns: race, gender, and sexuality in the speculative.
Description: Columbus : The Ohio State University Press, 2019. | Series: New suns: race, gender, and sexuality in the speculative | Includes bibliographical references and index.
Identifiers: LCCN 2019002157 | ISBN 9780814214015 (cloth ; alk. paper) | ISBN 0814214010 (cloth ; alk. paper)
Subjects: LCSH: American fiction—African American authors—History and criticism. | Vampires in literature. | Blacks—Race identity. | Racism in literature.
Classification: LCC PS374.V35 J46 2019 | DDC 813/.5409375—dc23
LC record available at https://lccn.loc.gov/2019002157

Cover design by Black Kirby
Text design by Juliet Williams
Type set in Adobe Palatino

♾ The paper used in this publication meets the minimum requirements of the American National Standard for Information Sciences—Permanence of Paper for Printed Library Materials. ANSI Z39.48-1992.

*Dedicated to Jerry Michael Jenkins (1946–2001)
and Beatrice Woodard*

CONTENTS

| | | |
|---|---|---|
| Acknowledgments | | ix |
| INTRODUCTION | The Vampire's Blackness | 1 |
| CHAPTER 1 | Blackness, Freedom, and the Staying-Alive Vampire in *The Gilda Stories* | 23 |
| CHAPTER 2 | Antizealot Atheism and the All-American Bourgeois Negro in *My Soul to Keep* | 55 |
| CHAPTER 3 | African American Manhood and the Masculine Africa Narrative in *Dark Corner* | 91 |
| CHAPTER 4 | Human Blackness, Transhuman Blackness, and the Black Body in *Fledgling* | 117 |
| CHAPTER 5 | Black Church Corporatism and the Black Gay Vampire in *Image of Emeralds and Chocolate* | 147 |
| CONCLUSION | Post-Black, New Black, and the Immortality of Blackness | 175 |
| Works Cited | | 181 |
| Index | | 193 |

ACKNOWLEDGMENTS

I WANT to give a big thank you to Susana M. Morris and Kinitra D. Brooks, the New Suns series editors, and Kristen Elias Rowley, Ana M. Jimenez-Moreno, Taralee Cyphers, and Rebecca S. Bender of The Ohio State University Press for their work on and belief in this project. To Black Kirby, thank you for producing a cover illustration that captures many of the tensions that I discuss in this book. I also want to thank the people who took time out of their lives to comment on various chapter drafts: Andrea Bell, Abbie Cory, Carlton Floyd, Brent Gowen, Bill Jahnel, Martin Japtok, Aundrey Jones, Yader Lanuza, Fergal O' Doherty, and Bruce Orton. In addition to these wonderful people, I want to acknowledge colleagues, friends, and mentors who have, over the years, provided valuable insights on the topics covered in this book: Luis Alvarez, Adrian Arancibia, Robert Cancel, Laura "LC" Choe, Hassan Dhouti, Ivan Evans, Rod Ferguson, Jack Halberstam, Rudy Jacobo, Danielle Jones, Joe Limer, Bennetta Jules-Rosette, George Lipsitz, George (Jorge) Mariscal, Moses Maddox, Kyndra Miller, Mychal Odom, Leonard Thomas, and Angelica Yanez. I am also very grateful for the comments provided by the anonymous reviewers, whose insights helped make this book better.

I want to thank the Hatley, Jenkins, Liddell, Woodard, Aaron, and Sciurba families for their loving support, and I want to give a big shout

out to Cheka Jenkins, Umayma Alexander, Andrew Jenkins, Adrian Jenkins, Allan Jenkins, and Michael Jenkins for being loving and supportive siblings. I also want to thank the Guardians of the Boneyard (i.e., my "bones"/domino colleagues) for being able to merge entertainment, intellectual debate, and community into an organic whole: Teahoen "Buu" Aaron, Lemuel "C-Cubed" Cabrera, Glenn "Crew Chief" Powell, Brian "B-Smoov" Starr, and Glen "G-Dub" Wilson. To my sons, Isa, Ras, and Nyo, thank you for your everyday reminders of why this book matters. Finally, and most importantly, I want to thank Katie Sciurba, for not only providing insightful comments on various chapter drafts of this project, but also for being an amazing parent, partner, and scholar.

Chapter 1 is based on an article that was first published in *African American Review* 46.2–3 (2013), 313–28. Reprinted with permission by Johns Hopkins University Press. Copyright © Johns Hopkins University Press and Saint Louis University.

INTRODUCTION

# THE VAMPIRE'S BLACKNESS

IN HIS 2007 BOOK, *The Dead Travel Fast: Stalking Vampires from Nosferatu to Count Chocula,* Eric Nuzum recounts his introduction to the "Van Helsing party," a group of self-professed vampires from Washington, DC. What made this group noteworthy is that they challenged Nuzum's expectations of what the typical self-declared vampire looks like. Before meeting them, Nuzum expected to see a group of people with "jet-black hair, pale skin, dark clothing, heavy makeup, and various metal things covering their clothes and skin" (31–32). In other words, Nuzum expected to meet a group of white goths, "people who, since the late 1970s, have used the figure of the vampire to inflect their readings and productions of music, philosophy, literature, film, dance, fashion, and sexuality" (Holmes 169). However, when Nuzum met the group at a chain restaurant in Laurel, Maryland, he had to rethink his plans because the group did not meet any of his expectations, except for the hair color. Indeed, the seven people sitting at the table were "all smiling," "all fairly normal-looking," and "all African-American" (Nuzum 32).

What stands out in Nuzum's premeeting expectations is the assumption that interests in vampires is a *white thing,* an assumption that appears to be shared by many scholars and critics. For example, in her insightful analysis of Jewelle Gomez's *The Gilda Stories* (1991), the first novel about a black vampire to be published in the US,[1] Ingrid Thaler treats the vampire as a "white trope," one that limits the vampire's literary-historical roots to nineteenth-century European literature and medieval Eastern European folk tales (46, 151–52 n. 7). For Thaler, *Gilda* is speculative fiction that "borrows its genre conventions from vampire fiction and black women's writings" (45). While I agree with Thaler's assessment of Gomez's novel and speculative fiction in general as fictions that rely on the mixing of genres, I question her decision to limit the vampire's literary-historical roots to medieval and nineteenth-century Europe. In my view, such a decision assumes that the vampire is not a black trope and overlooks the widespread presence of vampires throughout the ancient world, a presence that indicates that the fears and desires that these creatures stir up are deeply rooted in the human psyche, not just in the white psyche (Bartlett and Idriceanu 4).[2] Indeed, although African American vampire fiction is a late twentieth-century development, vampire myths are not foreign to Africa or the African diaspora.

In Africa, for example, the Yoruba of precolonial Nigeria referred to their vampires as "witch-wives," jealous women who "secretly sucked the blood of their husbands and of the children of their other wives," and the vampires of the Hausa tribe in Niger were referred to as "soul-stealing witches" (Allen vii–viii).[3] The *obayifo* and the *asasabonsam* were West African witches who attacked at night, sucked the blood of their victims, most often children, and were members of the community who lived incognito.[4] The *adze*,

---

1. Although Gomez's novel introduces us to the first black literary vampire, Hermine Pinson's 1988 poem, "All-Around Vampires," may be the first literary text about vampires penned by an African American.

2. As Christopher Frayling puts it, the vampire is "as old as the world" (qtd. in Beresford 8). Indeed, the belief in vampires existed during the time of primitive humans and was expressed in the customs and practices of everyday life, especially those pertaining to funeral rites and burial places (Summers, *Lore and Legend* xvii). According to Raymond McNally and Radu Florescu, the history of vampirism traces back to "man the hunter, who discovered that when blood flowed out of a wounded beast or a fellow human, life, too, drained away. Thus men smeared themselves with blood and sometimes drank it. The idea of drinking blood to renew vitality thereupon entered history" (117).

3. Vampires of the ancient world were not only believed to be real, but they tended to be female or lack male genitalia, their victims were primarily women and children, and they served as explanations for problems surrounding childbirth, agriculture, and unexpected deaths, particularly those that result from suicide, accident, or unknown illness (see, for example, Bartlett and Idriceanu 4–5; Beresford 19–30; M. Jenkins, *Vampire Forensics* 217–20, 222, 228; McNally and Florescu 117–18; Melton xxii–xxiii; Summers, *Kith and Kin* 189–98, 202–03).

4. Although, as Luise White notes in *Speaking with Vampires: Rumor and History in Colonial Africa*, the vampires of colonial East and Central Africa (e.g., the *wazimamoto*,

found in Ghana and Togo, could assume the form of a firefly, and it sat on the mouth of its victims while using a sucking apparatus that resembled an elephant's trunk. Like the obayifo, the adze consumed palm oil, coconut water, and blood (Bartlett and Idriceanu 4; Gomez, "Recasting the Mythology" 87). Moreover, many of these vampires would make their way to the West via the slave trade and would become, for example, the *loogaroo* of Haiti and Grenada, the *asema* of Surinam, and the *sukuyan* of Trinidad. Born from West African slaves appropriating European demonology and synthesizing it with West African vampirology, these Afro-Caribbean vampires were used to help comprehend the evils of new world slavery (Melton 4–5, 431, 632, 657).[5]

In Europe, the nineteenth-century play *Le Vampire* (1851) made Alexandre Dumas, the grandson of a Haitian slave and French aristocrat, the first black writer in the West to pen a version of the vampire myth and, for some, the "father of black horror." What makes Dumas's play a noteworthy text in the European vampire literary tradition is that it has "the first dark-skinned character to appear in a vampire story, a woman he described as 'Moorish' and cast in the role of a pagan witch" (Allen vii).[6] In the US, there are a few

---

*banyama,* and *batumbula*) were not witches, these vampires, who were primarily men and representatives of the colonial bureaucracy (e.g., game rangers, mine managers, firemen, and Catholic priests), were constructed partly from ideas about witchcraft as well as those about colonialism (18, 29).

5. For example, the loogaroo, asema, and sukuyan, like their West African ancestors (e.g., the obayifo, the adze, and the aziman of Dahomey), are not revenants; instead, they are living human beings, most often witches and elderly women, who have gained the ability to leave their skin at night, travel in the form of fire or light, and extract blood from their neighbors, particularly their neighbors' children. For example, in Nalo Hopkinson's short story "Greedy Choke Puppy" (2000), the *soucouyant,* a different form of sukuyan, is the black Caribbean version of the vampire myth: "'Soucouyant,' or 'bloodsucker,' derives from the French verb 'sucer,' to suck. 'Ol' Higue' is the Guyanese creole expression for an old hag, or witch woman. The soucouyant is usually an old, evil-tempered woman who removes her skin at night, hides it, and then changes into a ball of fire. She flies through the air searching for homes in which there are babies. She then enters the house through an open window or a keyhole, goes into the child's room, and sucks the life from its body. She may visit one child's bedside a number of times, draining a little more life each time, as the frantic parents search for a cure, and the child gets progressively weaker and finally dies. Or she may kill at once" (106).

6. It seems that Sheridan Le Fanu followed Dumas's lead, as evidenced in his *Carmilla* (1872), where we find a "hideous black woman" who wears a "sort of coloured turban" and has "gleaming eyes," "large white eye-balls," and "teeth set as if in fury" (*Carmilla* 98–99). Bartlett and Idriceanu argue that the role of the "hideous black woman" in *Carmilla,* as in Le Fanu's "The Child That Went with the Fairies," is to hint to the "terrible nature of the foe incarnated in the innocent looking Carmilla" (153). Although Allen does not tell us how Dumas's black character fits into the play's narrative, Le Fanu's use

reports of vampires by African Americans living in the South during the late nineteenth and early twentieth centuries. For instance, there is an account from Tennessee of an old woman who would suck the blood of sleeping children to improve her health. In Louisiana, the *fifollet* or *feu-follet*, a derivative of the French *incubus/succubus*, was the soul of a dead person or a child who died before baptism. This soul was returned to Earth by God to do penance; however, instead of doing penance, the fifollet attacked people and, like its Caribbean and West African ancestors, occasionally "became a vampire who sucked the blood of people, especially children" (Melton 7). While these early vampires of African American culture retained some of their West African origins and had little influence on American adaptations of the vampire myth, the cinematic black vampires that emerged in the 1970s represent the beginnings of an African American vampirology and would play a significant role in America's departure from Bram Stoker's Dracula character, who defined the vampire in Western culture for most of the twentieth century.

The film that may have had the most influence on America's departure from Stoker's vampirology is *Blacula* (1972), the first Hollywood-produced film about a black vampire. Hollywood was so impressed with *Blacula*'s box-office success that American International Pictures, the studio that released *Blacula*, announced its plan to remake all classical Hollywood horror films with all-black casts (Benshoff 32).[7] However, *Blacula* not only engendered the blaxploitation horror genre, but it also helped shape the *Dracula* adaptations by John Badham and Francis Ford Coppola in 1979 and 1992, respectively, by making the vampire more human than monster.[8] Moreover, *Blacula*'s box-office success led to the production of Bill Gunn's *Ganja and Hess* (1973), the black vampire film whose "philosophical musings" would become the "cornerstone" of Anne Rice's *Vampire Chronicles* (Benshoff 45).[9] *Blacula* may

---

of the dark-skinned Moorish woman suggests that Dumas's black character may serve as a warning to his audience of the evil hiding under the skin of the vampire.

7. *Blacula* debuted at number twenty-four on *Variety*'s list of top films and became one of the highest-grossing films in 1972, even though it was released in August of that year (N. Lawrence, *Blaxploitation Films* 57; Martinez, Martinez, and Chavez 58).

8. As Benshoff notes, "central to [the blaxploitation horror film's] reappropriation of the monster as an empowering black figure is the softening, romanticizing, and even valorizing of the monster." For example, the African vampire in *Blacula* is portrayed more as a "lover than a fighter," and in the sequel, *Scream, Blacula, Scream* (1973), Blacula's inability to cure his vampirism portrays him as "more a doomed freedom fighter than a monster" (37–38). For more on *Blacula*, see Medovoi (1998), Jenkins (2005), and N. Lawrence (2009).

9. For a detailed discussion of *Ganja and Hess*, see, for example, Diawara and Klotman (1991) and David (2011).

have also inspired the creation of the 1970s Marvel Comics character Blade,[10] a half-human, half-vampire black warrior-hero who has been immortalized by Wesley Snipes in the *Blade* film trilogy (*Blade* [1998], *Blade II* [2002], and *Blade: Trinity* [2004]).

What the examples above indicate is that the vampire is also a black trope; that is to say, to treat the vampire as the sole property of whites is to ignore the history of this creature, a history which predates the word "vampire"[11] and the biological notion of race.[12] In this light, we should think of the vampire as a trope that expresses how a culture confronts human-

---

10. Blade first appeared in the July 1973 (No. 10) issue of Marvel Comics' *The Tomb of Dracula* and frequently reappeared throughout the seventy-issue history of the series. While Blade appeared in various Marvel Comics series (e.g., *Doctor Strange: Sorcerer Supreme, Midnight Sons Unlimited,* and *The Nightstalkers*), he did not receive his own series, *Blade, the Vampire-Hunter,* until 1994 (Melton 51–53).

11. Although vampires have existed in every culture throughout history, only a few have been called vampires (Nuzum 2). Indeed, the word *"upir,"* an early form of the word that would become "vampire," first appeared in a 1047 document that refers to a Russian prince as "Upir Lichy," or "wicked vampire" (Melton xxxi). Katharina Wilson argues that "the earliest recorded uses of the term 'vampire' appear in French, English, and Latin, and they refer to vampirism in Poland, Russia, and Macedonia (Southern Yugoslavia). The second and more sweeping introduction of the word occurs in German, French, and English, and records the Serbian vampire epidemic of 1725–32" (583). While some believe that the word entered the English language in the eighteenth century (e.g., Beresford 8; Chantrell 534; Melton xxxii), Wilson notes that the oldest written record of the word "vampire" in English is Paul Ricaut's 1679 *State of the Greek and Armenian Churches* (580). Wilson argues that this reference is "misleading" because "Ricaut does not mention vampires by name"; however, he is describing a figure that he believes his audience is aware of: "a pretended demon, said to delight in sucking human blood, and to animate the bodies of dead persons, which when dug up, are said to be found florid and full of blood" (Ricaut qtd. in Wilson 580). Ricaut's description of this "pretended demon" is similar to the definition of the vampire offered by Montague Summers (see, for example, *Kith and Kin* 7–12), whose work on vampires has been widely cited by critics and scholars.

12. According to Martin Bernal, while "racial prejudice" (i.e., the practice of treating people differently because they differ from the somatic or physical norm of a society) has existed in many cultures, the "racism" of today is a modern phenomenon that began in the fifteenth century, when "Portuguese ships started to outflank Islamic power by sailing around the coast of West Africa and immediately began kidnapping anybody they could find and taking them back to Portugal to sell as slaves" (82). For example, although "Asian and European attitudes towards Africans and skin color appear to have begun to change [from 'ambiguity' to 'evil'] around 500 BCE" (79), the absence of a monolithic notion of blackness indicates that these "new 'racial' attitudes" were "qualitatively different from the 'caste racism' found in the modern world" (80). In his words, "modern racism is particularly vicious because it maintains absolute lines of caste and insists that the worst white is better than the best nonwhite" (83). What can be deduced from Bernal's argument is that racism did not exist in the ancient world because the biological notion of race did not exist at that time.

ity's deeply rooted fears and desires at a particular historical moment. However, what are these deeply rooted fears and desires that vampires stir up? It appears that many of these fears and desires can be reduced to one fear and one desire: the fear of death and the desire for immortality. As Mary Hallab explains in *Vampire God: The Allure of the Undead in Western Culture* (2009),

> The vampire's most human quality—its infinite adaptability to people, place, and time—is a major reason for its persistence. This, along with its very un-human and ambiguous position between the flesh and the spirit, its mysterious comings and goings, and its variable forms and faces, allows it to be continually revived in different guises in our differing worlds. But as diverse as they may be, from the bloated peasant of folklore to the opera-caped Dracula to the bratty *Lost Boys* (1987), vampires address issues and attitudes about death and immortality that are meaningful in all times and places. (5)

Like Hallab, I am interested in examining the issues and attitudes about death and immortality that the vampire stirs up. However, I focus on a genre of Western vampire literature absent from Hallab's study: African American vampire fiction.[13]

This absence is somewhat surprising because the number of African American–authored vampire novels and short stories that have emerged since the publications of Hermine Pinson's "All-Around Vampires" (1988) and Gomez's *Gilda* (1991) is quite substantial. For example, African American speculative writers such as Tananarive Due, L. A. Banks, Brandon Massey, Linda Addison, Kevin S. Brockenbrough, Robert Fleming, K. Murry Johnson, and the late Octavia E. Butler have written vampire fiction, and non-speculative African American authors such as Zane, Omar Tyree, Donna Hill, and Monica Jackson have taken a stab at the genre. Since most of the works by the writers above were published before Hallab's study, it is even more interesting that none of them were included for analysis. However, Hallab's study is not the only contemporary study of vampires that excludes African American vampire fiction. For example, Wayne Bartlett and Flavia Idriceanu's *Legends of Blood: The Vampire in History and Myth* (2006), Matthew Beresford's *From Demons to Dracula: The Creation of the Modern Vampire Myth* (2008), and Mark Collins Jenkins's *Vampire Forensics: Uncovering the Origins of an Enduring Legend* (2010) briefly discuss the vampires of African

---

13. Although Gomez's *The Gilda Stories* appears in the "Works Consulted" section of Hallab's study (as does *Blacula*), there is no analysis of Gomez's novel or any other African American–authored vampire fiction.

cultures, with a particular focus on ancient Egypt, in their discussions of the origins of the vampire myth, but in their discussions of contemporary vampires, they do not mention any African American vampire fiction or even the contributions that *Blacula* and *Ganja and Hess* made in changing how late twentieth-century American audiences view the vampire. In addition to its absence from contemporary scholarship on vampires, virtually all the scholarly work on African American vampire fiction focuses on Gomez's *Gilda* or Butler's *Fledgling* (2005). Implicit in this focus is the assumption that there is not enough African American vampire fiction worthy of scholarly attention, an assumption that, as I noted earlier, lacks credibility. However, in spite of its limited focus, the scholarly work on these novels does identify some of the literary and political elements that one would find in most African American vampire fiction.

Beginning with the scholarly work on *Gilda*, Nina Auerbach (1995) situates Gomez's novel within Anglo-American culture's "mutating vampires" and argues that the novel is just like all other "Reaganesque" vampire fiction in which the vampire is "infected with the anesthetizing virtue of the 1980s" that purges lesbianism and vampirism of aggression. By doing so, according to Auerbach, Gilda becomes the stereotypical "good woman" who "confronts no powerful patriarchs" (1, 184–86). In contrast to Auerbach's evaluative claim, Miriam Jones (1997) argues that Gomez "inverts the historical metaphoric functions of the vampire" in *Gilda* to show us who the "real" monsters are. The real monsters are not Gilda, a black lesbian vampire who has escaped slavery, and her family of disenfranchised people, but the racists, rapists, pimps, and power-hungry rich who are trying to destroy Gilda and her family (153–54, 167). Lynda Hall (2000) and Shannon Winnubst (2003) examine the ways in which *Gilda* queers "the 'master narratives' of 'normal' traditional white, heterosexual, male power" (Hall 395) or what Winnubst calls the "Guises of Universality" that dominate the classic vampire narrative (5–7). For Cedric Bryant (2005), Gomez's novel is an example of how the African American Gothic "politicizes a nexus of issues" such as race, gender, sexuality, power, family, and sharing (550), and Christopher Lewis (2014) offers a reading of *Gilda* that "seeks to move critical conversation about neo-slave narratives into [a] queer-positive territory by highlighting the novel's positioning of gender and sexual normativity as regimes of enslavement and queer gender and sexuality as means of liberation" (449). In the same vein as Bryant and Lewis, Thaler focuses on how Gomez's novel negotiates time and genre to rework vampire fiction through the Black Atlantic memory of slavery and to use vampire fiction as a literary tool to revise the Black Atlantic imaginary (46–47). Susana M. Morris

(2016) adds to the critical conversation on *Gilda* by locating the novel within an Afrofuturist discourse and arguing that *Gilda* "exposes the potentially radical ways of (re) envisioning embodiment and identity in regards to race, gender, and sexuality that is at the heart of Afrofuturist feminism" ("More Than Human" 33–34).

As suggested by the scholarship on *Gilda*, one of the defining features of African American vampire fiction is queering. According to Siobhan Somerville, a "queer" critique does not focus solely on questions of what constitutes "normal" sexuality; instead, it is an "antinormative project" that challenges "identity categories that are presented as stable, transhistorical, or authentic." For example, since straight members of marginalized racial groups are defined as not "normal" by the dominant culture, a queer critique acknowledges that "heteronormativity itself must be understood . . . as a racialized concept," a concept that "shores up as well as depends on naturalized categories of racial difference" ("Queer" 190). Similarly, Lynda Hall contends that if we think of the term "queer" as a synonym for words such as "transgress, blur, and interrogate," then it is possible to "move beyond a strictly sexualized definition [of 'queer'] to address the deconstruction of diverse essentialized and 'naturalized' differences and to explore challenges to dichotomous thinking" (394–95). Situating this definition of "queer" within the scholarship on *Gilda*, we can view African American vampire fiction as an antinormative project that not only queers the traditional vampire narrative, the black literary imagination, and their guises of universality, but it also, as suggested by the scholarly work on *Fledgling*, has the potential to denormalize our disdain of hybridity, our boundaries of power, and our obsession with utopias.

In her retrospective on Butler, Stephanie A. Smith (2007) notes that Butler was a master at dealing with the "crossing of sexual hunger, domination across difference, and violence." However, Smith contends that Butler's treatment of enslavement and symbiosis in *Fledgling* is "more than a little problematic" because it not only tends to be "reminiscent of rape," but it may also lead readers to think of Shori, the black half-human–half-vampire protagonist, as reinforcing the nineteenth-century American stereotype of the sexually animalistic black woman (389–90). In contrast to Smith, Morris (2012) argues that the novel offers a "black feminist Afrofuturist epistemology" that "radically reimagines identity, kinship, and intimacy through nonmonogamous queer human-vampire hybrid families that have a variety of configurations." Yet, as Morris continues, "by ambivalently regarding the concepts of free will and symbiosis," the novel also problematizes our search for "utopian panaceas" ("Black Girls" 146–47). Similarly, Ali Brox (2008) argues that although Butler was critical of utopian narratives, Shori is a hybrid vampire figure who "exemplifies the characteristics of a utopia." However, the utopian world offered in *Fledgling* is not static or free of problems; rather, it is a world where problems are dealt with, fixed categories and boundaries are challenged, and human agency is a source of change (392–93). For Lauren J. Lacey (2008), *Fledgling*, like Butler's *Parable* novels (1993 and 1998), requires its black female protagonist to take power for herself so that she can develop responses to power that range from "direct confrontations with damaging dominant discourses to the construction of alternative communities" (381). However, like Brox and Morris, Lacey argues that the alternative communities that Butler offers in *Fledgling* (e.g., Ina society and Shori's created family) are less than ideal, even though they function as critiques of mainstream society (386).

Marty Fink (2010) examines how Butler's novel interrogates the practice of narrating illness, specifically the narrating of HIV/AIDS by mainstream society. Although HIV/AIDS is not mentioned once in *Fledgling*, Fink submits that the novel addresses a host of issues concerning illness, sex, queerness, and racism in such a way that it "reworks the metaphorical connections between the vampire and the HIV-positive subject, challenging the narrative practices of racialization and homophobia that continue to fuel the pandemic today" (416, 422). Instead of examining how illness is narrated in *Fledgling*, Melissa J. Strong (2010) is interested in how the novel narrates hybridity. Strong applies critical race theory to *Fledgling* to reveal the ways in which the novel "mirrors legal storytelling" to facilitate an understanding of the hybrid subject's status and of those who would oppose hybridization (11). Expanding this discussion of hybridity, Pramod K. Nayar (2011) argues that in *Fledgling* human-vampire "species miscegenation," a form of "domestication" that allows a species to "erase their characteristic 'essences' in order to fit in better with their ecosystem," leads to a "posthuman interracialization" (pars. 1–2). Ultimately, Nayar concludes, *Fledgling* is "the fantasy of 'species interdependence' . . . where animal, human, and other species distinctions become blurred" (par. 7).

Like the scholarly work on *Gilda* and *Fledgling*, I am also interested in examining how African American vampire novels queer identities and genres to celebrate the hybrid subject, to question dominant discourses and boundaries of power, and to warn against the search for no-problem utopias. Unlike the scholarly work on these novels, I am primarily interested in connecting the queer/antinormative practices of African American vampire novels to the notions of death and immortality that its black vampires embody. Indeed, *The Paradox of Blackness in African American Vampire Fiction* is not only a challenge to the tacit assumption that there is a lack of quality African American vampire fiction to study besides *The Gilda Stories* and *Fledgling,* but it also proposes that an analysis of African American vampire fiction might provide new insight into the link between *our* vampires and our fear of death and desire for immortality. Since vampires, as Hallab puts it, appear in "variable forms and faces," these different forms and faces imply that there may be significant differences in how groups within a culture, as well as between cultures, conceptualize death and immortality. Stated in slightly different terms, since identity itself is fundamentally about "desire and death" (i.e., the desire for recognition, association, and protection, and the willingness to die or kill others in order to satisfy that desire) (West, "Identity" 163–64), the vampire always tells us, on some level, a story about the issues and ideologies that a group associates with the life and death of its identity. This means, among other things, that what one group sees as a path to immortality, others might see as a path to death. It is this understanding of the relationship among identity, death, and immortality that guides my analysis of African American vampire fiction's black vampires. To be more specific, I am interested in addressing the following questions: Which notions of death and immortality do the black vampires of African American vampire fiction embody, and what does this tell us about African American conceptions of blackness at the dawn of the twenty-first century?

My central argument in *The Paradox of Blackness in African American Vampire Fiction* is that the African American vampire novels examined herein offer black vampires who represent various responses to the following questions: Is there more to being black than having a black body, and what might the answers to that question mean for African Americans in the twenty-first century? My interest in these questions derives from recent criticisms of the idea that there is *one* black America. For example, Eugene Robinson contends in *Disintegration: The Splintering of Black America* (2010) that there are at least four, distinct black Americas, and the only time these communities become one is when they are "lumped together, defined, and threatened solely on the basis of skin color" (5–6). Similarly, Touré argues in *Who's Afraid of Post-Blackness* (2011) that if there are an infinite number of ways to be black, then the idea of authentic blackness is "bankrupt" and "fraudulent" (11). The arguments by Robinson and Touré represent the paradoxical tension surrounding questions of blackness in the early moments of the twenty-first century. On the one hand, they suggest that the idea of one black America is impossible because having a black body does not automatically determine what one will think, enjoy, or do. On the other hand, they also imply that the idea of one black America is inevitable because the belief that "the physical body offers transparent evidence of its history, identity, and behavior is a deeply held cultural fiction in the United States" (Somerville, *Queering* 9). The African American vampire novels under examination in *The Paradox of Blackness* suggest that the solutions to that paradox can be found in the fates of their black vampires. Put in more specific terms, the black vampire's immortality narrative not only represents a set of demands for those African Americans seeking eternal life, but it also informs that vampire's approach to being black in the twenty-first century.

According to Stephen Cave, to understand the human quest for immortality, we must begin with what he refers to as the Mortality Paradox, the theory that death for humans is both inevitable and impossible: "On the one hand, our powerful intellects come inexorably to the conclusion that we, like all other living things around us, must one day die. Yet on the other, the one thing that these minds cannot imagine is that very state of nonexistence; it is literally inconceivable" (16). To solve this paradox, we have created four immortality narratives that account for every human attempt at achieving everlasting life. Although Cave concludes that these narratives are "illusions" that will not enable us to live forever (250), they are important because they shape our everyday lives by driving our civilizations. For instance, the first and most straightforward immortality narrative is the Staying Alive Narrative, the dream of avoiding death forever. That dream, according to Cave, has sustained whole religions and shaped the idea of scientific progress (4). What is perhaps most noteworthy about the Staying Alive Narrative is that it is not concerned with life-after-death questions. Instead, this narrative is concerned with "staying alive here and now"; that is, it is concerned with acquiring a steady flow of the basics of survival such as food, drink, shelter, and defenses. Since civilizations are, at their core, a "collection of life-extension technologies" that refine the ways in which we acquire the basics of survival, they also represent our first attempts to stay alive forever (35). Unlike the Staying Alive Narrative, which disputes the notion that all living things must die, the Resurrection Narrative accepts the fact that death is inevitable. However, this narrative's followers also proclaim that "one day, with the selfsame bodies, we can rise to live again" (89). Central to this narrative's appeal is the belief that it is possible to undo the processes of death and decay by magically binding the "linearity" of human fates to the "cycles of nature" that promise "life, death, and life again" (93). The third immortality narrative, which is the backup plan for the first two, is the Soul Narrative, the belief that "the real you is separate from your body and can outlive it." This narrative not only makes the body irrelevant in the quest for immortality, but it also provides an authentic, transhistorical self that belongs to the "unchanging realm of the divine" (144–45). Finally, the Legacy Narrative contends that we can become immortal in the world of the symbolic (i.e., the world of language and culture) or in our offspring (208, 230). Unlike the previous immortality narratives, the Legacy Narrative is the only one that is bodiless and soulless, the only one that does not require individuals to have a body or a soul to live on indefinitely.

It is surprising that Cave dedicates an entire chapter to Mary Shelley's *Frankenstein* as a critique of the Resurrection Narrative but does not mention one vampire myth because the immortality narrative that most vampires in Western culture embody is the Resurrection Narrative. As noted in J. Gordon Melton's *The Vampire Book: The Encyclopedia of the Undead*, the typical dictionary definition of the vampire depicts the creature as "a reanimated corpse that rises from the grave to suck the blood of living people [and] thus retain a semblance of life." However, as Melton warns us, while that definition describes Stoker's Dracula, it is "inadequate" because it does not describe all vampires (xx). Since all vampires are not bloodsucking revenants, to use Dracula as the starting and ending points on what constitutes a vampire is to racialize the vampire as a white figure. Indeed, that notion of vampirism ignores the fact that creatures who consume the blood or life-force of humans or other animals for survival, who were once human or belong to a humanlike species, and who are undead or immortal but are not demons nor ghosts—traits that all vampires share—have existed in the human imagination long before Stoker created his iconic character. Moreover, what makes Dracula a problematic starting point for my project is that only one of the black vampires examined in *The Paradox of Blackness* is a resurrection vampire, and the rest are staying-alive vampires, vampires who do not need to die to achieve immortality. Even the black staying-alive vampires are not the same—some embody the Staying Alive Narrative's elixir version, while others embody its scientific version. As I intend to show throughout this book, the variety of black vampires in African American vampire fiction implies that these vampires offer not only several ways to grapple with the Mortality Paradox but also several ways to be black.

It is important to note that none of the black vampires examined in *The Paradox of Blackness* are soul or legacy vampires because this absence suggests that bodiless or conscious-less forms of immortality are devalued in

African American vampire fiction. To understand that absence, it is helpful to begin with Cave's critiques of the Soul and Legacy Narratives. The Soul Narrative claims that the *real you* is "immaterial in nature" and is, therefore, able to continue when your body finally succumbs to decay and destruction (Cave 144). The problem with the Soul Narrative is that "everything the soul was supposed to explain—thoughts, consciousness, life itself—has been shown to be dependent on the body"; therefore, when the body dies, so does the soul (195). Moreover, even if we could achieve immortality as immaterial beings, that form of immortality would be unappealing if we could not interact with the physical world. As Cave notes in his discussion of the skepticism surrounding the Legacy Narrative's ability to make us immortal, many people believe that "true" immortality is "living forever as a full person—that is, continuing indefinitely to enjoy life something like the one [we] have now"; therefore, a notion of immortality in which the full person does not survive is not desirable (204–05). For example, the cultural Legacy Narrative tells us that we can live forever in the hearts and minds of people by permanently fixing our names into the culture through some extraordinarily bad or good act; however, one is not only reduced to an idea in this narrative (e.g., a theory, philosophy, style, technique, martyr, or legend), but one also needs to be kept alive in the memories of the people who knew one and their descendants. The problem here, as Cave puts it, is that "memories are not forever," since it is estimated that the "length of time for which most of us can expect to be remembered [is] seventy years" (224). In this light, our chances of achieving cultural immortality are slim because once we are forgotten, we cease to exist.

Similarly, the biological Legacy Narrative is unable to grant us an immortality that we would be happy with because we would lack our individual consciousnesses. The biological Legacy Narrative claims that "we live on in our offspring [because] we and they are connected in a profound way that makes us in some crucial sense the same being" (Cave 230). However, if the parent lives on in the body of his or her offspring, then does that body belong to the parent or the offspring? In other words, is the parent or the child doing the thinking for that body? Supporters of the biological Legacy Narrative have responded to such questions by arguing that we are not distinct individuals, but a collection of cells that is part of "a widening chain of life that is billions of years old and has no end in sight." Thus, it is not our bodies, but the cells in our bodies that are immortal because those cells have been around since life itself began; therefore, we are nothing more than a "direct continuation of the original" (233–35). According to this version of the Legacy Narrative, because we were born when life began in the universe and will die only when the universe ends, we have lived and will continue to live most of our existence unconsciously, since we have no memory of our existence before the one we have now. What makes that image of eternity dreadful is that it is akin to being in a "permanent vegetative state" in which your cells live on but your consciousness does not (238).

For African American vampire fiction, the problem with the Soul and Legacy Narratives is that they not only offer paths to immortality that are undesirable because one will either spend eternity as an immaterial substance or in a vegetative state, but they also conflict with what it means to be a vampire. Since "the true vampire is corporeal"—that is, "the vampire has a body, and it is [its] own body" (Summers, *Kith and Kin* 12)[14]—black soul vampires cannot be vampires precisely because bodily immortality is a prerequisite for being a vampire. Similarly, black legacy vampires do not exist in African American vampire fiction because the vampire has its own body and, therefore, does not need the body of its offspring to guarantee its immortality, nor does it require other people's permission to exist, since its immortality is not dependent on the memory of others or their belief in vampires. Furthermore, the vampire's immortality is not conscious-less; indeed, vampires are not ghouls, but beings who have "intelligent control" (Melton 707). What is perhaps the most important reason why we do not find black soul and legacy vampires in African American vampire fiction is that such narratives do not allow an ideological space to engage the black vampire's blackness, since racial difference in US culture, as Shannon Winnubst notes in her discussion of how the traditional vampire "haunts" straight white male subjectivity, is "signified through visual markers on the body" (8). In other words, black soul and legacy vampires do not make sense in African American vampire fiction because blackness is not determined by one's soul, reputation, or cells, but by how one looks. At the same time, the African American vampire novels examined in *The Paradox of Blackness* acknowledge that how one looks is not always a reliable indicator of one's blackness, since black people in America have skin colors that range from the very light to the very dark due to the persistency of the debunked *one-drop rule*, the racist

---

14. According to Melton, there is a theory of vampirism that treats the vampire as an immaterial substance—psychic vampirism. This theory of the vampire, developed to explain "the persistency and universality of vampire myths," emerged in the nineteenth century on the heels of psychical research and traced its origin to "folktales that identified the vampire entity as a ghostly figure rather than a resuscitated body." However, in all the instances of psychic vampirism discussed by Melton (e.g., astral vampirism, vampiric entities, and magnetic vampirism), these ghostly or immaterial vampires only become a threat when they are inhabiting a body because this is the only time when they can exert their power on the material world (see 546–48).

belief that one drop of black blood makes a person black. In this light, these novels ask not only what makes a body black but if the body is the issuing source of blackness.

The novels that I have chosen for examination—Jewelle Gomez's *The Gilda Stories* (1991), Tananarive Due's *My Soul to Keep* (1997), Brandon Massey's *Dark Corner* (2004), Octavia Butler's *Fledgling* (2005), and K. Murry Johnson's *Image of Emeralds and Chocolate* (2012)—are a *first* for the author or in African American vampire fiction. Gomez's novel is not only the first African American vampire novel to be published in the US, but it also offers the first staying-alive and black lesbian vampire in African American vampire fiction. Due's novel is the first of what is now a four-book series—which includes *The Living Blood* (2001), *Blood Colony* (2008), and *My Soul to Take* (2011)—and its Life Brothers are African American vampire fiction's first black resurrection vampires. Johnson's novel is the first African American vampire novel to feature a black gay vampire, and the novels by Massey and Butler are the authors' first vampire novels, and their novels, like those by Gomez, Due, and Johnson, offer black vampires who have "a broader, more ancient cultural frame of reference" than the vampires of European tradition (Gomez, "Recasting the Mythology" 87–88). Indeed, none of the black vampires in the selected texts trace their lineage to Stoker's Dracula or to medieval Eastern European folklore.[15] In fact, when Dracula is mentioned in these texts, he tends to be treated as a mythical caricature of the vampire. At the same time, these black literary vampires are not modern versions of the vampire witches of West African and black Caribbean folklore, though some of them are from Africa. Instead, they can be read as a corrective to the "new" vampire that emerged in the US during the 1970s, when *Blacula* initiated America's departure from the vampirism of Stoker's Dracula.

According to Jules Zanger, unlike the "old" vampire, such as Dracula, the "new" vampire is "secularized," "socialized," and "humanized" (22). The new vampire is not a damned soul living a solitary life as one of the Devil's minions; instead, this vampire belongs to a community of vampires who are more human than monster in that they have free will. This means that the new vampire has the choice to be good or evil, a choice that is unavailable to Dracula. In Zanger's words,

---

15. This means that L. A. Banks's *Minion* (2003), the first novel of her very successful *Vampire Huntress* series, will not be a part of this study because Fallon Nuit, the novel's master vampire, is Dracula's "protégé" (268) and because the novel focuses on a black vampire huntress, not a black vampire.

> No longer embodying metaphysical evil, no longer a damned soul, the new vampire has become, in our concerned awareness for multiculturalism, merely ethnic, a victim of heredity, like being Sicilian or Jewish. Or, alternatively, vampirism can be understood . . . as a kind of viral infection, possibly like AIDS, without any necessary moral weight. It should be noted, however, that the new vampire, although "ethnic" in one special sense, does not come to us like Dracula from some mysterious foreign clime, preferably Eastern, but is resolutely American. . . . This new, demystified vampire might well be our next door neighbor, as Dracula, by origin, appearance, caste, and speech, could never pretend to be. (19)

While the new vampire is an American "ethnic," it is also resolutely white, as indicated by Zanger's examples (i.e., the New England Brahmin in the 1960s television series *Dark Shadows*, the Louisiana plantation owner in Rice's *Interview with the Vampire*, and the rural redneck and the white California teenager in the 1987 films by Kathryn Bigelow and Joel Schumacher, respectively). Moreover, Zanger assumes that the audiences for vampire fiction and films are also resolutely white, as evidenced by his claim that his list of new vampires could be the next-door neighbors of most Americans. Indeed, the history of antiblack segregation and discrimination in America, for example, would make it difficult for African American audiences to imagine Zanger's new vampires as their next-door neighbors or as merely ethnic. Thus, while the black literary vampires examined herein are, like their white ethnic counterparts, more human than monster in that they are communal and have free will, these vampires, unlike their counterparts, tend to belong to a multiracial or a black multicultural vampire community. By situating the black vampire within such communities, the African American vampire novels by Gomez, Due, Massey, Butler, and Johnson are not only de-whitening the vampire myth, but they are also suggesting that the question of whether there is more to being black than having a black body cannot be answered in a racially or culturally homogeneous vacuum precisely because blackness, like all racial identities, is about what black people think of themselves *and* what nonblack people think of black people (Japtok and Jenkins 6).

In addition to situating their black vampires in multiracial or black multicultural vampire communities, most of the African American vampire novels discussed in *The Paradox of Blackness* also ask us to consider the role that African American Christianity or the Black Church might play in the everyday lives of twenty-first-century African Americans. Such a question is noteworthy because the Black Church has historically played a crucial role in the

African American fight against antiblack racism during and after slavery. It is surprising, however, that an African American Christianity emerged, given how black people were treated by white Christians during slavery. For example, although black slaves could join the New England churches at the beginning of the eighteenth century, they were told by church leaders, such as the influential Cotton Mather, that serving their masters as God demanded would lead to eternal happiness (D. White, Bay, and Martin 62–63). Similarly, white Christian clergy and slave owners in South Carolina required slaves to take an oath before their baptism that offered the same message as Mather:

> You declare in the presence of God and before this Congregation that you do not ask for the holy baptism out of any design to free yourself from the Duty and Obedience that you owe to your Master while you live, but merely for the good of Your Soul and to partake of the Graces and Blessings promised to the members of the Church of Jesus Christ. (qtd. in Glaude 102)

Since slaves could be Christian and enslaved by Christians because of their blackness, "many slaves rejected Christianity out of hand as the religion of those who held them in bondage" (Glaude 101). Yet, the first "subordinate" black congregations, which were "usually headed by black ministers but subordinate to white church hierarchies," emerged in South Carolina and Georgia during the 1770s, and the first "truly independent black church" emerged between the 1780s and the early 1800s in Philadelphia (Hine, Hine, and Harrold 117).

Given the history of slavery and the hypocrisy of white Christian clergy and slaveholders, what led slaves and free blacks to create an African American Christianity? According to Eddie Glaude, Jr., the answer is the Great Revivals of the eighteenth and early nineteenth centuries, "when African Americans, particularly those in bondage, found in the Christian gospel as it was preached during the Great Revivals liberating possibilities—both in their personal experiences of conversion and in a vocabulary that enabled them to escape the psychical effects of slavery" (103). The Great Revivals, also known as the Great Awakening, began in New England in the mid-1730s and spread south during the Revolutionary era. While many of the New Lights, the white evangelical ministers who led these revivals, emphasized in their sermons that black people's belief in Christ could make them free and "fostered the education, conversion, and eventual manumission of several notable black northerners" (e.g., Phyllis Wheatley and Albert Ukawsaw Gronniosaw), only a few of the New Light ministers challenged slavery, and some were slave owners themselves who defended slavery on religious grounds (D. White, Bay, and Martin 96–98). Given these circumstances, as White, Bay, and Martin explain, many African Americans realized that they had to make Christianity their own, if they were going to be Christians: "[Black people] embraced Christianity's message that all men and women are equal before God, and they saw in the Bible's promises of spiritual deliverance some hope of eventually achieving freedom on earth as well as in heaven. In doing so, they crafted a distinctly Afro-Christian religious faith that helped them survive slavery while praying for freedom" (100). Since the black pastors of early African American Christianity became the "primary" leaders of the African American communities that they served and their churches became physical spaces that housed "schools, social organizations, and antislavery meetings" (Hine, Hine, and Harrold 117), African American resistance has historically been, as Sikivu Hutchinson puts it, "religious and secular humanist in orientation" (*Moral Combat* 9).

Thus, in one sense, it is not too surprising that recent studies report that "black Christians have the highest church attendance of any group in the United States" and that the Black Church continues to be "an influential institution with many positive benefits" (Van Camp, Sloan, and Elbassiouny 4). For example, Hutchinson references a 2009 study that reported that "92% of African Americans identified themselves as Christians and were more likely than whites to identify as 'born-again'"; it concluded that African American religiosity is becoming more aligned with conservative readings of the Bible (*Moral Combat* 4). That move toward the conservative helps to explain the tensions in the contemporary Black Church, since many of its churches preach a socially conservative message, maintain a patriarchal structure, practice staid rituals, lack social engagement, and have denounced or remained silent about nontraditional sexualities (Hine, Hine, and Harrold 660–61). While the black vampires in the novels by Due, Gomez, and Johnson confront those tensions directly, all the black vampires examined in *The Paradox of Blackness*, on some level, consider the role that the Black Church or God will play in the lives of African Americans as we move deeper into the twenty-first century.

In chapter 1, I examine the concept of black freedom in Gomez's *The Gilda Stories* and argue that Gilda is a staying-alive vampire who offers a queer critique of the "single-issue" view of black freedom, the idea that the only ism that affects the African American community is racism and that straight black men are racism's primary victims. That notion of freedom, as I demonstrate in this chapter, informed two movements that competed for the hearts and minds of African Americans during the 1970s and 1980s—Afrocentrism and multicultural conservatism. Although Afrocentrism's biology-determines-culture discourse and multicultural conservatism's color-blind capitalism are ideological adversaries, Gomez suggests in *Gilda* that both are problematic. What makes these ideologies problematic is that they support a conception of blackness in which black lesbians are constructed as those who are black in body only and, therefore, should never be representatives of black freedom. However, Gomez's depiction of Gilda and her vampire family suggests that to move toward a "full vision" of black freedom that can solve the paradoxical tension surrounding the question of blackness, African Americans must adopt Gilda's "a row of cotton is a row of cotton" philosophy of blackness and freedom, a philosophy that acknowledges that blackness is a myth that is treated as fact; therefore, the only requirement for being black is having a body that is defined as black.

Tananarive Due's *My Soul to Keep* is the focus of chapter 2, where I examine Due's depiction of the differences between African and African American blackness as represented by Dawit/David Wolde and Jessica Jacobs-Wolde, respectively. Jessica is a middle-class African American woman who was raised in the Black Church and is referred to by the narrator as an "all-American bourgeois Negro," and Dawit, Jessica's husband, is a resurrection vampire and an atheist from sixteenth-century Africa. I argue that Dawit represents what the all-American bourgeois Negro considers unthinkable for many late twentieth-century African Americans: being an atheist and being African. Since a large part of African American life, as implied by Due's depiction of the all-American bourgeois Negro, has historically revolved around the Black Church, Dawit's atheism makes his blackness suspicious and in need of salvation. I contend that such thinking is reminiscent of the *civilizing* discourse espoused by some nineteenth-century black nationalists in which African Americans must *save* Africa and Africans to form a unified African diaspora. As implied by Dawit's critiques of theistic religions and the monocultural blackness of the all-American bourgeois Negro, African Americans, like the all-American bourgeois Negro, need to develop a conception of blackness that is multicultural and absent of religion if they are interested in achieving *real* African–African American solidarity.

In chapter 3, I turn my attention to Brandon Massey's *Dark Corner* and argue that Diallo, a staying-alive vampire from late eighteenth-century Mali who is attempting to dominate an African American town at the end of the twentieth century, represents two late twentieth-century discourses of African American manhood that insist that masculinization must come from African, not African American, culture and that women should be excluded from the masculinization process: paternal Pan-Africanism and the contemporary heroic slave. Paternal Pan-Africanism represents the moment when Daniel Patrick Moynihan's problematic depiction of poor and working-class African American families as institutions of emasculated men and matriarchal women in his *The Negro Family: The Case for National Action* (1965) intersects with the equally problematic post–civil rights Pan-Africanism that not only agreed with Moynihan's depiction of the so-called emasculated man–matriarchal woman problem, but also argued that a cultural return to Africa could solve that problem. Similarly, the contemporary heroic slave represents the moment when post–civil rights Pan-Africanism intersects with whom Gregory Stephens refers to as the "heroic slave," an Afro-Caribbean figure of resistance who was alone in his fight against the system of slavery because he was "often betrayed by his own black brother—especially by brown-men—or by his black woman who has been sleeping with the white man" (128). While paternal Pan-Africanism and the contemporary heroic slave address different spheres of black male life (i.e., the former describes the manhood of the black father in the US, while the latter describes the manhood of the black male leader in the Caribbean), both presume that African American men are less black and less manly than their black counterparts outside the US. However, as suggested by Massey's depiction of Diallo, African Americans should be wary of black men espousing paternal Pan-Africanism or the rhetoric of the heroic slave because they are promoting a politics of black purity and restoration that is not only impossible and contradictory but also dangerous.

Octavia Butler's *Fledgling*, the last novel by Butler to be published before her unfortunate death in 2006, is the subject of chapter 4. The novel tells the story of the birth and rebirth of Shori Matthews, a staying-alive vampire who has amnesia and is, therefore, unaware that she is black, a vampire, and a genetic experiment. I argue that human-vampire miscegenation does not lead to "posthuman interracialization," as Nayar claims; instead, it represents Butler's conception of what I call *transhuman blackness,* in which every human, regardless of skin color, is born *black* because every human, except for the rare exceptions, has melanin. Unlike the staying-alive vampirisms of Gilda and Diallo, which represent the elixir version of the Staying Alive Narrative, Shori represents that narrative's scientific version, in which transhumanism, the belief that we should use technology to *improve* our species, is its latest manifestation. The difference between the transhuman and the posthuman is that the latter represents the moment when humans are no longer *human,* while the former represents the evolutionary stage between the human and the posthuman. As suggested by Butler's depiction of Shori, since transhumans are still human, they will also have melanin because they will need skin to help protect them from, among other things, the sun's ultraviolet radiation. Thus, unlike the novels above, which propose that the only requirement for being black is having a black body, *Fledgling* contends that the presence of melanin, regardless of the amount, is what makes a body black.

In chapter 5, I examine K. Murry Johnson's first novel, *Image of Emeralds and Chocolate*, which is the first black gay vampire novel by an African American author. Set in contemporary Louisiana, *Image* focuses on the romantic relationship that develops between Eric Peterson, a high school senior and closeted gay man who has been raised in the Black Church, and Emanuel Marquis LeBlanc, a gay man who was born a slave in 1800 and became a staying-alive vampire and a free man at the age of eighteen, the same age that Eric decides to stop being a virgin. I argue that the novel can be read as a critique of what I call *Black Church corporatism*, the idea that the Black Church should be the single corporate person who has the authority to speak for all African Americans. One of the main problems with Black Church corporatism, as suggested by Johnson's *Image*, is that many Black churches conceptualize salvation and blackness in ways that marginalize black gay men by implying that there is more to being a black man than having a black body. Johnson not only demonstrates in *Image* that since most of the Black Church does not allow for differences in black male sexuality, it is unable to speak for all African American men, but he also argues that to remove the homophobia that pervades the Black Church will require treating the Bible as a literary text, not as *book knowledge*.

In the conclusion of *The Paradox of Blackness in African American Vampire Fiction*, I focus on whether the black vampires in the novels by Gomez, Due, Massey, Butler, and Johnson represent a "post-black" or a "new black" notion of blackness. Glen Ligon, the visual artist who, along with Thelma Golden, coined the term "post-Blackness" to describe what they saw happening in art (Touré 16), defines it as "a more individualized notion of Blackness": "I just think we're getting beyond the collective notion of what Blackness was. Blackness was about group definitions so there could be Black leaders who spoke for Black people in total. And I think we've moved beyond that and we're entering the space where more individualized conceptions of Blackness will be the rule and not the exception" (qtd. in Touré 25). While "post-blackness" describes the shift from collective to individualized notions of blackness, the "new black," as defined by Lani Guinier and Gerald Torres, describes the shift from an individualized to a super-collective notion of blackness. The new black is "a cross-racial coalition of disenfranchised groups that mobilize under the umbrella 'political race,'" in which "a group of people are ultimately defined by their politics rather than by their physiognomy." For Guinier and Torres, new-black blackness makes political sense because, as they put it, "if blacks are going to make a meaningful difference in the socioeconomic hierarchy that so far defines the twenty-first century, it will not be due solely to a mobilization that only includes other phenotypically black people" (20). In light of Ligon's definition of post-blackness and Guinier and Torres's notion of the new black, I want to examine where Gilda, Dawit, Diallo, Shori, and Marquis fall in the post-black versus new-black debate because such an examination can offer us insight into which notion of blackness will most likely prevail in the twenty-first century and why this will matter to all Americans.

CHAPTER 1

# BLACKNESS, FREEDOM, AND THE STAYING-ALIVE VAMPIRE IN *THE GILDA STORIES*

IN "BUT SOME OF US Are Brave Lesbians: The Absence of Black Lesbian Fiction," Jewelle Gomez contends that speculative fiction featuring black lesbians may be politically more useful than academic writings on black lesbian identities and cultures:

> It is the *representation* of black lesbian lives, not simply its analysis and deconstruction that has the most immediate, broad-based and long-lasting cultural and historical impact. Only by telling our stories in the most specific, imagistic, and imaginative narratives do the lives of black lesbians take on long-term literary and political significance. This representation, especially as created by black lesbians, continues to occupy an inordinately small space in the world of literature. (290)

Gomez reminds us that fiction helps to construct the meanings of what it is representing and, therefore, helps us make reality meaningful by challenging or reinforcing the sets of "truths" that we live by (see Storey 5–6). She also reminds us that fiction may be more effective in challenging or

---

This chapter is a revision of an earlier article published in the *African American Review* 46.2–3 (2013).

reinforcing these "truths" than academic studies simply because fiction reaches more people than peer-reviewed articles or books. Moreover, since speculative fiction is a "work that postulates a time and circumstance as yet unknown" (Gomez, "Speculative Fiction and Black Lesbians" 949), speculative fiction is also asking us to consider what the future would look like if certain ideas about an individual, group, or being are discredited or maintained. However, if black lesbians are barely visible in the world of fiction, as Gomez notes, then how can the "truths" about black lesbians be discussed in African American communities and in the US as a whole? Her answer is for black lesbians to write the "most specific, imagistic, and imaginative narratives" possible, narratives that feature black lesbian characters who live in "many worlds, not just the heterosexual one" ("But Some of Us" 293–94). As I attempt to show in this chapter, Gomez's *The Gilda Stories* (1991) is one of those narratives.

In the afterword to the 2004 edition of *Gilda*, Gomez states that her fascination with Dracula started at fifteen years old, when she began watching classic horror movies with her neighborhood friends on Saturday nights. She recognized later in life that her attraction to the legendary vampire was due to the link she made between the loneliness she felt as a child of divorced parents and Dracula's "doomed pursuit" of a companion who would live with him forever. Although Gomez was never "quite comfortable with the dead bodies that littered Dracula's path to fulfillment," she believed during her adolescent years that "[she] was the only one who could understand Dracula's suffering." As a "lesbian feminist of mixed race," however, Gomez states that she needed to "excavate and reshape" the mythology of the vampire before she could claim vampires as her own.[1] In other words,

---

1. According to Winnubst, the "white straight male viewer/reader" of the classic male vampire story (e.g., Stoker's *Dracula*) is able to identify with the victim, the vampire, or both because whiteness, maleness, and heterosexuality are invisible in contemporary American culture (6). Consequently, readers/viewers who are not white, straight, and male are limited in their identification because they are "constantly placed in the role of victim, identifying easily with the victim taken by the vampiric powers" (10). It appears, however, that Gomez's own reflections about what attracted her to Dracula interrogate the notion that readers/viewers of the classic male vampire story who are not white, straight, and male automatically identify with the victim. Indeed, in spite of the dead bodies that litter Dracula's "path to fulfillment," Gomez identifies with Dracula, not his victims. Moreover, Gomez's identification with Dracula is not shaped by her race, sex, or sexuality; instead, her identification with the legendary vampire appears to be based on a shared "suffering," a "suffering" that transcends, at least in Gomez's teenaged mind, their social identities. Thus, while Gilda may be a revision of Stoker's Dracula, it does not seem to be a revision that is shaped by Gomez's identification with Dracula's victims; rather, it seems to be shaped by her identification with Dracula's powers as well as his "doomed pursuit" for an eternal companion.

to claim vampires as her own, Gomez had to create a vampire with a cultural frame of reference that is older and more diverse than Dracula's. To do so, Gomez's vampire had to be a "heroic figure" who embodied and interrogated the activism reflected in, for example, the poems of the Black Arts Movement, the songs of the feminist movement, and the literary journals of lesbian activists. What made these poems, songs, and journals produced during the "highly active political period" of the 1970s and 1980s inspirational for Gomez is that in the process of converting "the pain of oppression into art," they became "calls to action," calls that shape her vampire's actions, observations, and personal development (*Gilda* 256–57). While Gomez acknowledges that black vampire films of the 1970s, such as *Blacula* (1972) and *Ganja and Hess* (1973), attempted to claim the vampire myth for African Americans, she also notes that these films rely on a "formulaic design" in which the black woman functions as either "handmaiden" or as "temptress/bait" ("Recasting the Mythology" 89). Thus, Gomez needed to de-whiten, de-straighten, de-male, and de-pain the vampire myth to claim vampires as her own and to give long-term literary and political significance to the lives of black lesbians.

I argue in this chapter that Gilda not only satisfies Gomez's need to recast the vampire as a black lesbian who is not doomed to loneliness, but she also offers a queer critique of the "single-issue" view of black freedom, a view that informed two movements that competed for the hearts and minds of African Americans during the 1970s and '80s—Afrocentrism and multicultural conservatism. As I noted in the introduction of this book, a queer critique is an antinormative project that challenges identity and genre categories that are presented as authentic or as transcending time, space, and culture. Consequently, a queer critique of the "single-issue" view of black freedom—the idea that the only ism that negatively affects the African American community is racism and that straight black men are racism's primary victims (Gomez, "Speculative Fiction and Black Lesbians" 951)—is concerned with interrogating not only the normalization of heterosexuality in this view of black freedom but also the normalization of the straight black male as *the* image of black freedom. Indeed, what makes Afrocentrism and multicultural conservatism problematic is that they foster notions of blackness and freedom in which black lesbians are constructed as those who are not really black and, therefore, should never be viewed as representatives of black freedom.

According to Molefi Asante, Afrocentrism is a philosophy of blackness that seeks to liberate African Americans from the "intellectual plantation" of Eurocentric thinking that constrains their economic, cultural, and intellectual development by offering an African-centered perspective on the world ("Afrocentricity, Race, and Reason" 20–21). A crucial element of Afrocentrism is preventing "Eurocentrism from imposing itself as universal" by demonstrating that Eurocentrism is "only way to view the world" (*Afrocentricity* 89). Thus, Afrocentrism does not call for a physical return to Africa, as some black nationalist movements have done in the past; rather, it calls for a cultural return to Africa in which African Americans see the world through African eyes instead of European ones. However, Afrocentrism also treats the body as the site where identities become complete. As Asante puts it, the so-called "non-Afrocentric [black] person" or "Eurocentric African" is "contradictory" and "destructive" to themselves and to black people because they embrace "images, symbols, lifestyles, and manners" that contradict what their bodies tell them about how they should think and live (*Afrocentricity* 1). According to that logic, since one cannot *truly* leave or enter another race, one cannot *truly* leave or enter another culture because one's body prevents one from doing so. However, as Gilda learns from her family members, if all humans trace their origins to Africa, then all humans are black; therefore, blackness, whiteness, and all other racial identities are figments of the human imagination, not facts of nature.

In contrast to Afrocentrism's body-equals-culture discourse, multicultural conservatism, according to Angela Dillard, holds that any individual or group can be *American* as long as they embrace assimilation, individualism, and free-market capitalism; therefore, one's body is not an indicator of one's culture or the primary determinant of one's socioeconomic fate. In the context of race, multicultural conservatives claim that being color-blind will move our nation toward an America where people are judged by their character, not by their skin color. Ironically, as Dillard notes, multicultural conservatives (i.e., conservative African Americans, Latino Americans, Asian Americans, women, and LGBTQ people) do not support multiculturalism; instead, they believe that being "white" (i.e., adopting white middle-class standards) is the only way to be American (90). As such, multicultural conservatives mistakenly view Afrocentrism as a form of multiculturalism, as an intellectual development that champions political correctness, silences free speech, teaches illiberal education, and encourages individuals who are not white, male, and heterosexual to engage in an identity politics in which they are always victims or oppressed.[2] In other words, while multicultural

---

2. The multicultural conservative link between Afrocentrism and multiculturalism is inaccurate because the former is invested in racial homogeneity and the latter is concerned with cultural diversity. As Donald E. Collins puts it, "even with its roots in mul-

conservatives support the study of how racial minorities, women, and gays and lesbians have contributed to America's development, "they are fiercely opposed to such efforts if they threaten notions of our common heritage in favor of attacking 'dead white men' of the past and white heterosexual men of the present" (88).[3] However, as Gilda reveals in her discussion of why she remains connected to the mortal world, the multicultural conservative's call for color-blindness is highly problematic at best because one cannot be color-blind in a society where economic forms are racialized and pain is colored black.

Although Afrocentrism and multicultural conservatism are ideological adversaries, Gomez suggests in *Gilda* that both rely on the single-issue view of black freedom. Before discussing how Gilda and her vampire family discredit the notions of blackness and freedom put forth by Afrocentrism and multicultural conservatism, I provide an overview of Gilda's staying-alive vampirism. I begin with Gilda's vampirism because not only is it the source of her immortality, but it also allows her to create a family that represents what a "full vision" of black freedom might look like and that offers a worthwhile answer to the question of whether there is more to being black than having a black body. As I noted in this book's introduction, the Staying Alive Narrative is the dream of avoiding death forever, a dream that is not concerned with life-after-death questions, but with staying alive here and now. This focus on the present is ultimately concerned with acquiring a steady supply of the basics of survival, such as food, drink, shelter, and defenses. Since one does not need to be supernatural in order to acquire a

---

ticulturalism, Afrocentric education asserts that Western culture is inherently inferior to African (particularly ancient African) cultures" (18–19). Thus, as I suggest in this chapter, Afrocentrism is not a form of multiculturalism, but a *blackened* version of Eurocentrism.

3. This discourse informed the proponents of the Arizona bill to ban ethnic studies, which was signed into law in 2010. In response to a letter in which a student complained that the only literary texts offered in his or her English classes were primarily by "dead white people," Tom Horne, Arizona's school superintendent at the time and author of the bill that banned ethnic studies, assumed that this student had been taught the "wrong things" about literature; that is to say, this student had been taught to judge literature by the race or gender of the author, not by its content. However, as Katie Sciurba notes, Horne blatantly disregarded the "irrefutable fact" that texts written by and about racial and ethnic minorities, women, and the LGBTQ community continue to be absent, or at least grossly less present, in America's public schools (126). Horne's disregard for the absence of women and nonwhite American authors in America's classrooms highlights the problem with multicultural conservatism—it assumes that the real American is the straight male WASP. Thus, as Sciurba contends, "until educators can introduce students to curriculum that adequately reflects their between-, across-, and within-group diversity, we will have no choice but to consider 'race and gender' when considering what literature to teach" (129).

continuous supply of survival basics, this also means that one does not have to be supernatural to be immortal. Thus, Gomez severs the link between immortality and monstrosity found in the narrative of the resurrection vampire, which I discuss in more detail in chapter 2, by creating a vampire who is both immortal and human. By doing so, Gomez not only creates the first black staying-alive vampire of African American vampire fiction, but she also offers a vision of black freedom that expands our understanding of blackness and freedom beyond the single-issue view.

## Gilda's Elixir of Life

*The Gilda Stories* begins in 1850 with Gilda as an unnamed black girl who has recently escaped slavery and ends with her as a black vampire who achieves *real* freedom in 2050. During her escape from the Mississippi plantation where she was born, her father was sold, and her mother died, Gilda kills a white man "wearing the clothes of an overseer" who was "stiff for conquest" (*Gilda* 9–11). Hiding in the cellar of a farmhouse in Louisiana, Gilda is discovered and taken in by Miss Gilda, a white female vampire who owns a brothel near New Orleans. Eventually, Miss Gilda and Bird, a Native American woman who is Miss Gilda's partner, give Gilda, who is called "the Girl" at this point in the novel, the gift of vampirism, a gift that will allow her to travel across the US in search of the moment when she is "no longer fleeing for her life," the moment when she is truly free (252). However, Gilda realizes very early in her life as a vampire that her search for freedom is not an individual journey, but a communal one; therefore, she builds a family of vampires that consists of three black lesbians (including herself), a straight black man, two gay white men, and a Native American lesbian. In spite of being free from slavery for over forty years, Gilda tells one of her future vampire family members that killing the overseer or the end of slavery did not make her feel free: "It soon became clear that although the institution of enslavement was no longer sanctioned, our world had not become a more hospitable place for me or my people. Often it was only the gift that I acquired in this new life [as a vampire] that saved me from those we call civilized" (82). As suggested by the passage above, one of the first lessons that Gilda learns as a freewoman and as a vampire is that freedom, as well as oppression, cannot be achieved or maintained without violence or the threat of it. Indeed, Gilda's "gift" has saved her from being lynched, raped, beaten, and exploited by the so-called civilized of Reconstruction, the barbarians of white supremacy. Although Gilda killed the bounty hunter as a human, implying that she was destined to be free long before she became a vampire, she admits that she would not have maintained her freedom if it were not for her vampirism. In this way, as Thaler argues, the novel "signifies on contemporary vampire culture by inverting the vampire from a trope connoted with death to a positive, life-affirming figure" (55).

In *Gilda*, vampirism functions not only as a pathway to attaining and maintaining freedom but also as a deathless pathway to immortality. Indeed, given Gomez's desire to reimagine the vampire and to give long-term literary and political significance to the lives of black lesbians, Gilda could only be a staying-alive vampire because the resurrection vampire embodies the idea that freedom and immortality can only be obtained after death. This point is alluded to in Miss Gilda's explanation of the human-to-vampire process and vampire feeding practices to Gilda:

> We draw life into ourselves, yet we give life as well. We give what's needed—energy, dreams, ideas. It's a fair exchange in a world full of cheaters. And when we feel it is right, when the need is great on both sides, we can re-create others like ourselves to share life with us. It is not a bad life. (*Gilda* 45)

It is noteworthy that death is completely absent from the discussion of vampiric transformation and feeding because it parallels the Staying Alive Narrative's dismissal of the first part of the Mortality Paradox, the idea that death is inevitable.

Some readers might argue, however, that Gilda is indeed a resurrection vampire because her transformation from human to vampire is no different from the resurrection vampire's transformation process. For example, Miss Gilda begins the transformation process by biting the Girl on the neck to remove the human blood from her body. To complete the transformation, the Girl drinks the "red life that seeped from [Miss Gilda's breast]" and settles into Miss Gilda's lap until the "fire died" (*Gilda* 46). These same readers would also note that when Gilda saves Ermis, a black New Mexican woman born in the twenty-first century, from suicide by transforming her into a vampire, Gilda tells Ermis after she awakes that her plan to kill herself has been "half-fulfilled" (245). While it appears that the Girl dies during her human-to-vampire transformation, as alluded to by the fire reference, her ability to feed from Miss Gilda suggests otherwise. Indeed, the Girl could not be dead when she begins to drink the "red life" from Miss Gilda's breast precisely because she would have lacked the drive and the motor skills to do so. Similarly, the problem with reading Ermis's transformation as a resurrection is that Gilda is not telling Ermis that she is undead, one who is both dead and alive; instead, she is telling her that only part of her has died, the part of her that had "chosen death rather than wait for death to choose her" (244). What the examples above suggest is that the human-to-vampire transformation in *Gilda* is closer to a blood transfusion than a resurrection. In this light, vampiric blood in *Gilda* can be read as an example of the mythical version of the Staying Alive Narrative that transforms humans into immortals without the need of death or science. However, Gomez makes it clear in the novel that being a vampire, like being immortal, is not for everyone.

Unlike the scientific version of the Staying Alive Narrative, which began during Europe's Enlightenment period and focuses on the use of science to avoid death, the mythical version is as old as recorded history and refers to the magical elixir of life. The elixir is "the legendary substance that, when consumed, will halt the usual processes of decline and decay, elevating the imbibers above the fate of mortals, making them what the Chinese call *hsien*—transcendent, celestial, immortal." The elixir is not just a pill or potion, but "whatever help[s] to stave off aging and death for a little bit longer" (Cave 44). What is perhaps the most important aspect of the elixir legend, which is abandoned by its scientific counterpart, is the idea that immortality is only for a select few, the "wise and virtuous" (46). While this caveat addresses the overpopulation problem that could emerge as a result of individuals living indefinitely,[4] it does not tell us how to become wise and virtuous. Nevertheless, Cave suggests that there are two questions that wise and virtuous mortals consider before drinking the elixir, questions that the foolish and fainthearted apparently ignore or answer incorrectly: "what we want to *have* [and] who we want to become" (48). Thus, what distinguishes the wise and virtuous from the foolish and fainthearted is that the former acknowledges that to be mentally fit for eternity, our desires, which shape who we really are or want to become, must be transformed. In other words, since the legend of the elixir embodies the "desire for transformation" (44), the wise and virtuous are those individuals who acknowledge that to be mentally fit for eternity and, therefore, eternally happy, our post-elixir selves cannot be a mere extension of our pre-elixir selves.

Like the mythical elixir, vampiric blood in *Gilda* can make one physically fit for immortality, but not mentally fit. For example, right before Gilda saves Ermis from suicide, the narrator notes that Gilda's time since the late twentieth century has been spent "learning to be more than human." This means,

---

4. For example, India's overpopulation problem, a population that jumped from 439 million in 1960 to 1.2 billion in 2012, "is not due to any increase in the birth rate but to a decline in the mortality rate" (Parrillo 258).

as the narrator continues, "[Gilda] saw more deeply into life, further into the past and through lies. But the future was as much a mystery to her as to anyone—a delicious reason for being, she thought" (243). According to the narrator, to be mentally fit for immortality and, therefore, eternally happy, one must become more than human. To reach this state, one is required not only to examine the past in order to distinguish between the *truths* and "lies" of history but also to embrace the future as the great unknown. This understanding of being more than human is very similar to the mythical approach to finding the elixir. As Cave explains,

> Broadly speaking, early civilizations [in search of the elixir] aspired mostly to maintain the gains they had made—to defend themselves against the onslaught of the barbarians and prevent a collapse into chaos. This is reflected in the form of their immortality narratives: they looked backward to their founding fathers . . . who were thought already to have found the elixir. Their ambition was to maintain or rediscover past glories, not to move toward something new. (58)

Like these early civilizations, Gilda looks to the past to learn how to become mentally fit for immortality and eternally happy. Indeed, by viewing the future as a "mystery," as an exciting but unknown time, Gilda suggests that the future should not be too important for those considering immortality because the *real* utopias are in the past. However, since Gilda is a staying-alive vampire, the past that she invokes must lead to a utopia that can make today's Gilda as well as tomorrow's unknown Gilda eternally happy.

To find this utopia, Gilda, unlike most early civilizations, who deferred to their founding fathers, looks to her *founding mothers*. What Gilda learns from looking backward is that she, her mothers, and her family belong to America's *cheated*, those who have been historically disempowered because of *who* they are, not because of *how* they are. By giving her family members long life, what Ermis calls "the most valuable commodity on the planet" (*Gilda* 247), Gilda transforms disempowered mortals—such as blacks, poor whites, Native Americans, and LGBTQ people—into empowered immortals. However, Gilda learns on her journey to real freedom that immortality is not for all disempowered people because disempowerment alone does not make one mentally fit for eternity. As suggested by the monsters that Gilda defeats on her way to freedom, although Afrocentrics and multicultural conservatives come from groups who have been cheated in the US, they are not fit for eternity because they rely on ideologies and practices that would result in an eternity of disempowerment for people like Gilda and her family.

## Blood, Family, and Racialized Biopolitics

Paul Gilroy reminds us in *Against Race: Imagining Political Culture Beyond the Color Line* that there is an African American philosophical tradition that conceptualizes freedom as both a bodily *and* an intellectual matter. In this view of freedom, the black body can never be truly free until the black mind is free. As Gilroy explains, "organic intellectuals from Frederick Douglass to George Clinton suggested that the most valuable forms of freedom lay in the liberation of the mind. Dr. Funkenstein's prescription was 'Free your mind and your ass will follow.' The dualism was problematic, but it could be forgiven because, against the expectations of raciologists, it was the mind that came first!" (*Against Race* 185). Raciologists are the missionaries of biopolitics who define people only in terms of their bodies and whose prescription for freedom is "free the body and the mind will follow," a prescription that essentially eradicates the mind-body dualism from the discussion of freedom. Thus, as Gilroy puts it, racialized biopolitics establishes the "limits of the authentic racial community. . . . almost exclusively through the visual representation of racialized bodies" in which "politics becomes an exclusively aesthetic concern with all the perils that implies" (185). Consequently, by treating the body as the site where one's identity becomes complete, the raciologists assume that the body dictates what we should think, how we should behave, and whom we should love and/or get along with.

Like the prescription for black freedom given by Dr. Funkenstein, a stage persona created by Clinton for his 1970s funk group Parliament/Funkadelic, Gomez's prescription for black freedom in the post–civil rights era is Gilda's vampire family, a *black* family that is free of racialized biopolitics. In contrast to the virtually all-white, male-headed vampire families and communities of the "new" vampire discussed in the introduction of this book, such as the family created by Lestat, Louis, and Claudia in Anne Rice's *Interview with the Vampire* (1976), Gilda's vampire family is a female-headed, multiracial, multisexual, multigenerational, and multicultural group. This means that to be a member of Gilda's family, one must reject the racist, sexist, and homophobic understanding of blackness created by Eurocentrism and reinforced by Afrocentrism. As I noted earlier in this chapter, the primary goal of Afrocentricity is to liberate African Americans from the intellectual plantation of Eurocentrism, "a variation of ethnocentrism in which the content, emphasis, or both, in history, literature, and other humanities primarily, if not exclusively, concern Western culture" (Parillo 14). It is, therefore, not too surprising that Asante claims that Eurocentric black folks or non-Afrocentric blacks are destructive to themselves and to the African diaspora because they embrace ways of seeing the world that do not come from "one's own center" and, therefore, lack a "true sense of destiny" (*Afrocentricity* 1). Indeed, since one's biology dictates one's "center" and destiny, the problem with non-Afrocentric African Americans is that they are not listening to what their bodies are telling them to think, do, and desire.

To get back to one's center, Asante contends that African Americans must embrace Afrocentricity, "the belief in the centrality of Africans in post modern history" (*Afrocentricity* 6). Once African Americans embrace Afrocentricity, they will realize that it "supersedes any other ideology because it is the proper sanctification of [their] own history." While Asante acknowledges the diversity of local histories within the African diaspora, the history that he is referring to in the quote above is the history of African people. Since the "roots" of African people, regardless of "present locations," are in East Africa, African Americans cannot be Afrocentric until they rid themselves of "all fantasies" that do not emerge from those roots. In this light, Afrocentricity can be viewed as a theory and practice of "conversion," "reconstruction," "renunciation," and "recovery" in which African Americans learn their "proper" ideology (7).

It appears, despite Asante's claim to the contrary, that present locations do matter because contemporary Africa does not appear anywhere in Asante's *Afrocentricity*. In fact, none of the people whom he identifies as the "essential grounds" of Afrocentricity are African or women (see *Afrocentricity* 7–30). This is partly why Gilroy refers to Afrocentrism as another form of "Americocentrism," an Americanized understanding of ethnicity and cultural difference in which the family functions as the "approved, natural site where ethnicity and racial culture are reproduced" ("It's a Family Affair" 197). In other words, family functions in Afrocentrism's biology-determines-ideology discourse as the "connective tissue of black experience and history" and, therefore, stands for community, race, and nation (203). What is suggested by Gilroy's critique of Afrocentrism is that its "dubious appeal" to the family as a site of black solidarity is impractical, ahistorical, and extremely selective because it not only distances itself from contemporary Africa, but it also attempts to construct a black "sameness" (i.e., an American blackness) across national identities (195). As Gilroy sees it, there is no "proper" ideology for black people because blood is not the connective tissue of the family or the race.

Gomez's portrayal of Gilda's vampire family shares Gilroy's critique of the link between race and family in Afrocentrism. Unlike Gilroy, who believes that the trope of the family is not useful as a foundation for black solidarity, Gomez contends that the concept of family is useful for moving toward a "full vision" of black freedom. Indeed, instead of thinking of family as a biological product, Gomez offers us a vampire family that is defined by choice, not blood. For example, one of the most important lessons that Gilda learns during her time with Sorel and Anthony, a vampire couple who will become members of Gilda's family, is that families, like friends, are matters of choice. As Anthony explains,

> Sorel is correct, I think, in believing that to choose someone for your family is a great responsibility. It must be done not simply out of your own need or desire but rather because of a mutual need. We must search ourselves and the other to know if it is really essential. To do otherwise is a grave error, the result of which can only be tragedy.... These are not the families that bring solace or that last in harmony. (*Gilda* 69)

According to Lynda Hall, "family" in *Gilda* focuses on "the individual's ability to choose and 'create' the 'family'" (401). Such a focus, as noted by Anthony, acknowledges that the foundation of familial solidarity is not blood, but "solace," "harmony," "desire," and "mutual need." If blood is not the foundation of familial solidarity, this suggests that blood is not the foundation of racial solidarity. This is a lesson that Gilda learns during her time with Miss Gilda and that is reinforced during her time with Sorel and Anthony.

When Miss Gilda found Gilda, who is called "the Girl" at the time, in the cellar of her farmhouse, Gilda immediately recognizes that she is not like most white people. For example, Miss Gilda has "dark eyes and pale skin," but she can "talk without speaking," a skill that the Girl "never expected a white to be able to do" (*Gilda* 13). Moreover, like the Girl, whose birth name is unknown, Miss Gilda's familial origins are unknown, except that she is "Creole" and the "mistress" of the "Woodard house," a "well attended" brothel. For some in the black community, this lack of a known past is what makes Miss Gilda unlike "regular" white people. According to Bernice, "the dark, wary cook" of the Woodard house, "after all the time I been here I still don't know who Miss Gilda is. Inside I don't really know what she thinkin' like you do with most white folks. I don't know who her people is. White folks is dyin' to tell each other that. Not her" (36). Although Miss Gilda may keep quiet about her "people" because she does not want to reveal that she is a vampire, her silence on the issue also suggests that she might not be purely white. As one of the white women who works at the Woodard house warns the Girl, "there's lots of folks down this way believe in ha'nts and such like. Spirits. Creoles, like Miss Gilda, and Indians, they follow all that stuff" (35). What makes Miss Gilda's whiteness up for question is that her skin color tells the community that she is white, but her actions and beliefs tell them that she is not. Indeed, Miss Gilda challenges the *what you see is what you get* approach to racial identity, which Afrocentrism and Eurocentrism rely upon, by thinking and living in ways that are supposedly not white. This uncertainty about the racial purity of white people becomes more certain during Gilda's first discussion with Sorel.

When Gilda enters Sorel's bar, he introduces her to his "genteel" patrons, who objected to Gilda's "well-traveled clothes" and "dark skin," as a "family" member who has returned "home" (*Gilda* 59). After Anthony brings a bottle of champagne to celebrate Gilda's "return," he informs her that he would like to welcome her by honoring the ancestors as it is done in "the homeland of [her] mother's people." As he pours the champagne or "first libation" onto the floor, Anthony says, "I honor your ancestors. I honor our ancestors" (60). In honoring the ancestors, Anthony does not make a distinction between his ancestors and Gilda's, even though Anthony is an eighteenth-century European with "immense deep, blue eyes." Similarly, when Gilda tells Sorel that some of the women at the Woodard house begin to attribute her youthful looks to her "blackness" because they believed that "the African has a magical power over the appearance of youth," he replies that the African's magical power must explain his "enduring good looks." As Gilda stares more closely at Sorel's "pale skin and dark eyes," she asks if there are "strains of Africa in [his] blood." With laughter, Sorel answers with another question: "In what great, civilized nation are there not?" (79).

Sorel suggests that every human has African blood in them; therefore, *white* people are also *black*. Consequently, if white people are black, then it follows that blood does not unite a race. In this view, since blood makes us part of the same race, it is our ideas about blood that group us into races. The comments by Sorel and Anthony problematize the expectations of raciologists such as Asante. For Asante, blackness is not an ideology but a physical fact, as indicated by his statement "the African continent gave birth to Africans." However, since all humans trace their origins to East Africa, what Asante refers to as "the cradle of human history" (*Afrocentricity* 7), then all humans are African, regardless of their continent of birth. Even though 100,000 years ago there were at least six human species on the planet and there was some interbreeding among them, approximately 88,000 years later every human species on the planet became extinct, except for us, the Homo sapiens (Harari 12–19). Given this context, what Sorel's comments imply is that since our blood makes all humans *black*, all notions of blackness, as well as whiteness, are arbitrary precisely because our ideologies about our bodies, not the bodies themselves, determine how we view and treat our bodies and the bodies of others. In other words, what Sorel is telling Gilda is that shared ideas, not shared blood, are what unite families and races.

## Race, Pain, and Color-Blindness

Although Gomez treats race in *The Gilda Stories* as an ideological phenomenon instead of as a biological fact, she does not subscribe to the color-blind politics of multicultural conservatism. According to Dillard, multicultural conservatism can be viewed as a "'counterrevolutionary' effect" of the leftist movements of the 1960s and 1970s in which conservative racial minorities, women, and homosexuals represent themselves as "poster children for the American Dream of individual mobility, proof positive that merit and determination can produce success." It is, therefore, not too shocking that multicultural conservatives view Afrocentrism (as well as feminism, Chicano studies, and queer theory) as a "radical" and "dangerous" academic trend because, in their view, it advocates an "[identity] politics engendered by conceiving of individuals as members of oppressed and victimized groups" (2–3). What makes the existence of multicultural conservatives "fascinating" is that "the conservative tradition in America was shaped by racialist and outright racist doctrine, by heterosexual-patriarchal notions of gender and family, and by xenophobic influences" (xii). In spite of that tradition's influences, multicultural conservatives see themselves as "reclaiming a lost 'Golden Age' of politics, an age dominated by a supposed consensus around the desirability of assimilation not as members of an artificially contrived cultural minority but as individuals, as citizens, as Americans" (14). This turn to the Golden Age of politics, in other words, means being body blind (e.g., blind to a person's skin color, sex, or age) and developing a blind faith in the free market. Although multicultural conservatives "want" to speak only as individual Americans, Dillard writes that "they are constantly forced to concede that the power of their critiques relies heavily on their socially constructed identities. . . . They speak not only as conservatives but, more important, as *conservative African Americans, Latinos, women, and homosexuals*" (14). Moreover, since the "economic forms" of capitalism (e.g., "money, labor, labor power, surplus labor, profits, capital, capitalists, enterprises") demand the "performance of specific, historically and socially constructed meanings and identities" (Ruccio 36), the multicultural conservative's call for color-blindness seems disingenuous precisely because one cannot be color-blind in a society whose economic forms are racialized.

Gilda's experiences in twentieth-century America indicate that the call for color-blindness is also problematic because the color of pain in America is black. In other words, while critical of Afrocentrism's racialized biopolitics, multicultural conservatism is also grounded in a racialized biopolitics in which the black body, unlike its white counterpart, has to prove its Americanness because it is viewed and treated as the embodiment of pain. Consequently, as Debra Walker King suggests, if one has a black body that is not in pain, then one is not really black: "Black bodies in pain have a history of being the most 'visible' objects for pain's public consumption. In fact, the popular and recurring images of black bodies in pain as a normalized representation of suffering in photos, film, and other cultural products has come to position those bodies as material representations of pain. This misrepresentation of the black body ultimately assists in building the mythology of who is and who is not 'American'" (15). Since being American means being "pain-free," the black body in pain functions within "a negative symbolic index of social worth defining what an American is *not*" (17). These conceptions of the pained black body and the pain-free American are what make Gilda's staying-alive vampirism even more appealing—it offers those with black bodies the opportunity to live pain free forever. However, while Gilda's vampiric blood solves the Tithonus problem—the idea that if we could stay alive indefinitely, we would not end up with a "utopia of strong-bodied demigods but a plethora of care homes and hospitals filled with the depressed, the diseased and the incontinent old" (Cave 67)—it cannot solve the problem of black pain entirely because this pain has physical *and* symbolic origins.

The difference between "symbolic" violence and physical or "overt" violence is that the latter often ends in injury or murder and the former addresses one's complicity in the violence. As King puts it,

> While overt violence is often bloody, symbolic violence manifests itself through individual or communal acceptance of naturalized racial markings. In this way, symbolic violence works to legitimize strategies of exclusion and build the political, economic, cultural, and social capital of the status quo. It can also act as a mechanism to encourage containment of anything or anyone, group or individual, that the established social order deems unsavory or unwanted. (34)

Thus, when one views the black body as only an image of pain, one is committing an act of symbolic violence, a metaphorical and rhetorical act that attempts to keep the black body contained in the categories of unsavory, unwanted, and un-American. King calls the black pain engendered by symbolic violence "blackpain." Blackpain occurs when the black body functions in literature and popular culture as a "metaphor for suffering, injury, and pain" that symbolically unmakes black people as human beings, as individuals, and as American citizens. In the eyes of those committing blackpain, because black people are held by pain's unparalleled grip, they can never be "true" Americans, virtually pain-free individuals who can help others transcend "the painful realities of unfortunate circumstances" because they are economically and politically able to do so (48–49). Read against this background, Gomez's notion of black freedom in *Gilda* is concerned with not only keeping the black body free of pain but also freeing the American imagination, black and nonblack, from the view that the black body is a representation of pain and un-Americanness.

According to Elaine Scarry, examining the body in pain is essentially an examination of how other people become "visible to us, or cease to be visible to us" (22–23). This means that a body's relationship to violence is an indicator of that body's value in society, especially in a consumer capitalist society shaped by racialized biopolitics such as the US. Looking at the role that pain plays in marking the black body in American culture, Elizabeth Alexander observes the following:

> Black bodies in pain for public consumption have been an American national spectacle for centuries. This history moves from public rapes, beatings and lynchings to the gladiatorial arenas of basketball and boxing. . . . White men have been the primary stagers and consumers of the historical spectacles I have mentioned, but in one way or another, black people also have been looking, forging a traumatized collective historical memory which is reinvoked at contemporary sites of conflict. (82–83)

As suggested by Scarry and Alexander, what makes black people in the US both visible and invisible is pain. On the one hand, the black body in pain becomes visible when there is an opportunity to profit from its presence. In this instance, having death be the eventual resolution of the pained black body is not desired because such an end would entail killing a means of making money for those putting this body in pain and, in some cases, for the black person who is experiencing this pain. Thus, black bodies in pain are only visible in America when they generate money, pleasure, and power for the producers and consumers of these suffering bodies (see King 44–46). This explains why the bounty hunter tried to rape Gilda instead of kill her— her pained body would be worth more alive than dead.

When the black body in pain is made invisible, on the other hand, it is because its visibility is no longer profitable and, more important, no longer a symbol of blackpain. This point is captured in Gilda's explanation of why she will remain connected to the mortal world:

> The inattention of her contemporaries to mortal questions, like race, didn't suit her. She didn't believe a past could, or should, be so easily discarded. Her connection to the daylight world came from her blackness. The memories of her master's lash as well as her mother's face, legends of the Middle Passage, lynchings she had not been able to prevent, images of black women bent over scouring brushes—all fueled her ambition. (*Gilda* 180)

Gilda's references to slavery, rape, lynching, and the Middle Passage—practices designed with the intention to produce, consume, and profit from black bodies in pain—suggest that even though blackness is an artificially contrived identity, it has been made real by the history of black pain. Even though Gilda has been a vampire at this point in the novel for a little over 120 years, she is still forced to pay attention to questions of race because the black body in 1970s America continues to be viewed and interpreted as a sign of pain, "a sign to be feared, hated, and avoided, particularly when confronted outside the protected arena of popular culture and literature" (King 29). For example, while contemplating Julius's lack of siblings, Gilda compares the production and consumption of black pain in slavery with that during the civil rights and Black Power movements. She reasons that while she, like Julius, is inspired by the progressive movements of the 1960s, the death of George Jackson, one of the Soledad Brothers, and Angela Davis's short stint as a fugitive were signs for Gilda that the "horror of slavery" yields "endless returns" (*Gilda* 180).[5] While the "returns" of slavery during

---

5. Angela Davis was the first African American woman to be on the FBI's Ten Most Wanted list due to her work on behalf of the Soledad Brothers and overall involvement in the prisoners' rights movement. George Jackson, along with John Clutchette and Fleeta Drumgo, were accused of killing a white guard at California's Soledad Prison. In August of 1970, Jackson's younger brother, seventeen-year-old Jonathan Jackson, attempted a one-man raid on a northern California courthouse to capture and trade hostages for the release of the Soledad Brothers. The shootout that resulted from this raid left Jonathan Jackson, a judge, and two prisoners dead, and Angela Davis was accused of supplying the weapons for this raid. Davis escaped and lived as a fugitive, but she was captured, spent over a year in prison, and was eventually acquitted by a jury (Hine, Hine, and Harrold 612).

slavery were pained black bodies, the returns of slavery in the 1970s were dead or imprisoned black bodies.[6]

Thus, Auerbach's claim that Gilda "shed[s] her identification with mortals" and "exists entirely apart from antagonism" to live exclusively among her "virtuous" vampire family (185) is unfounded because Gilda cannot, even if she wanted to, distance herself from black people or conflict precisely because violence and the black body are inextricably linked in American culture. Indeed, Gilda's frustration with the color-blind politics adopted by some of her vampire peers derives from their disregard for the fact that she still lives in a society where skin color is viewed as transparent evidence of how people think, live, and love, and where people are punished for behaving in ways that blur, interrogate, or transgress this so-called evidence. What makes color-blindness even more frustrating for Gilda is that nonblack people are largely responsible for why blackness matters and for why violence and the black body are linked in American culture. This is a lesson that Gilda learns from Bernice of the Woodard house.

In her explanation of why Gilda should not be "shamed" by the "creamy-colored quadroons" who treated Gilda and Bird as if they were invisible, Bernice makes the following observation: "What you shamed about is them folks thinkin' they white and they ain't. Thinkin' being nasty to dark folks is gonna help make them white. That's a shame alright. Not yours . . . theirs, so just go on 'bout your business" (*Gilda* 28). According to Bernice, although the quadroons, a derogatory term used to describe people with one black grandparent and three white grandparents, will never become "white" because they have visible traces of blackness, they assume that the path to whiteness requires "being nasty to dark folks." Thus, what Gilda learns from Bernice is that even if black people stop identifying themselves as black, they will continue to be black as long as quadroons, whites, and other nonblack people define them as such. This insight about blackness is

---

6. Jerome G. Miller notes in *Search and Destroy: African American Males in the Criminal Justice System* that "until the late 1970s, most criminologists accepted the proposition that racial bias was an important element to be considered in studying the justice system" (54). This changed by 1980s and 1990s, when the "war on drugs" began in earnest and when researchers started to conclude that "more blacks were in the criminal justice system because they committed most of the crimes. . . . Concomitant with these developments, we saw the reintroduction of the proposition that genetic racial differences might be a major contributor to criminal behavior" (56). However, as Miller shows, that proposition is highly problematic because, for example, "while African-Americans and Hispanics made up the bulk of those being arrested, convicted, and sentenced to prison for drug offenses, in 1992, the US Public Health Service's Substance Abuse and Mental Health Services Administration estimated that 76% of the illicit drug users in the United States were white, 14% were black, and 8% were Hispanic" (81).

what makes the multicultural conservative's call for color-blindness highly problematic—it ignores or downplays the ways in which notions of individualism, upward mobility, and assimilation have been and continue to be racialized in American culture as not black:

> One point on which Latino, Asian-American, women, and homosexual conservatives seem to agree is the desire, to restate the matter bluntly, not to be like blacks—members of a group that persists in pressing for collective redress from the government rather than pursuing the path of individualism, upward mobility, and assimilation. . . . If Toni Morrison is even partially correct in asserting that previous waves of immigrants have embraced a (white, middle-class) American identity "on the backs of blacks," then there is reason to fear that new immigrants will seek to replicate this pattern. . . . That some African American conservatives, a contingent that remains predominately middle and upper class, appear to follow suit—to assimilate on the backs of poor blacks—is doubly disturbing. (Dillard 182)

If the path to the American Dream has been and continues to be "on the backs of blacks," then it is also the case that audiences of black bodies in pain do not learn anything about the people experiencing pain; rather, they learn, among other lessons, how that body can be exploited to achieve the American Dream. As King writes, "the constant 'truth' about interpretations of black pain in America is that black people disappear while their bodies are constantly renewed as memorials to suffering and as tools for lessons benefiting systems of American acculturation" (9). Ultimately, what Gilda takes away from her time with Bernice is that there will continue to be a market for black pain and blackpain precisely because part of the process of becoming *American* is exploiting and terrorizing black bodies.

While Gilda is unwilling to discard the history of black pain from her sense of blackness, she does not let that history define who she is or what she should think, enjoy, or do because it can only lead to "soul murder," the moment when one's spirit becomes so broken by the pain caused by antiblack racism that he or she cannot emerge "safely" from it. Indeed, soul murder can sometimes engender a "hopelessness" and "death of desire" to such a point that victims or witnesses of black pain are reduced to being "members of the walking 'dead,' unmotivated and afraid (or, at least, unwilling) to engage life" (King 40). Soul murder, in other words, produces zombies, not vampires. Indeed, while the zombie and resurrection vampires, who will be discussed in detail in chapter 2, are both revenants, the zombie lacks control of its mind and body, whereas the resurrection vampire has free will and a free body. Thus, as a black staying-alive vampire, Gilda can never die of soul murder because her blackness keeps her connected to the mortal world and her vampirism provides her the tools to emerge safely from black pain. However, what allows Gilda to avoid soul murder is not just her vampiric strength, speed, and immortality, which give her the ability to subdue, injure, or kill all "beasts on two legs" (*Gilda* 67), but also her realization that one does not have to be a monster to be a vampire, nor does one have to be a capitalist to avoid black pain.

Karl Marx once noted that capitalists are "vampire-like" because they can only live by exploiting or "sucking" the "blood" of "living labour" (qtd. in Halberstam, *Skin Shows* 102). Although capitalism is different from earlier forms of social and economic organization, such as feudalism and slavery, it is, like its predecessors, "based on class exploitation, defined as one group (feudal lords, slaveowners, and capitalists) appropriating the surplus labor of another (serfs, slaves, and wage-laborers)" (Ruccio 33). Like Marx, Bird's explanation of fair exchange and Anthony's concept of the ghoul treat capitalism as a social and economic system that must be tamed because it produces monsters whose paths to profits are filled with pained bodies. For instance, the very first lesson that Gilda learns as a vampire is "fair exchange," how to "partake of life" while being careful "not to take life" (*Gilda* 49). Although Miss Gilda introduces this concept to Gilda in her pre-vampire life (45), it is Bird who gives clarity to this philosophy: "As you take from them you must reach inside. Feel what they are needing, not what you are hungering for. You leave them with something new and fresh, something wanted. Let their joy fill you. This is the only way to share and not rob. It will also keep you on your guard so you don't drain life away." Before Gilda asks for an explanation, Bird concludes with the following: "You'll move faster than anyone, have the strength of many. It's that strength you must learn to control. But we will talk more of these things later. It is better to begin before there is pain" (50). To avoid pain, as Bird acknowledges, Gilda must feed on the blood of others, but she must not cause pain when taking the blood of others; otherwise, she will become a monster. For Bird, a monster is one who takes blood from others without leaving them something of value. Indeed, since vampires are stronger and faster than humans, it is tempting for vampires to rob humans of their blood. This is why Bird warns Gilda that she must learn to control the means by which she satisfies her hunger—if not, she will become another beast on two legs.

Gilda is reminded of Bird's lesson during her discussion with Anthony about the difference between monstrous and nonmonstrous vampires. According to Anthony, there are many vampires "who enjoy the terror we can bring to others. They live as much for that as for the blood. . . . Some here are certainly [ghouls]. What else can we call one who thrives on ripping out another's throat, or on deceiving people into ruin or servitude. I would say they are ghouls" (*Gilda* 67). Anthony, like Bird, suggests that there is very little difference between the ghoul and the capitalist because both use terror to ruin people or subject them to servitude. This link between the capitalist and the monster is confirmed by Gilda's pre- and postvampire lives. For instance, during Gilda's prevampire life "on the road" after her escape from the plantation, she recalls what her mother once said about "white [men] wearing the clothes of an overseer": These men not only represent "danger," but they are "not fully human" (9–10). Indeed, the monsters that Gilda defeats in her vampiric and prevampiric lives are, as she puts it, "beasts on two legs" (67). Although Gilda remembers very little about the "beasts" she has killed over the years (e.g., the white overseer in Louisiana; the black pimp in Boston named Fox; and the "Hunters," twenty-first-century bounty hunters who are paid by the rich to capture vampires to rob them of their blood), she does remember their "preying eyes and the surprise when she struck" (134). As suggested by Gilda's encounters with the beasts on two legs, the "real" monsters in the novel and in everyday America are, as Miriam Jones puts it, the "racists," "rapists," "pimps," and "power-hungry rich" who "literally feed off others" (166–67). These are the people who tend to profit from black pain, the ones whom Anthony refers to as ghouls and whom Gilda's mother would describe as not fully human. Indeed, the monsters that Gilda has defeated in her pre- and postvampire lives all seem to believe that black women are easy prey and that exploiting their bodies is one way to satisfy one's hunger for profits.

Thus, in contrast to the black conservatives of early 1990s, who claimed that a "cultural revival of the Protestant ethic in black America" that promotes "vigorous 'free market' strategies" and requires "fundamental changes in how black people live and act" (instead of how all Americans live and act) could solve the social and economic problems that negatively affect poor and working-class African American communities (see West, "Nihilism" 18), Gomez suggests in *Gilda* that the conservative's faith in the market ignores or downplays the ways in which economic forms are racialized in American culture. For Gilda, since black women are the primary prey of America's racists, rapists, pimps, and power-hungry rich, promoting vigorous free market strategies within the African American community will not result in black freedom, but in black cannibalism, as symbolized by Fox, the black pimp who exclusively exploits black women. As Marx noted in *Das Kapital*, "one capitalist always kills many" because the capitalist's desire for and process of accumulating private property not only leads to the "expropriation of many capitalists by few," but it also "grows the mass of misery, oppression, slavery, degradation, exploitation" of wage-laborers (293–95). The critique of capitalism represented by Gilda's vampirism is unlike the "monstrous anticapitalism" of Stoker's Dracula, who disrupts "the natural ebb and flow" of money and blood that the capitalist, the vampire, and their victims rely upon by only taking and never giving (Halberstam, *Skin Shows* 102). While Dracula disrupts capitalism's ebb and flow, he also produces and consumes bodies in pain to satisfy his hunger for blood and capital. In this context, Dracula's fight against the defenders of capitalism is really a fight between capitalists. In contrast to Dracula's monstrous anticapitalism, Gilda embodies a critique of capitalism that is grounded in the idea of fair exchange, the idea that if you take, you must replace. Such thinking holds that it is possible to satisfy one's hunger without being a monster, without producing or consuming bodies in pain.

Since Gomez suggests in *Gilda* that what makes blackness partly real in American culture is the production and consumption of black bodies in pain, it would seem that the novel would have one scene in which Gilda is attacked because she is a lesbian. Indeed, when Gilda is attacked by the beasts on two legs, she is attacked because she is identified as black, female, or a vampire, not because she is identified as lesbian. According to Auerbach, Gilda's lesbianism and vampirism are "purged of aggression," "conflict," and "confrontation"; therefore, Gilda does not present a "threat to the established power." Moreover, this lack of confrontation "defangs" Gilda into the "paralyzing stereotype" of the "good woman" who "confronts no powerful patriarchs" and is "segregated from anger and power" (185–86). Implicit in that reading of *Gilda* is that the lack of homophobic violence directed at Gilda reinforces the view that black lesbians are outsiders to the black community and its history because their sexuality somehow puts them in less danger than straight black people. However, as the concluding pages of this chapter attempt to demonstrate, Gilda's notion of "a row of cotton is a row of cotton" calls for a full vision of black freedom that acknowledges that black lesbians have been and will continue to be what Gomez refers to as "uplifters of the race" (Gomez and Smith 54) and, therefore, threats to the established power.

## Homophobia and the Arrested Development of Afrocentrism and Black Conservatism

Marlon Ross reminds us that before the "open and autonomous culture of gays and lesbians began to form in America's urban centers during the late

1960s," there was already an "established and visible tradition of homosexuality" within the African American community (498). Similarly, Barbara Smith notes that "the cultural and political leadership of the Black community has always had a very high percentage of lesbian and gay men. If they want to destroy all Black lesbians and gay men then they would alter the entire history of the race. Though closeted in many cases, Black lesbians and gays have been central in building our freedom" (Gomez and Smith 54). In spite of this history, black conservatives and Afrocentrics embrace the ahistorical view that homosexuality is a "white thing" that is destructive to the African American community. For example, Asante claimed in 1980 that homosexuality "does not represent an Afrocentric way of life" (qtd. in Nero, "Toward" 401). In 1988, Asante not only associated homosexuality with "European decadence," but he also claimed that homosexuality "makes the person evaluate his own physical needs above the teachings of national consciousness"; therefore, "homosexuality cannot be condoned or accepted as good for the national development of a strong people." Moreover, by reducing homosexuality to the "African American male's psyche," Asante's Afrocentrism assumes that black lesbians do not exist and that the "real and complicated" issues that affect the African American community pertain only to men (*Afrocentricity* 57). This sexist and homophobic logic explains the exclusion of women from the theoretical foundations of Afrocentrism—it is naturalized as a sacrifice for the "advancement of the people." According to Asante, a "woman's time" is to "create" art, music, dance, and literature, while the "man's time" is to "produce" science, technology, and industry (52). Since Asante views Afrocentrism as a "science" (80–82), it is not a woman's job to spend her time engaging in the theorization of Afrocentrism; rather, her job is to focus on its implementation, to focus on becoming a creative implementer instead of a creative producer.

Similar to Afrocentric homophobia, as Dillard notes, "black social and religious conservatives share the widespread view among African Americans that homosexuality is essentially a 'white thing'" (142). Unlike Afrocentric homophobia, black conservative homophobia is primarily concerned with questions of political agency and religious doctrine, instead of questions of history and nation-building. Although there are some black conservatives, like Ward Connerly, who do not appear to have a problem with gays and lesbians in the conservative movement, many black conservatives, such as Elizabeth Wright, have "greeted their homosexual counterparts with hostility and invective" (142). For instance, Wright, who at the time of the following comments was the editor of the black conservative newsletter *Issues and Views*, argued in her 1997 article that "[homosexuals] should not be allowed to equate inborn characteristics of ethnicity with what is nothing more than a behavior pattern—a way of doing sex" (qtd. in Dillard 162). According to that logic, homosexuality is not natural, and therefore, homophobia is less serious than racism and sexism because the fear of gays and lesbians is a response to a group's choices, not its biology. In addition to their politically driven homophobia, black conservatives also espouse what Elijah G. Ward calls "theologically-driven homophobia" (493). For example, Joseph E. Broadus, who, at the time of the following comments, was a member of the Virginia Council on Equal Employment, claimed in 1995 that the appropriation of civil rights strategies by gays and lesbians is "an affront to many black Americans, who with their strong religious roots and traditional view of family stand against the normativity of homosexuality" (qtd. in Dillard 163). Comments like those made by Broadus point to the significant role that the Black Church plays in the "genesis," "legitimation," and "weekly reinforcement" of homophobia in the African American community (E. Ward 493). Indeed, such comments not only define homosexuality as foreign to black life, but they also give cultural, ideological, and spiritual legitimation to notions of masculinity in which being a "real man" means engaging in "bullying, misogyny and gay-bashing" (498).

In addition to problematizing the racialized biopolitics of Afrocentrism and multicultural conservatism, Gomez's prescription for black freedom in *Gilda* can also be read as a cure for the homophobia that plagues these approaches to blackness and freedom. In "Talking About It: Homophobia in the Black Community," a dialogue between Gomez and Barbara Smith, Smith argues that "being homophobic," like being a "rabid and snarling racist," is not a "healthy state" for people because it is a "sign of arrested development." Since there have been gays and lesbians "as long as there've been African people," black homophobia, like antiblack racism, is an irrational and ahistorical view of the "human family." Indeed, because homophobes claim that "a certain segment [of the human family] is expendable because of their sexual orientation," they represent those who have not "grown up" as a people or a culture (Gomez and Smith 47–48). Gomez suggests in *Gilda* that if homophobia is a sign of "arrested development," then Afrocentrism and black conservatism reinforce that arrested development through their support of the single-issue view of black freedom. The link between homophobia and the single-issue view is best illustrated by Gilda's explanation to Julius about why a black theater company in New Orleans "folded":

> Most of the men we marched with ran out of liberation ideas. They had a big dream about black men being free, but that's as far as it went. They

really didn't have a full vision—you know, women being free, Puerto Ricans being free, homosexuals being free. So things kind of folded in on top of themselves. (*Gilda* 170)

Frustrated by Gilda's critique of these men, Julius asks, "Shit, who the hell's got the time for all that?" Julius's question inspires a passionate tongue-lashing from Gilda:

> You think these companies breeze through life on righteousness? I had a friend, a brilliant woman, who devoted her life to a little black company, doing the scut work, the kind that's just got to get done and nobody's willing to pay for it. She figured the brothers would be ready when nation time came. She worked like crazy: grant applications, giving advice backstage when directors got stuck, and housecleaning when they said they were too busy to get to the theater in time. But when nation time came she might as well have been wearing a sheet! Grant money went to every brother in the place but not to her. A row of cotton is a row of cotton, so if you think she felt any different from how you feel, you haven't been really thinking. (170)

Julius's frustration with thinking of black freedom as something beyond "black men being free" highlights one of the central problems with the single-issue view—it defines the black lesbian as the "Other of the Other," one who is excluded not only from the possibility of being free in America but also from the possibility of being free in the African American community. As Shannon Winnubst explains, whiteness, maleness, and heterosexuality maintain their power in American culture by "erasing themselves as anything particular," by "silently" and "invisibly" parading themselves as universal, normal, and natural (6). Since Gilda is not straight, male, or white, "[she] is, in every way possible, the opposite of Stoker's Count, which is the vampire-norm"; therefore, she is "the opposite of the desired opposite, the Other of the Other" (9). However, Gilda is not just the other of the straight white male's desired other, but she is also the other of the straight black male's desired other within Afrocentrism and multicultural conservatism—the black queer man. Indeed, Afrocentrism's and multicultural conservatism's heteropatriarchal approaches to black progress, as symbolized by Julius's frustration with thinking of black freedom as something beyond black men being free, allows gay black men to become "uplifters of the race," while black lesbians are doubly othered. As Gomez puts it, black lesbians within the African American community "straddle the fence that says [they] cannot be the uplifters of the race and lesbians at the same time" (Gomez and Smith 54).

For example, while Asante states that black gay men "can be and must be tolerated" until the development of Afrocentric schools, schools that can "redeem" black manhood (*Afrocentricity* 57), such schools, tolerance, and redemption are not necessary for black lesbians because they do not exist in Afrocentrism. Thus, as Melba Joyce Boyd argues, Afrocentrism's rise to prominence in the early 1990s is not based on a counter-hegemonic explanation of or solution to the "chaos" that exists in black urban communities. Instead, Afrocentrism became popular because it provides a "conventional explanation" for why this "chaos" exists—the lack of an authentic black identity and the need for black male role models (26). Read in this context, Gilda's vampire family not only challenges the idea that heterosexuality, patriarchy, and procreation define the *real* family (L. Hall 401; Thaler 58), but it also problematizes Afrocentrism's sexist homophobia by offering a black lesbian as an image of resistance for black girls. For instance, almost a century after Miss Gilda decides to die, Bird decides that she and Gilda "should lie together" as lovers, not as mother and daughter. It is this act of desire, what the narrator describes as "not unlike lust but less single-minded," that "cement[s] their family bond" (*Gilda* 138–39). Here, as Thaler notes, incest functions as a "trope for alternative 'family' structures that returns in vampirism" (59). Indeed, the bond between Gilda and Bird eventually leads to parenthood. When Gilda decides to give "birth" to Julius, a heterosexual black male whose "vision of the future" is "fueled" by the black cultural and political movements of the 1960s (180), she sends a telepathic message to Bird stating the following: "We've finally delivered a brother for me" (194). As suggested by Gilda's transition from daughter to parent and sister, the creation and reproduction of the vampire family is more about choice than biology. In each stage of Gilda's vampiric development, Gilda chooses and is chosen to be a daughter, parent, and sister; therefore, these roles are not determined by Gilda's biological relationship to her vampiric mother, brother, or son, but by her ideological relationship to these people. Such an approach to the black family, as Gilda's transition from vampiric daughter to vampiric mother suggests, can lead to the normalization of the free black family, a family that, as defined in an article by QUASH (Queers United Against Straight-Acting Homosexuals), "promote[s] sexual choices and liberation rather than sexual oppression" (qtd. in C. Cohen 30).

This approach to the family also positions Gilda as a role model for black girls who, as Gomez puts it, were only given two images of black womanhood during the early moments of the post–civil rights era: "the well-groomed *Essence* girl who pursues a profession and a husband" or "the snappy baby machine" (Gomez and Smith 49–50).[7] In both cases, the *normal* black woman is the straight black woman whose straightness and blackness is confirmed by having a black man or having children. This notion of the normal black woman, as I suggested above, is repackaged as the creative implementer in Afrocentrism, as one who sacrifices her own interests to the will of the people and to the will of men, since men are the ones who produce ideas that she will implement into her everyday life. In this context, Gilda functions as an alternative to the *Essence* girl, snappy baby machine, and creative implementer, an alternative that does not require black women to define themselves via children, a man, or the people. Indeed, by depicting Gilda as a black lesbian who makes a "conscious decision to be out and have children," a decision that will prevent her from becoming a "long-suffering" victim, Gomez suggests that black lesbian mothers can function as "models" of resistance for young black girls, straight or queer, who are pressured to have children or marry a man to prove that they are "grown up" (Gomez and Smith 49–50).

Unlike Afrocentric homophobia, black conservative homophobia is primarily concerned with questions of political agency and religion, instead of questions of history and nation-building. For instance, influenced by the homophobic rhetoric of the Catholic Church and conservative evangelicals as well as by their own homophobia, a number of African American and Latino parents, activists, and educators in New York during the early 1990s believed that the multicultural curriculum recommended by *Children of the Rainbow* was being imposed on their kids by a white elite. For these parents, gays and lesbians are a group of "rich white . . . men" who are "over-represented" in positions of power and whose political agenda puts the struggles of black and other nonwhite communities on "the back burner." In the words of one African American parent/activist, "Gays and lesbians are not a culture; being lesbian or gay [should not] be a political identity. Racial and ethnic identity should be primary and therefore part of the multicultural education" (Lee, Murphy, and North 13).[8] Thus, the primary issue for these

---

7. For a content and contextual analysis of the images of black womanhood in *Essence* between the 1970s and 1990s, see Woodard and Mastin.

8. Besides some of the parents' existing homophobia, another reason why religious conservatives were able to influence these parents was due to the invisibility of gays and lesbians of color as "vital actors in the histories and cultures of our communities" (Lee, Murphy, and North 15). This invisibility was partly due to the way in which sex education was taught during that period. As Janie Victoria Ward and Jill McLean Taylor noted in 1991, when *The Gilda Stories* was published, most sex education programs in the United States isolated human sexuality from other human relationships by emphasizing

parents was not the naturalness or unnaturalness of homosexuality, but the racial politics of the homosexual community. Since the prevailing view of that time was that homosexuality was essentially the sexuality of rich white men and that multiculturalism was anything not dominated by whites, it is not too surprising that some African Americans would see homosexuals as representing the political interests of privileged white men. However, black homophobia during that period was not only a political issue, it was also a religious issue due to the Black Church's reinforcement of homophobia in African American communities. Even for those African Americans who no longer attend church nor embrace the religious principles and imagery of the church as adults, many of them have been so profoundly influenced by the church that its principles and imagery continue to shape their beliefs and practices (E. Ward 493–94). One of the principles preached by many African American ministers is that homosexuality is "unnatural" for black people because it is a "white disease" (P. Collins 108). Thus, even though the homophobia of the African American parents, activists, and educators who were critical of *Children of the Rainbow* was articulated in political terms, the ideology that supports that homophobia derives largely from the Black Church.

Ironically, the Black Church's heteropatriarchy allows gay black men to become uplifters of the race, while black lesbians are doubly othered, othered as women and as lesbians. As Gomez puts it, "there have always been acceptable places for gay Black men to retreat and escape (relatively speaking) from the danger [of homophobia], i.e., the choir queen or the Black gay man who embraces the white gay male community" (Gomez and Smith 54). Although several black ministers preach outright homophobic rhetoric to their congregations, a considerable number of these ministers who refer to homosexuals as "fags," "sissies," "punks," and "bulldaggers" are gay themselves (E. Ward 497). According to Rev. Juan Y. Reed, "I've been in churches where the preacher's gay, much of the choir is gay, and much of the congregation is gay, and the preacher's condemning homosexuality as an abomination, and nobody [in the church] thinks there's anything wrong with it" (qtd. in E. Ward 497). Thus, even in institutions that have been historically

---

the mechanics of reproduction over the "feelings, expectations, fears, passions, cultural values, and beliefs [that] affect sexual decision making." Moreover, these sex education programs were ethnocentric, culturally biased, heteronormative, and based on theories about the white, middle-class, male experience of adolescent development (62). Thus, by separating human sexuality from human relationships, these sex education programs avoided not only discussions of why people choose to be or not to be intimate with others or themselves, but also discussions of people who are not white, heterosexual, male, or middle-class and how these people view and express their sexualities.

homophobic, such as the Black Church, black gay men can become uplifters of the race so long as they choose to be "straight-acting" homosexuals, gay men and women who search for "opportunities to integrate into dominant institutions and normative social relationships" (C. Cohen 29). However, as Gomez warns, even if a black lesbian chooses to be a straight-acting homosexual, she would be prohibited from being a leader in the Black Church because she is a woman. This exclusion is noteworthy because, as Johnetta Betsch Cole and Beverly Guy-Sheftall suggest, it was engendered by the collision between the "more fluid gender ideology [and] dual-sex political systems" found in most West African societies and the "more static gender ideology of the West, especially Christianity, where a woman's place was more clearly defined as in the home and outside the pulpit." While there were a few black women preachers in the early days of the Black Church, black women "lost access to pulpits" around the beginning of the twentieth century due to the notion that God made women inferior to men, which helps to explain why patriarchy became "a protected modus operandi, a visible if unacknowledged tradition, and one of the most cherished and tenacious values in the Black Church." While black women have always resisted biblical arguments that called for them to be subservient to men, preaching continues to be an overwhelmingly male practice and discourse (106–9).

As a response to the politically and religiously driven homophobia of black conservatism, Gomez creates Gilda's vampire family as a vision of black freedom that includes women and queer folks being free and being leaders. However, for Gilda and her family to represent such a vision, they had to reject many of the principles and imagery of Christianity found in the Black Church. In other words, Gilda's response to the heteropatriarchy of Christianity is to "vote with [her] feet" (see Cole and Guy-Sheftall 113–14); that is, Gilda's vampire family represents her walking away from the idea that Christianity can attend to her material and spiritual needs. For example, when Bird began teaching Gilda how to read during their time at the Woodard house, she started with the Bible and the newspaper. However, "neither of them could see themselves reflected there," so Bird began to use stories from her Lakota childhood to teach Gilda how to write (*Gilda* 21). As suggested by Gilda's development as a reader and a writer, identities forbidden to slaves, Christianity cannot teach real freedom to people who are absent or are made absent in its sacred text. In fact, Gilda was taught by her African-born mother that Christianity is a religion for white people. For example, while searching through her trunk of personal belongings, Gilda finds the "rough cross" given to her by her mother. According to the narrator, "[Gilda] knew it was a Christian symbol although her mother had not really believed in their God. She had clung to the dim memories of the gods of her homeland. The cross was more a signpost. It marked a time in life, like the signs erected at crossroads" (95). Gilda is reminded of this understanding of Christianity at the end of the novel, right before she achieves real freedom and after she saves Ermis from suicide by giving her the gift of vampirism. While making their way to Machu Picchu, where Gilda's family is waiting for her, Ermis begins humming a gospel tune. Ermis tells Gilda that her mother was not the "religious sort," but she believed that gospel music was "pure" and made her think of "the history." Indeed, Ermis's parents treated "Steal Away to Jesus" not as a religious song, but as a "romantic ballad" that marked their time together as a couple and as black people in America (252).

In each of the examples above, Christianity is not thought of as a path to secular or spiritual salvation for black people; rather, it functions as a historical signpost of African American history, a signpost of when Africans in America became African American. Although Gilda acknowledges that the Black Church played a significant role in black people's struggle to free themselves from slavery, the absence of Christianity as a unifying ideology for Gilda's family suggests that Gomez is questioning the future of the Black Church as an institution that can adequately serve the needs of all African American women, since many of its churches continue to reinforce the single-issue view of black freedom. In this light, when black conservatives and other multicultural conservatives argued during the 1980s that poor and working-class African Americans could achieve the American Dream if they became *good* capitalists and Protestants, they were also arguing that this group of African Americans had to become *good* sexists and homophobes as well. In other words, Gomez proposes that the vision of freedom offered by black conservatism, a vision shaped significantly by the sexism and homophobia of the Black Church, is not freedom for Gilda and her family because freedom in that vision is straight and male.

Gilda's call for a full vision of black freedom can be read as a response to one of the problems that Afrocentrism and black conservatism share—they, like the black nationalist movements of the 1960s and 1970s, offer visions of black freedom that assume that the only ism that affects the African American community is racism and that straight black men are racism's primary victims. While the Afrocentric and the black conservative differ on the relationship between race and culture, both exclude black lesbians from their conceptions of black freedom and leadership by racializing homosexuality as white and defining *real* homosexuals as men. Therefore, as Gilda indicates in her tongue-lashing of Julius, to move toward a full vision of black freedom, the African American community must adopt the expression "a row of cotton is a row of cotton." This expression proposes that all black bodies, regardless of how they are identified, are the same in the eyes of those who seek to produce and consume black bodies in pain. In this view, even though Gilda is never attacked because she is a lesbian, she is a lesbian who has been attacked because she is black; therefore, she is, using Smith's words, "as Black as anybody ever thought of being" (Gomez and Smith 54). However, Gilda is not only trying to show Julius that black lesbians are authentically black because their skin color puts them in danger of being harmed; she is also trying to show him that thinking of black freedom as black men being free is an example of how black men can be the oppressed and the oppressor at the same time (Ferguson 130). For instance, when Gilda kills the white overseer, who is trying to rape her and return her to slavery, and the black pimp, who is terrorizing and exploiting the bodies of black women, Gomez is showing that black sexism is just as dangerous as white racism—both isms produce black pain. Thus, the expression "a row of cotton is a row of cotton" offers a vision of black freedom that is not concerned with the sex or sexuality of the black bodies in pain, nor is it concerned with the race, sex, or sexuality of the people liberating these bodies. Instead, this vision of black freedom is focused on the effectiveness of the strategies used to liberate pained black bodies, and, as Gomez suggests in *Gilda*, Afrocentrism and multicultural conservatism are ineffective strategies.

In addition to functioning as a corrective to the single-issue view of black freedom put forth by Afrocentrism and multicultural conservatism, Gilda's row-of-cotton theory also offers an answer to one of the questions that is at the heart of blackness: Does being black mean more than having a black body? According to Gilda's row-of-cotton theory, to answer that question requires acknowledging that being black and black freedom are separate issues. On the one hand, Gilda's theory argues that since all human bodies are black but all human bodies are not defined as black, being black simply means having what is considered a black body.[9] Unlike the notion of blackness championed by Asante's Afrocentrism in which biology determines ideology, Gilda's theory is a critique of the myth of race, the myth that ignores the fact that variations in human skin color and other racialized traits do not reflect significant biological differences, but gradations of the same. At

---

9. Because of the "one-drop" rule, the racist belief that one drop of black blood makes a person black, the color of the black body in the United States ranges from the very light to the very dark and all that falls in between. Although this belief has been debunked, most black and nonblack Americans continue to identify mixed-raced people who are part black as black, as in the case of Tiger Woods, Lisa Bonet, Mariah Carey, Lenny Kravitz, and President Barack Obama.

the same time, Gilda's theory is also a critique of the multicultural conservative's color-blind politics, which ignores the ways in which the myth of race significantly shapes the realities of those who are considered black and not black in America. Thus, Gilda's row-of-cotton theory of blackness is one that acknowledges that blackness is a myth that is treated as fact; therefore, the only requirement for being black is having a body that is defined as black. Here, since one's body determines if one is or is not black, the myth that black lesbians are either inauthentic blacks or inauthentic lesbians is beyond irrational precisely because all lesbians are not white and because one cannot stop being black because one is lesbian.

On the other hand, Gilda's row-of-cotton theory of blackness offers a vision of black freedom—as represented by her multicolored, multisexual, multigenerational, multicultural vampire family—that includes those who are not defined as black. Since Gilda's theory considers those who are not defined as black as simply black people who are not defined as such, black freedom is an ideological project to unify all black people, both those with bodies that are defined as black and those whose bodies are not. Indeed, since it is our ideas about bodies, not the bodies themselves, that make one black or not black, Gilda's row-of-cotton theory implies that there is more to black freedom than just black people being free. As suggested by her vampire family who helped her achieve real freedom, Gilda's row-of-cotton theory insists that the ultimate goal of black freedom should be the creation of a community, culture, or nation where bodies of different colors are no longer viewed and treated as transparent evidence of one's blackness or nonblackness, but simply as gradations of the same.

CHAPTER 2

# ANTIZEALOT ATHEISM AND THE ALL-AMERICAN BOURGEOIS NEGRO IN *MY SOUL TO KEEP*

I ARGUED at the end of chapter 1 that the Black Church in *The Gilda Stories* is treated as incapable of attending to the material and spiritual needs of Gilda and her vampire family because it reinforces the single-issue view of black freedom, the idea that the only ism that affects the African American community is racism and that straight black men are racism's primary victims. In that notion of freedom, black lesbians, unlike black gay men, are invisible and not assumed to be leaders or representatives of black freedom because they are women and queer. Thus, for Gilda and her vampire family, Christianity is not an ideology of black freedom, but a historical signpost for when Africans in America became African American. In contrast to Gomez's *Gilda*, Tananarive Due's *My Soul to Keep* (1997), like Stoker's *Dracula*, treats African American Christianity as a crucial component of black freedom. According to Christopher Herbert, a critical reading of *Dracula* must acknowledge that it may be the "most religiously saturated popular novel of its time" and that Dracula is "an emanation of the world of superstition and an image of a terrible menace posed by the superstitious mentality to decent Christian existence" (101). I intend to demonstrate in this chapter that *My Soul to Keep* is a religiously saturated novel that portrays the Life Brothers, a group of African immortals, as a threat to the Christian mentality embraced by those whom the narrator refers to as the "all-American bourgeois Negro," an example of the multicultural conservative discussed in chapter 1.

Like *The Gilda Stories*, *My Soul to Keep* revises the mythology of the traditional literary vampire to address late twentieth-century notions of blackness in the US by focusing on the relationship between an African immortal and a late twentieth-century African American. The immortal's birth name is Dawit, who was born in Abyssinia, what is now Ethiopia, during the early sixteenth century. As a child, Dawit was kidnapped by Muslims who killed his parents and sold him to a Christian nobleman who used him as a slave. When he obtained his freedom as an adult, Dawit converted to Islam, but his religious allegiances were, as described by the narrator, "fickle." For instance, Dawit killed Christians and Muslims as a mercenary, and his conversion to Islam was not based on a spiritual calling; instead, it was based on his desire to trade Indian silks and clothing (*My Soul* 58). Dawit's life as a trader and his belief in God comes to an end in 1540, when he meets Khaldun, who will become his immortal father. Khaldun, whose name means "eternal," became immortal by stealing and then drinking the blood of Jesus, what he calls the "Living Blood." Because Khaldun equates the consumption of the "Living Blood" with the story of Adam and Eve's consumption of the "forbidden fruit," he believes that the primary purpose of the "Life Brothers," those who agreed to undergo his ritual of immortality, should be the pursuit of knowledge (61).

In late twentieth-century America, Dawit has become Dr. David Wolde, a professor of music history who also teaches Spanish at the University of Miami. David is married to Jessica Jacobs-Wolde, an African American journalist and one of his former students, and they are the parents of an intelligent and beautiful daughter named Kira. In other words, as the narrator informs us, David appears to be just like Jessica, an "all-American bourgeois Negro" (*My Soul* 9). While David may look and sound like an all-American bourgeois Negro, Jessica, her sister Alex, and her mother Bea remind him that he will never be one of them until he discards what the premarried Jessica referred to as his "unusual blackness." Although Jessica Jacobs, the college student, was "absorbed" by David's "face" and "startling beauty," she also thought that he looked "unusual." She was "certain" that David was "black" because of his "rich clay-brown" skin and "tightly curled hair" that is "kinky if somewhat wispy," but his "forehead," "nose," and "lips" somehow made him look "nearly Middle Eastern, or some mix from somewhere far from the United States" (24–25). In fact, Jessica reasoned that David's beauty is the result of being Ethiopian, since one of her college classmates told her that "many Ethiopians [are] exceedingly handsome" (35). In addition to his beauty, Jessica's "history with black men" made David seem like a "godsend" (50). She describes the African American men she had intimate relationships with as "sloppy, adult-sized children" (33). Thus, Jessica welcomed David's unusual blackness because it gave her the opportunity to date and possibly marry someone who is black, but not African American.

While Jessica Jacobs was attracted to David's unusual blackness, Jessica Jacobs-Wolde becomes terrified by it. For example, one of the questions that is pondered throughout the novel is first posed in one of Jessica's dreams: "Are there good monsters, too?" (*My Soul* 75). The answer to that question comes to Jessica in a daydream, where her deceased father insists that she tell Kira that "there are no good monsters" (103). The warning from Jessica's deceased father foreshadows the moment when David fatally poisons Jessica and Kira in an attempt to keep his family together by making them Life Sisters. While Jessica emerges from death as a Life Sister, Kira does not, and the novel concludes with David returning to Lalibela, the stone city in Ethiopia where the other fifty-eight Life Brothers live, and with Jessica, along with her mother, her sister, and Beatrice, the daughter whom Jessica was pregnant with when David made her a Life Sister, healing the sick in South Africa.

As I noted in the introduction of this book, *My Soul to Keep* is the first novel of Due's *African Immortals* series, which includes *The Living Blood* (2001), *Blood Colony* (2008), and *My Soul to Take* (2011). Along with her first novel, *The Between* (1995), which has been hailed by some as "the first major commercial horror work by an African-American writer" (Guran par. 9), *My Soul to Keep* was nominated by the Horror Writer's Association for a Bram Stoker Award and received a 2004 American Book Award.[1] Although Due's speculative work has been described as "literary horror" (Glave 700), there is very little literary criticism on her work. However, the scholarship that exists provides some groundwork for understanding how *My Soul to Keep* addresses the question of whether there is more to being black than having a black body. For instance, Kinitra Brooks argues in her comparison of L. A. Banks's *Vampire Huntress* series and Due's *African Immortals* series that

---

1. *The Between* was nominated for Superior Achievement in a First Novel, and *My Soul to Keep* was nominated for Best Novel (Glave 695). Due is also the author of *The Good House* (2003), *Joplin's Ghost* (2005), and *Ghost Summer: Stories* (2015). She has coauthored, with her mother Patricia Stephens Due, *The Black Rose* (2000), a historical novel about Madam C. J. Walker (1867–1919), the first African American millionaire, and the civil rights memoir *Freedom Family: A Mother-Daughter Memoir of the Fight for Civil Rights* (2003). Due is also the coauthor, along with her husband Steven Barnes and actor Blair Underwood, of the Tennyson Hardwick novels: *Casanegra* (2007), *In the Night of the Heat* (2008), *From Cape Town with Love* (2010), and *South by Southeast* (2012).

Banks and Due "rewrite and revamp history by focusing on black women's bodies as sites of reality-changing power" (2). Addressing Due's *My Soul to Keep* and *The Living Blood*, Brooks contends that "Due empowers Jessica with a commitment to help her community with the gifts she bears from her body" (10). Similarly, Tonja Lawrence applies what she calls an "Africentric reading protocol" to examine the first three books of the series. According to Lawrence, "the names of characters, history, and acts of resistance [in the *African Immortals* series] take on added meaning that is apparent only when an Africentric reading protocol highlights Due's concentration on naming and power" (91). When this protocol is applied to Due's work, we discover, according to Lawrence, that "Due concentrates most of her authorial energy on the spiritual connections with West African religion" (104). Like Brooks, Sandra Grayson argues that central to Due's *My Soul to Keep* and *Living Blood* are "black women who become activists," who become "positive forces of social change devoted to helping the community" (73). However, Grayson's argument is based more on conjecture than analysis, and, therefore, does not show how Due constructs Jessica and the novel's other black women characters as forces of change (see 74–75).

While I am interested in Jessica's representational significance as an image of change and in the role that religion plays in *My Soul to Keep*, I am equally interested in Dawit's representational significance, since most of Due's speculative novels feature male characters and are set in the present (Thaler 15). Moreover, as Due noted in a 2002 interview, because the "memory of slavery is fresh in [Dawit's] mind," he is the "mouthpiece" for those aspects of slavery that "too many of us, blacks included, do not like to think about" (Glave 699). By making Dawit the voice for the unthinkable aspects of slavery, Due suggests that the all-American bourgeois Negro has either forgotten or moved beyond that history. However, Due's depiction of Dawit as a resurrection vampire from Africa who threatens the Christian mentality of the all-American bourgeois Negro suggests that he is more than just an unwelcome reminder of slavery's unthinkable history. I argue that Dawit represents what the all-American bourgeois Negro considers unthinkable for late twentieth-century African Americans: being an atheist and being African. Since a large part of being African American, as implied by Due's depiction of the all-American bourgeois Negro, has historically meant being a member of the Black Church, Dawit cannot be accepted into the African American community as is precisely because he is an atheist. For the all-American bourgeois Negro, Dawit's atheism, "a non-belief or rejection of a personal, supernatural god or deity" (Fonza 185), is evidence not only that he is "unusual" but also that Africa is a land of superstition inhabited by primitive-thinking people. I contend that such thinking is not only reminiscent of the *civilizing* discourse espoused by some nineteenth-century black nationalists, in which African Americans must *save* Africa and Africans to form a unified African diaspora, but it is also useless as a solution to one of the questions that haunts movements for black solidarity: Is there more to being black than having a black body? As implied by Dawit's critiques of theistic religions and the monocultural blackness of the all-American bourgeois Negro, the answer to that question is no. Thus, to achieve *real* black solidarity, according to Dawit's antizealot atheism, African Americans need to develop a multicultural approach to blackness and a unifying ideology absent of religion.

Since *My Soul to Keep* offers us the first resurrection vampires in African American vampire fiction, Dawit and the Life Brothers, I begin my examination of the novel with a discussion of Dawit's resurrection vampirism with a particular focus on the roles that rituals and deities play. Indeed, Dawit's conception of his resurrection largely explains why he is an atheist and why he breaks the Life Brothers' Covenant. Next, I analyze the ways in which Dawit's atheism complicates the all-American bourgeois Negro's assumptions about the role that religion should play in black solidarity. Finally, I conclude this chapter with a discussion of whether Dawit's antizealot atheism offers a viable solution to the paradoxical tension surrounding the relation between the black body and the meaning of blackness.

## Resurrection Rituals and the Problem of the Covenant

I suggested earlier in this chapter that Khaldun's immortality is a product of theft and death. He not only steals the Living Blood, but he also kills the man who performed the ritual that is required to complete one's transformation from mortal to immortal. Prior to becoming immortal, Khaldun was a nomad who joined a group of shepherds during the time of Jesus's crucifixion. After joining the group, they met another nomad, whom Khaldun refers to as the "dreamer," who did not follow the teachings of Jesus, but claimed that he learned in a dream that Jesus was "among the prophets chosen to rise." They all decided to attend the crucifixion of Jesus, and the "dreamer" helped Jesus's followers clean the dead body, while secretly stealing its blood. The vial in which the blood was contained remained cold for two days, then became warm at the time of Jesus's supposed resurrection. While the blood is necessary for resurrection, the dreamer informed them that it was inadequate to make one immortal. According to Khaldun, the dreamer "learned an incantation in his dream, a Ritual of Life for the Living Blood. He held up a vial of poison. Only through death, he said, could life return" (61–62). Implicit in Khaldun's transition from mortal to immortal is that the resurrection vampire lives in a world of rituals. Indeed, the Living Blood does not function as an elixir of life as vampire blood does in *The Gilda Stories*; instead, it is just one part of an extravagant ritual. Moreover, as suggested by Khaldun's path to immortality, for the Resurrection Narrative to be believable and the resurrected vampire to exist, "a great deal of faith in powerful magical intervention" is required, faith that our rituals can reverse the processes of death and decay (Cave 93). Although the "apocalyptic" and the secular versions of the Resurrection Narrative share the same goals, "the mastery of nature and conquest of mortality," they offer very different explanations for the resurrectionist's faith in powerful magical intervention. While the secular version contends that science is behind that faith, the apocalyptic version, the version that the Life Brothers and most traditional resurrection vampires represent, contends that a deity or some other supernatural force is responsible for the rituals that can bring the dead back to life (116–17).

What is also noteworthy about Khaldun's path to immortality is that it highlights the fact that rituals are always about control and transcendence. On the one hand, rituals are very often impractical actions that are designed to control our social and natural environments and to bolster the belief that "everything will be all right," that the necessary steps have been taken to avoid a particular threat. On the other hand, rituals also allow us to transcend "the smallness and frailty of our lives." For the resurrectionists, their rituals not only can guarantee life after death, but they are so powerful that they provide some humans the opportunity to "attain cosmic significance, to become one with their gods and so to attain immortality" (Cave 90–91). For example, the Life Brother's human-to-immortal transformation process is "highly rule-bound"; that is, it "must be performed by certain people, at certain times, in certain places, in certain ways" (Cave 90). When Khaldun transforms Dawit into a Life Brother, he follows the same steps that the dreamer used to transform him into an immortal: He invites Dawit to a holy space (Lalibela), convinces him to commit suicide, injects the Living Blood into Dawit's dead body, and concludes the process by reciting the Ritual of Life over the dead body. By following these steps, Khaldun develops the power to control the processes of death and decay. Indeed, by acquiring the Living Blood and the Ritual of Life, Khaldun usurps God's power to decide who shall be resurrected and who shall remain dead, as indicated by his decision to watch the dreamer die: "I had a vision that he would become a monster, perverting the blood to harm scores of men and make himself a god. After he drank the poison, I stood over him with the pouch of Living Blood in my hand, but I gave him none" (*My Soul* 62). Khaldun's refusal to resurrect the dreamer suggests that he believed not only that the Living Blood and the Ritual of Life were meant for him alone, even though the dreamer apparently received this information directly from God, but also that his resurrection made him one with his deity, since he is now capable of resurrecting the dead and determining a person's nature via his divine visions.

While it appears that Khaldun has become one with his deity, he later acknowledges in his description of his post-resurrection loneliness that such thinking was foolishly arrogant because God, not the individual performing the ritual or the ritual itself, determines who is cosmically significant: "I have lived much like a hermit for many years, asking God to forgive me. But He does not hear my prayers because I have stolen from one of His favored children. So, I no longer seek redemption. I seek knowledge instead, because knowledge is infinite" (*My Soul* 62). While Khaldun's loneliness leads him to forsake redemption, he still believes that God is the power behind the Living Blood, the Ritual of Life, and the knowledge that he seeks. Khaldun does not become an atheist after his resurrection or after God refuses to answer his prayers; instead, he continues to work at becoming one with his deity through his pursuit of knowledge. What Due seems to be suggesting here is that while religious rituals promise to make their believers one with their deities, they can never deliver on that promise because the believers have convinced themselves that they can never be one with their deities, even though their rituals are designed to accomplish such a task. For example, although Khaldun constantly reminds the "Khaldunites," the Life Brothers who are "convinced" that Khaldun is a deity, that "his gifts could be attained by any of them, given enough time and study," Dawit is the only Life Brother who is an atheist (95–96). If Khaldun does not see himself as a deity, why are the Khaldunites convinced that he is? The answer seems simple: They, unlike Dawit, do not believe that they could ever attain Khaldun's gifts, even though they completed the same ritual as Khaldun. Due's point seems to be that being a god means more than being immortal and having the power to resurrect the dead, and part of that *more* is being omniscient. By believing that they can never know as much as their gods, Khaldun and the Khaldunites give justification for their gods' existence. Indeed, if Khaldun and the Khaldunites thought like Dawit, if they believed that they can achieve the gifts of their deities, then what role would their gods play in their lives since they could become gods themselves? In this light, religious rituals are more than a believer's attempts to become one with his or her god; they are also designed to prove that this god exists and explains why things are the way they are in the universe.

In addition to living in a world of rituals, the resurrection vampire, unlike its staying-alive counterpart, is not concerned with re-creating the past or looking backward for utopian models of existence precisely because he or she has risen from the dead. Instead, the resurrection vampire is future-focused. For example, Jessica cannot always deal with David's "ramblings" about the past because she feels like a "moron," since her "knowledge of the world [is] limited to Spain sending Columbus to 'discover' America in 1492." She complains that although David is a "history whiz," his indifference to "current events, pop culture, and even racial issues" has created a "barrier" between them that is "getting harder to ignore" (*My Soul* 48). David's indifference has become so bothersome that Jessica admits to herself that she may "crave" the opportunity to "bond" with Peter—her white, closeted, gay coworker—because he, unlike David, "[gives] a damn about the things everyday folks talked about at the beauty shop and on their lunch breaks." As Jessica sees it, David chooses to live in "a world of books and jazz music," a world that makes him unable and unwilling to deal with discussions about contemporary African American politics and culture (49). Here, Dawit, like Gilda, is unwilling to discard the history of black pain from his sense of blackness, but he is also unwilling to let that pain define his future, as suggested by the reasoning for his half-truths to Jessica about Mahmoud.

When Mahmoud unexpectedly shows up at David and Jessica's home to warn David that Khaldun wants him to return to Lalibela, they began to argue as Jessica walks into the doorway. Jessica is unable to understand the argument because they are speaking in Arabic, but she knows that Mahmoud is not a former student upset about a grade, as David initially told her. However, before revealing the truth to Jessica, David tells her that Mahmoud grew up with him in the missionaries in Egypt. They had a falling out over his father's money, and he had not heard from Mahmoud until his unannounced visit to their home. When Jessica asks why he did not tell her about Mahmoud before, David says that unlike Americans, who "enjoy living in their unhappy pasts," he does not like to live in his. This way of thinking, as Jessica notes, is consistent with David's views on therapy and America's self-help television talk shows: "He derided the thought of most therapy, insisting that people should learn to grow past traumas and rely on inner strength to become reborn" (*My Soul* 163). These comments contrast with Jessica's critique of David as a history whiz who is unable to deal with the present world. Indeed, David's disengagement with contemporary America is due to contemporary America's disengagement with the present.

For Dawit, who has been a victim and producer of black pain, to live in the past is to live in pain, which can lead to soul murder. As I noted in the previous chapter, King defines soul murder as the moment when the spirit/soul of a person who witnesses or experiences black pain becomes so broken that it engenders a hopelessness that can reduce one to a member of the walking dead, those who have become unmotivated, afraid, or unwilling to engage life. Put in simpler terms, if one lives in the past, and the past is filled with pain, then there is no incentive to engage life. To avoid soul murder, as Dawit sees it, he must devote his energies to creating a future absent of pain, as suggested by his critique of television talk shows and his vision of life with Jessica if she became the first Life Sister: "He and Jessica could have dozens of children together—and, once immortal, might Jessica pass the Living Blood to their offspring, as Khaldun believed? What a blessing if that could be so! Their future children would be immortal without the price of the Ritual; lasting life without the pain of death" (*My Soul* 209). According to Dawit's vision of a pain-free future, one does not forget or dismiss the black pain of the past; instead, one attempts to rethink the ideologies and practices that allowed that pain to exist and that inhibit one from imagining a future of "lasting happiness." It is this line of thinking that appears to influence Dawit's decision to break the Covenant that Khaldun established with the Life Brothers—to avoid soul murder, Dawit must create, as he puts it, a "new covenant" (209).

In exchange for the gift of immortality, Khaldun asked each of the Life Brothers to make the following pledge: "No one must know. No one must join. We are the last" (*My Soul* 93). Therefore, by telling Jessica that he is a Life Brother and making her a Life Sister, Dawit not only violates the Covenant, but he also violates one of the golden rules that all immortality narratives share—immortality is not for everyone. For Khaldun, as indicated by the composition of the Life Brothers, all women are unfit for immortality. David's recollection of Khaldun's discussion of the Covenant explains why there are no Life Sisters:

> Khaldun had made the Covenant the clearest lesson of all. Passing on the Living Blood was a defiance against God, or Allah, or Yahweh, the Life Force who made the blood live. Large numbers would be dangerous to all, Khaldun said, inviting the scrutiny of outsiders. They might all find themselves imprisoned, studied, exploited. Moreover, any newcomer not first approved by Khaldun might be reborn as a monster to humankind.

> And absolutely no women could receive the blood, he said—because women might carry it in their wombs, passing it on to children. Immortals must not become a race ungoverned, Khaldun said. They would remain a select few. (93)

Khaldun's demand that women should be excluded from receiving the Living Blood presumes that women are not only responsible for the *monsters* in the world, but they are also more monster than human. Indeed, it is not the Living Blood or semen that can produce monsters, as Khaldun claims, but the mother's womb that carries the Living Blood. Thus, for Khaldun, to give women the gift of immortality is to threaten humanity with the emergence of an "ungoverned" race of monsters.[2] Implicit in that claim is that the Living Blood is also a gift of freedom, freedom from the limitations of mortal living and thinking. In other words, since the Agricultural Revolution, beginning approximately 10,000 years ago, most human societies have been patriarchal societies (Harari 152); therefore, to give women the freedom to transcend their mortality is to free their minds and bodies from male policing.

In addition to its problematic assumption that women could threaten humanity if they are given the gift of immortality, Khaldun's demand that women be excluded from receiving the Living Blood also suggests that God *himself* has made women unfit for immortality. For example, the three Abrahamic religions that Khaldun references (Christianity, Islam, and Judaism) contain sacred texts that encourage sexist beliefs and practices by evoking what Parrillo calls "supernatural justification for male supremacy":

> Islam's Koran states, "Men are superior to women on account of qualities in which God has given them pre-feminineness." In the New Testament, Saint Paul proclaims, "Let the woman learn in silence with all subjection. But I suffer not a woman to teach, nor to usurp authority over man, but to be in silence . . . she shall be saved in childbearing, if they continue in faith and charity and holiness with sobriety." Finally, the morning prayer of male

---

2. By linking women's bodies to chaos and monstrosity, Due implies through Khaldun that the doctrine of prenatal influence—the belief that *monstrous* births were caused by their mothers' imaginations—is much older than that which was dominant during Europe's Enlightenment period and is steeped in Abrahamic religious thought. As implied by the story of Jacob, who placed stippled rods before sexually excited sheep to make his ewes give birth to spotted and streaked lambs, the doctrine of prenatal influence as the cause of monstrous births had "divine sanction" as well as intellectual and scientific support (Todd 47).

Orthodox Jews includes the line, "Blessed art Thou, oh Lord our God, King of the Universe, that I was not born a woman." (433)

While Khaldun believes, like the passages above, that giving the Living Blood to women would be an act of defiance against God because the quest for immortality is a male quest, Dawit's decision to break the Covenant and replace it with a new one—"Love that which is constant, like yourself" (*My Soul* 209)—implies that lasting happiness cannot be achieved in a patriarchal society. Dawit's decision to include women in the world of immortals is a betrayal to Khaldun, the Khaldunites, and whoever created the Living Blood, but he seems to believe that allowing women, such as his wife and daughter, to exist in a world where their minds and bodies are free from male policing is more important than breaking a covenant with men. Such thinking helps to explain why Dawit is the only Life Brother who imagines the future as one populated by Life Brothers and Sisters and why he is the only Life Brother who is an atheist.

In her depiction of Khaldun's path to immortality, Due suggests that while rituals may promise their participants that they will become one with their deities because the power of the rituals comes from those deities, such a promise can never be fulfilled precisely because the deity, not the rituals, decides who is cosmically significant. Moreover, as represented by Khaldun's postresurrection loneliness and the Khaldunites' insistence that Khaldun is a god, the participants themselves do not believe that their rituals will make them one with their deities because if they did, they would have no need for their deities since they could become deities themselves. What Due seems to be getting at here is that if rituals are unable to make the believer one with his or her deity, then why does the believer continue to follow his or her religion, since rituals are "the physical manifestations of a particular religion or mythology" (Cave 90)? To be more specific, why is the all-American bourgeois Negro more like Khaldun and the Khaldunites than Dawit with respect to the issue of religion? Due appears to address that question in her depictions of Dawit's atheism and the all-American bourgeois Negro's African American Christianity. While the all-American bourgeois Negro treats African American Christianity as a solution to the Mortality Paradox and as an African American cultural practice, Dawit views the Abrahamic faiths and theistic religions in general as incapable of attending to black people's material needs. As Due shows in *My Soul to Keep*, Dawit's and the all-American bourgeois Negro's views of religion also shape how they address the question of blackness.

## Black Christianity, Black Atheism, and the Question of Real Tolerance

I have suggested that what distinguishes Dawit from Khaldun, the Khaldunites, and resurrection vampires such as Dracula is that Khaldun defers to God, the Khaldunites defer to Khaldun, and Dracula defers to the devil, but Dawit defers to no supernatural deity. Indeed, Dawit's decision to break the Covenant is informed by the fact that Khaldun, not a god, resurrected him and by his desire for Jessica and Kira to become Life Sisters. On the one hand, by breaking the Covenant and creating a new one, Dawit is declaring that the Living Blood and Ritual of Life are for men *and* women precisely because God cannot be the god of all humans if it is just the god of men. In this instance, Dawit is like Christianity's St. Paul, the apostle whose promise of resurrection attempted to resolve one of Judaism's main contradictions: the claim that Yahweh was simultaneously the god of the Jews and the god of everyone else. Paul declared, as Cave puts it, "through the death and resurrection of Jesus, [Yahweh] had sent his message to Jews and Gentiles alike, who were both now free from the old law" (Cave 110). On the other hand, unlike Paul, who would view Dawit's resurrection as an act of god, Dawit sees it as a direct result of Khaldun's use of the Living Blood and the Ritual of Life. It is Dawit's interpretation of his resurrection and the Living Blood that explains, in part, why Alex refers to Dawit as "The Brother from Another Planet" (*My Soul* 48).[3]

It is noteworthy that Alex's nickname for Dawit is "The Brother from Another Planet" because it suggests that if Jessica was not blinded by her desire for Dawit, she would realize that skin color, hair texture, and beauty cannot overcome the differences between her and Dawit. As Alex sees it, the differences between Jessica and Dawit are not only insurmountable, but they could result in harming Jessica. For instance, after meeting Dawit for the first time, Alex tells Jessica that Dawit is "running a game" on her and that he will "never really care about anybody but himself." Though Alex admits that Dawit is "fine," "intelligent," "a model father," and "good" to Jessica "most of the time," she also believes that he is "so different" from

---

3. Dawit's nickname is an obvious reference to John Sayles's *The Brother from Another Planet* (1984), a film about a black extraterrestrial alien, played by Joe Morton, who comes to Harlem after escaping slavery on a planet more technologically advanced than ours. However, unlike the "Brother" in the film, who receives the "active support of [Harlem's] black, Latino, and welfare white inhabitants" (Guerrero 45), Dawit cannot, at least in Alex's eyes, be a part of the African American family because his alien blackness has not been domesticated.

their father, who is seen by Alex, Jessica, and Bea as the epitome of African American manhood, that he should be distrusted. Although Alex could not give Jessica a "concrete reason" for her first impression of Dawit, she has held on to this image of him ever since (*My Soul* 50–51). Thus, while the term "brother" implies a familial bond between Dawit and African Americans that transcends history, ideology, and geographical boundaries, the words "another planet" indicate that Dawit's blackness is strange, foreign, out of place.

What makes Dawit strange in the eyes of the all-American bourgeois Negro is that he is an atheist. For the all-American bourgeois Negro, Christianity is not only the solution to the Mortality Paradox, but it is also "seen as a defining characteristic of African American life" (Mattis et al. 387). For example, during their first date, Dawit tells Jessica that he is a "misanthrope," a word that bothers her because it reveals his brilliance and her ignorance, not because he admits that he has a general hatred of humans (*My Soul* 32). When Dawit tells Jessica after their first night of premarital sex that he does not believe in God, she thinks to herself that "Christ might find him" (34). However, after several years of marriage, Jessica realizes that Dawit and Christ will never find each other. Moreover, if Jessica "trusted her Scriptures," she must accept that Dawit would never be "saved"; therefore, she would "spend eternity without him" (42). Jessica tried for one night to imagine what life would be like without believing in heaven, since Dawit is able to heal his body and spirit without medical or spiritual council, but she felt "swallowed by the vast barrenness" of believing that a "better place" does not exist after death (42–43). On the one hand, Christianity, for Jessica, solves the Mortality Paradox by promising the believer that faith in Jesus Christ as God or the son of God will guarantee a "better place" after death. Thus, while death is inevitable, it can be conquered by simply believing that Jesus's teachings are absolute truth, that he rose from the dead, and that heaven is for those who believe in his resurrection. In Jessica's description of why being an atheist frightens her, she alludes to a problem in Christianity's Resurrection Narrative—if she can be resurrected after death, why does she need to believe in a "better place"? Moreover, if her body is in the ground, then what part of her is going to heaven? These questions are answered, sort of, by Christianity's incorporation of the Soul Narrative into its promise of resurrection.

As I noted earlier in this book, the Soul Narrative claims that the *real you* is "immaterial in nature" and, therefore, can continue after your body dies. However, if one believes that the soul can outlive the body, then one must also believe that the soul goes somewhere after the body dies. For Christian theologians, heaven, as well as its counterpart hell, is where the soul goes once it leaves the body; however, these theologians have not agreed on where this extraterrestrial place is located or what it looks like. Historically, according to Cave, there have been two basic visions of heaven in the Christian world—the theocentric and the anthropocentric. The theocentric heaven, the heaven of Christian intellectuals and ascetics who borrowed the idea of the soul from Plato, is a paradise "centered on the adoration of God to the exclusion of almost everything else." In this heaven, carnality is despised, and "eternal happiness" is contemplating and worshipping God. In contrast, the anthropocentric vision of heaven is "one centered on the human." Like the Vikings' Valhalla and the Muslims' "Garden," the anthropocentric heaven is "very much like this world, only better." This is the heaven of milk and honey in which the saved will have a room in God's mansion where the departed are reunited with lost loved ones. Thus, it is not too surprising that the anthropocentric heaven became the dominant version in the Western world after the period between the US Civil War and World War One. As Cave explains, "the advent of industrialized warfare left behind millions of bereaved wives, mothers and fathers, and they had clear expectations of their religion: to give them their boys back." This would mean that for preachers to keep their congregations, they had to promote the anthropocentric vision of heaven (160–61). In this light, Jessica's belief in the Resurrection and Soul Narratives allows the dead Jessica to enjoy her afterlife in a better version of the world that she now lives in until she is resurrected to live in the "new earth," the city, as described in the Bible's "The Revelation of Jesus Christ," that descends from heaven after God sends the devil, nonbelievers, and false prophets into the "lake of fire" (Rev. 20:10–21:2).

On the other hand, since African American Christianity has played a significant role in African American struggles for freedom and against racial terrorism, Jessica's identification as a Christian can also be viewed as a cultural practice. For example, the turn from a theocentric to an anthropocentric vision of heaven came much earlier for African Americans than it did for the most of the Western world. As I noted in the introduction of this book, African American Christianity emerged as a response to white evangelicals who believed that white people had access to heaven on earth and in the afterlife, while black people were restricted to heaven in the afterlife. Thus, black church leaders preached a version of Christianity that addressed black people's material and spiritual needs by promising freedom on earth as well as in heaven. The adoption of the anthropocentric vision of heaven may help to explain why Christianity has functioned as a "liberating force" in the African American community since the 1700s, when "Black slaves publicly and politically declared that Christianity and the institution of slavery were incompatible," and why some of the first institutions that African Americans "created and owned" were Christian churches (Nero, "Toward" 407), even though resistance to slavery was a "global theme" in "New World Black Islam" during the eighteenth and nineteenth centuries (Turner 446). Moreover, according to Glaude, many Christian slaves in America believed that they were a "unique" or "chosen" people due to their relationship with God, a relationship that "allowed them to step outside of the master-slave relationship, which defined them as a mere extension of a white master's will, and to see themselves as self-determining agents" (Glaude 103). Since slavery was both a relation of "violent, coercive power" and a "hegemonic relation" in which "the consent of the dominated was constantly won and rewon," African American Christianity is a consequence of "ideological contestation" between slaves and masters, not just an "accommodation to slavery" (105). Thus, for the all-American bourgeois Negro, being Christian not only reaffirms the cosmic significance of African Americans, but it is also an African American cultural practice of resistance and freedom.

In addition to serving as a cultural practice of resistance and freedom and making African Americans feel cosmically significant, African American Christianity is supposedly more tolerant than other religions or Christian sects. Such thinking, as Anthony Pinn points out, is partly grounded in the idea of the Beloved Community, a concept that originates with Josiah Royce and was popularized by Dr. Martin Luther King Jr. and the civil rights movement. This community is not only the "final resolution to social problems" and "a signifier of ultimate, collective harmony and purpose," but it is also "framed by the love of God," which will inspire us to care about the welfare of others (Pinn 33–34). The idea of the Beloved Community is implied by Jessica's friendship with Peter, a fellow journalist and, apparently, a closeted gay man. Before Jessica spots Peter at a music festival "walking closely beside a bearded younger man," she claims that she already knew he was gay, since Peter is "intensely private," never uses the word "we" in his discussions of his life from the newsroom, and does not ever mention "a social life, a domestic life, [or] any kind of life." Jessica is saddened by Peter's refusal to come out to her after seven years of friendship, but she reasons that he might think that "since she was a Bible toter, she'd fling passages on Sodom and Gomorrah at him." However, the narrator is quick to tell us that "Christians got a bad rap for intolerance, and she wasn't like that." Jessica not only welcomes Peter into her family, but she also lives by a philosophy of tolerance that focuses only on "her own conduct, no one else's, and she trie[s] to live a good example if anybody cared to notice" (*My Soul* 20). The link that Jessica makes between her actions and her faith alludes to what makes the Beloved Community possible—it is composed of members who realize, through their faith in God, that one's actions are not the sole determinant of one's goodness or evilness, since humans are weak and frail, but also the intent behind these actions. Such thinking helps to explain why Jessica can welcome Peter into her family, even though Peter is gay and unwilling to welcome her into his—the members of the Beloved Community can always forgive others and themselves for solitary *mistakes* or *evil* actions because what matters most to God is that their hearts are in the *right* place, that the intent behind their actions is the building of a community where we live as brothers and sisters under God's rule and rules (see Pinn 35).

Given the history of African American Christianity, it is understandable why a black atheist would seem strange to the all-American bourgeois Negro or to most Americans. Although there has been a rise in the number of African American "nones," those who "clearly articulate disbelief in the basic premises of theism, including the notion of God" (Pinn 27), only a "scant 1% of African Americans identify as atheists" (Hutchinson, *Moral Combat* 24). However, there was a small but notable agnostic, atheist, or secular humanist presence in twentieth-century African American culture. For example, Jon Michael Spencer notes that there were Harlem Renaissance artists and intellectuals who were, "or perhaps seemed to be," atheists (e.g., Nella Larsen, J. A. Rogers, Alain Locke, Langston Hughes, Zora Neale Hurston, James Weldon Johnson, and W. E. B. Du Bois), but he argues that many of them were not atheists in reality, "as is often the case with artists and intellectuals who appear to be (or even claim to be) atheists" (454–56). Instead, they reflected the ways in which the "social gospel" of the Black Church shaped their works. As Spencer sees it, "the black churches that practiced the social gospel themselves comprised a component of the Renaissance, a component containing its own corpus of intellectuals," who were in dialogue with their secularist counterparts (457–58). Michael Lackey argues, however, that Hughes, Hurston, and Larsen did write "Touchstone narratives," which are the atheist's version of the traditional conversion narrative (15). According to Lackey, Larsen's *Quicksand* (1928), Hurston's *Dust Tracks on a Road* (1942), and Hughes's *The Big Sea* (1945) represent the "morphology" or stages of the Touchstone narrative: "The first consists of the apostate's acknowledgment that he or she has not been able to take the leap of faith. Next, the religious community tries to convert the erring infidel. After undergoing a harrowing experience at the hands of the community of believers, the apostate emphatically rejects the God concept. The final and most significant stage is the writer's analysis of the destructive personal and political consequences of religious belief" (121). What these narratives share is the idea that "atheism makes possible personal and political freedom" (141).

The link between atheism and black political freedom was also present during the Black Power movement. For example, as Ashley Lavelle reminds us, Eldridge Cleaver contended that "atheism and revolutionary nationalism were *sine quibus non* in any future program for Black emancipation" because neither the Christian God nor the Muslim one has come to the aid of black folks in the US (77). The notion that God does not help black people is also expressed in the plays of August Wilson, who once declared that "God does not hear the prayer of black people" (qtd. in Shannon 128). According to Sandra Shannon, who fears that Wilson's plays are challenging or totally ignoring Christian ethics, "the African American men who dominate Wilson's plays discard Christianity in favor of more flexible, man-made commandments" because they have been "consigned to a life of subjugation" (142). However, Cynthia Caywood and Carlton Floyd would argue that Wilson's Aunt Ester, an offstage character who is introduced in Wilson's *Two Trains Running* (1992) and has lived since 1619 as an embodiment of African wisdom and tradition, represents "an ancestral response to [the] demand, petition, and cry for divine intervention" by Wilson's African American characters (76). However, they also note that her statement "If you drop the ball, you got to go back and pick it up" was Wilson's critique of African Americans who are "always looking for something to come from outside of themselves in order to effect their salvation or change their condition in the world" (qtd. in Caywood and Floyd 74–75). What seems clear in this debate about the religiosity of Wilson's plays is that they, like African American atheists, question the tacit belief among African Americans that "blacks are by nature religious" (Lackey 146).

Like the African American atheists, or nones, discussed above, Dawit's critique of theistic religions not only serves as a critique of the myth that blacks are religious by nature, but it also points out that theistic religions are inherently intolerant and are, therefore, ill-equipped to foster real solidarity between and within groups. For instance, when Dawit tells Jessica that he is an atheist and reassures her that he is not an "antireligion zealot" because he is not "vain enough to profess to know absolute truth" (*My Soul* 34), he is also implying that all religions produce an arrogance within their followers by claiming that their image of God and knowledge of the world are absolute. As Dawit sees it, even though the members of a religion may claim that they respect the beliefs of others, they are ultimately convinced that all nonbelievers lack absolute truth and are doomed to an eternal hell if they do not convert. Such thinking explains why Dawit breaks the Covenant and why he could never convert to Christianity or any religion. For example, during an argument between Mahmoud and Dawit over Dawit's temptation to break the Covenant, Dawit recalls that Mahmoud has become a Searcher, a group of Khaldunites who monitor the lives of Life Brothers living away from Lalibela. The Searchers treat their work as a "religion" and strictly adhere to Khaldun's words: "As immortals, we are this planet's only true inhabitants. The others are only visitors, and our place is not with them. Their concerns are not our concerns. As the sun shuns the night, so too shall we be separate" (153). However, as Dawit emphasizes to Mahmoud, if the only difference between the Life Brothers and humans is the ability to not die, then the Life Brothers are nothing more than human beings with a gift: "We are humans, all of us. The Life gift does not make us other than human. We were born to mortal humans. We bleed and hurt like humans. We are immortal, but human still!" (159). In this instance, Mahmoud and the African American Christian are the same in that both assume that they have absolute knowledge about God and the world and that those who lack this knowledge are doomed to hell. Although the Covenant prohibits Mahmoud from creating more Life Brothers, Jessica's desire to convert Dawit and Peter is grounded in the same thinking as the Covenant: Immortality should not be available to everyone, only to the believers.

Although Jessica's relationships with Dawit and Peter are genuine and give the appearance that Christianity is a doctrine of tolerance, her belief that she lives a life that should be emulated paints Christianity (and religion in general) as an ideology of intolerance precisely because "real tolerance doesn't mean permitting other people to be like us; it means permitting them to be different" (M. Cohen 132). Stated in slightly different terms, Jessica's decision to marry and stay married to David, even though she believes that they will not spend eternity together because he is an atheist, and her decision to befriend Peter, who is considered by her religion a sinful person, are influenced by her desire to convert David and Peter. For example, while Jessica's friendship with Peter represents a critique of the homophobia preached in the Black Church,[4] she also suggests that Peter, like Dawit, needs to be saved from the "vast barrenness" of his life. However, Jessica's

---

4. As Nero noted in 1991, some Black Churches and their ministers have "adopted" heterosexist policies and practices (e.g., the practice of exorcism) that oppress black gay men in an attempt to "prove" the Black Church's worth to the middle classes (Nero, "Toward" 408–10). Given this background, the pain that Jessica feels as a result of Peter not coming out to her is a critique of the homophobia that plagues black theology in particular and Christian theology in general.

perception of Peter as alone not only reinforces the myth that gay men are doomed to a life of loneliness, but it also implies that the solution to his loneliness is to become a straight-acting homosexual by emulating Jessica, a self-proclaimed "Bible toter" who is in a heterosexual marriage and has a child. Like her decision to welcome Peter into her family, Jessica's decision to marry and stay married to Dawit is as much about converting him as it is about loving him. For instance, by concluding that Dawit is an atheist because he grew up as a Muslim child raised by Catholic missionaries who were "bent on converting rather than consoling" (*My Soul* 42), Jessica is also insisting that Dawit does not believe in Christ because he was exposed to the *wrong* truths about God and the world via Islam and Catholicism. Consequently, Dawit's disbelief in Christ can be solved by simply noticing the way Jessica lives her life as a "good example" of her faith. However, Jessica's belief that Dawit must convert to ensure their eternal bond as well as his salvation indicates that her faith prohibits her from practicing real tolerance.

Dawit's experiences as a slave offer another reason why he believes that theistic religions are incapable of real tolerance—they are at the root of Western racism. According to George Fredrickson, racism is a set of beliefs and practices that "directly sustains or proposes to establish *a racial order*, a permanent group hierarchy that is believed to reflect the laws of nature or the decrees of God." Furthermore, racism is primarily, if not exclusively, a Western product that originated, at least in prototypical form, in the fourteenth and fifteenth centuries and "was originally articulated in the idioms of religion more than those in natural science" (6). For instance, the growth of "religious racism or racialized religiosity" in Europe during the sixteenth and seventeenth centuries can be seen in the application of the Curse of Ham, the myth that may have provided the rationale for enslaving Africans regardless of their faith. According to this legend, Ham and his descendants, Canaan and the Canaanites, were punished by God to be servants of his brothers and their descendants because Ham saw Noah, his father, naked and mocked him. While the ancient Hebrews used that curse to justify their conquest and subjugation of the Canaanites, medieval Arabs who were importing slaves to the Middle East from East Africa shifted the curse's emphasis from Canaan to Ham, who was "widely believed to be the physical ancestor of all Africans, and the physical result of the curse became a blackening of the skin." In medieval Europe, the curse was applied to various Asian and European groups, but it was not thought of as a serious explanation for black servitude until the middle of the fifteenth century, when the Portuguese reached West Africa (43). What is noteworthy about the curse is that it identifies God, not humans, as the originator of antiblack racism.

Thus, it is not too surprising that race trumps faith in American identity politics. As Janet Jakobsen reminds us, "U.S. racial categories grew out of what was originally a religious distinction between Christians and 'strangers,' a categorization that differentiated between Christian indentured servants and African slaves" (202). It is the history of American racism that informs Mahmoud's refusal to travel to nineteenth-century America with Dawit. According to Mahmoud, "America will be worse than death for [Dawit]" because white Americans "slaughter" Native Americans and Africans for "sport." Nevertheless, Dawit arrives in America in 1844, and while touring Philadelphia, he decides to visit a slave plantation in the South to see "what became of the children of Africans he has seen sold, traded, and kidnapped over so many years," since it has been reported in Europe that American slaves are "pampered and content" (*My Soul* 136). However, when attempting to board a boat in Missouri to visit a plantation, Dawit offends a poor white male by simply being wealthier and more intelligent than he is and ends up as the slave of Lowell Mason, a gambler who has lost most of his wealth. What Dawit, who is called Seth at the time, finds repulsive about Mason, besides him and his son being "weak-willed cowards," is that he thought of himself as "pious" because he *gave* Adele to him: "If I had a way of thinking like my neighbors, I would take her for my own bed. Or leave her to Gil. But I'm a pious man, and I don't allow that here" (142). However, while "pious" white men like Mason do not engage in interracial sex, they do allow the selling and enslaving of children whose parents were forced to produce them by pious white men, as indicated by Mason's comments before he leaves Adele with Dawit: "I want her belly big by winter" (143). Mason's comments and actions are informed by the Curse of Ham; that is to say, Mason believes that black and white Christians are not equal in the eyes of God.

For Dawit, who has been kidnapped by Muslims, enslaved by Christians, and paid to kill both, theistic religions inspire their believers to dominate or exterminate all nonbelievers and all believers who do not believe in the *right* way or who do not *look like* believers. As Dawit discovered firsthand during his time as an American slave, since Christian doctrine was the theological justification for slavery in the US, where whites and blacks were not viewed as brothers and sisters under God but as masters and slaves, it is not only ill-equipped to provide an ideological basis for interracial unity, but it also fails as a unifying ideology for intraracial solidarity, as suggested by the all-American bourgeois Negro's view of Africa and Africans.

## Africa in the All-American Bourgeois Negro Imagination

Kevin Gaines notes that although many of the schools, churches, and other institutions established by northern free blacks during the eighteenth century bore the name "African," that name would be largely abandoned by the middle of the nineteenth century. Gaines writes that the "demands for U. S. citizenship, the dwindling population of African-born blacks, and an acknowledgement, at some level, of a black community 'whitened' by the sexual oppression of enslaved women" were some of the reasons why free African Americans during the nineteenth century "held an ambivalent attitude toward all things African." However, he also notes that "African" embodied "the stark conditions of exile" faced by African Americans as a result of being excluded from US society and being deprived of "an affirming connection" to their African homelands. It is, therefore, not surprising that the appeal of Africa would reemerge after emancipation, when African Americans were violently excluded from Southern politics (13). For Gaines, these shifts in African American attitudes toward Africa would not only continue throughout the twentieth century, but they also indicate that the appeal of Africa grows in times when African Americans are excluded from national citizenship and lessens when they are included (12).

Gaines's argument helps us to understand a late twentieth-century debate within the African American community over the term "African American": Should Americans of African descent be referred to as "African American," "Black American," or something else?[5] For example, Mary Church Terrell's 1949 call for the editors of the *Washington Post* and Americans in general to use "African American" or "colored people" in place of "Negro" was virtually repeated by Jesse Jackson in 1988.[6] Jackson declared that Americans of African descent should henceforth be referred to as "African American" because the term carries more "cultural integrity" than the word "black" (Norrell 320). Despite Jackson's claim, Kathy Russell, Midge Wilson, and

---

5. As Russell, Wilson, and Hall point out, American blackness has been largely shaped by a history in which Americans of African descent have been referred to as "Negro," "Colored," "Black American," "Afro-American," "People of Color," and "African American" (71).

6. According to Terrell, the word "Negro" is a "misnomer" because it does not "represent a country or anything else except one single, solitary color. And no one color can describe the various and varied complexions in our group" (548). Moreover, Terrell suggests that the word "Negro" also implies that Americans of African descent are not really American: "It is a great pity that the word 'Negro' was not outlawed in the Emancipation Proclamation as it certainly should have been. After people have been freed, it is a cruel injustice to call them by the same name they bore as slaves" (549).

Ronald Hall argued in the early 1993 that the term "African American" may be "politically correct," but it is not embraced by most of the people it describes. As an example, they reference a 1991 survey of 759 Americans of African descent in which "72 percent reported that they still preferred to be called Black, while only 15 percent wanted to be called African American. The remaining 13 percent were undecided or preferred Afro-American or even Negro." One of the main reasons why many of the respondents embraced the term "Black" more than "African American" is that the latter "puts Africa before America," even though America is the "most immediate homeland" of Americans of African descent (71).[7] Although those who prefer "African American" might argue that the term is just a shortened version of "American of African descent," the all-American bourgeois Negro would contend that the term is a lie because it only applies to someone like Dawit, a person from the African continent who has voluntarily immigrated to America. Thus, the narrator's choice of "Negro" instead of "black" or "African American" in the description of Jessica as an all-American bourgeois Negro suggests that this African American privileges her Americanness over her Africanness. However, it is not shame of being African that makes all-American bourgeois Negroes distance themselves from Africa; rather, it is a response to the reality that all native-born black people in America have been, on some level, physically and/or ideologically "whitened."

What is also shaping the all-American bourgeois Negro view of Africa is religious bias. Indeed, Bea views Africa and Africans in the same way that Johnathan Harker views Transylvania's Gypsies and Transylvania itself—both are "without religion, save superstition" (Stoker 49). For example, after discovering that Jessica is planning to move to Africa with Dawit, Bea warns Jessica to be "careful" because the "laws" in a "new place" (i.e., Africa) will not protect her; therefore, Dawit could take Kira away from her (*My Soul* 220). When Bea gets word that Jessica is attending Bible class, something that the adult Jessica rarely does, Bea asks Jessica if Dawit is "taking [her] to one of those Jim Jones cults" (222). While Bea's assumptions about Africa

---

7. For example, in his 1990 song "Tales from the Darkside," Ice Cube criticizes African Americans who "wanna free Africa" while his "homeboy" in urban America has just died because of a bad drug deal. Similarly, Dr. Dre states in his 1992 song "Let Me Ride" that gangsters do not wear or care about "[African] medallions, dreadlocks, or black fists" because what they symbolize are irrelevant to the "street[s]" of America, where the gangsters make their living. Even the early Afrocentrists, as Gilroy has pointed out, developed a concept of blackness that excluded contemporary Africa and was America-centered ("Family Affair" 197). What the examples above suggest is that by the end of the twentieth century, many African Americans began to develop a notion of blackness in which Africa has very little influence.

and Africans are grounded in her distrust of Dawit, they are very similar to those embraced by white Christians who supported slavery. As Katie Geneva Cannon notes,

> North American Christians credited themselves with weaning Africans of savage barbarity. Their joy in converting Africans was that they were giving to the "heathens" elements of Christian civilization. Being enslaved in a Christian country was considered advantageous to Africans' physical, intellectual, and moral development. Slavery exposed Africans to Christianity, which made them better servants of God and better servants of men. (416)

Given this historical backdrop, the term "cult," as uttered by Bea, does the ideological work that the word "fundamentalism" does in contemporary American culture by "positing some 'religions' as reasonable and others as threatening" (Jakobsen 204). What makes a religion or any belief system reasonable or threatening, in this context, is its ability or inability to "see the light of Christianity" (202). Thus, Bea's use of the word "cult" serves as a warning to Jessica: Africa is a land without Christianity's "light"; therefore, it is a place for African Americans to visit, but not to live.

While Jessica and Alex are not nearly as extreme as Bea, they do share some of her views of Africa. As I noted earlier in this chapter, Jessica's knowledge of world history begins with Columbus coming to the Americas in 1492, and her knowledge of that history is expanded only through her marriage to Dawit. Since Jessica's baseline knowledge of world history was one in which Africa is on the margins, it is not too surprising that she sees Africa as unsafe and unfamiliar. For example, when Dawit proposes the idea that the Wolde family should take a trip abroad to visit France and parts of Africa, Jessica is excited about the opportunity. However, while she believes that "Europe had culture, variety, freshness, and Africa even more" (*My Soul* 147), she also felt that Africa is strikingly different from the US or France. For Jessica, traveling to Africa, especially to Ethiopia, is traveling to an "exotic" place, while Alex describes Miami as "safe," "comfortable," but "boring." Moreover, even though Jessica and Alex have never been to France and do not speak French, Alex suggest that they are *closer* to France than Africa: "But, heck, James Baldwin went to France. All the writers go to France. Maybe it's a rite of passage for you" (150–51). Even though there is a history of African American artists and intellectuals spending time in parts of Africa (e.g., Nina Simone, Maya Angelou, Malcolm X, W. E. B. Du Bois, Richard Pryor, and recently, Dave Chappelle), Alex suggests that late twentieth-century African Americans are more familiar with French culture than African cultures. Even though Alex has been "talking about" traveling to South Africa since Nelson Mandela's election as president and has an application in her office drawer to direct a clinic in a South African township, she has yet to go because she needs "somebody to carry [her] tired butt out of here, to spur [her] on" (150–51). In other words, although Alex has the desire and opportunity to spend time on the continent, no one in her family or in the African American community has been willing to travel with her or has encouraged her to go. Apparently, this all changes once Jessica becomes a Life Sister and moves to South Africa with Alex and Bea to open a children's medical clinic, where they use Jessica's blood to heal children with life-threatening diseases.

Some have read Jessica's move to Africa as a sign of change in her ideas about home and community. For example, Grayson contends that Jessica's clinic is a symbol of her "activism" and her "journey of discovery." She not only uses her blood to heal others, but she also "defines her role as an immortal, a status she neither wants nor seeks, but one that is forced upon her." Instead of using her supernatural abilities for selfish ends, as Dawit does, "Jessica focuses on how she can help others" (73–75). Similarly, Tonja Lawrence argues that Jessica, like Dawit, undergoes a transformation in the novel, "a change of attitude and perspective by coming to realize her connection to Africa, not as an academic notion but as a personal journey that teaches her the benefits of cooperative socialism and community responsibility." Thus, as Lawrence continues, "returning to Africa allows Jessica to heal emotionally and spiritually, empowering her to become a meaningful contributor to the global village" (103). This connection to her roots, according to Brooks, is one way Due empowers Jessica to realize that her body is a site of "reality-changing power" that can help "her community." For Brooks, Jessica's willingness to use the blood to help those with the least amount of power in society is not done to satisfy "any need for reverence, but because of a necessity to serve" (10). Moreover, by foregrounding the experiences of an African American woman who is grappling with her faith, Due's portrayal of Jessica challenges the "standard and often patriarchal accounts of African American religion,"[8] what Jacquelyn Grant refers to as one of the

---

8. Glaude notes that since the 1960s, there have been three major trends in Black theology in America: "classical black theology" that begins with the work of James Cone; the Afrocentric "narrative turn" as expressed by the works of Dwight Hopkins and Peter Paris; and the works of black women theologians such as Katie Geneva Cannon, Jacqueline Grant, Evelyn Brooks Higginbotham, and Delores Williams. "By turning to the historical roles of black women in the religious life of black America," according to Glaude, "womanist theologians and historians unsettle the standard and often patriarchal accounts of African American religion by emphasizing and foregrounding the

"injustices" of Black theology—"treat[ing] Black women as if they were invisible creatures who are on the outside looking into the Black experience, the Black Church, and the Black theological enterprise" (430).[9] In this light, Due's depiction of Jessica as an African American woman grappling with her faith can be read as a reminder to the Black Church and the communities that it serves that there is a great deal to be learned from black Christian women about faith, injustice, and activism inside and outside the African American community.

While I believe that Jessica's activism is genuine, I do not believe that it is the result of a change in her ideas about Africa. Indeed, Due's depiction of Jessica in South Africa suggests that Jessica retains her all-American bourgeois Negro view of Africa because the all-American bourgeois Negro represents African salvation. For instance, while riding in a cab to the clinic, Dawit, who has been living in Lagos, Nigeria, since Kira's death, is holding in his hands an article about the clinic whose headline reads "Miracle Workers." When Dawit asks the cab driver if the clinic is organized by the government, the cab driver responds with the following: "The government! Don't talk crazy. The government clinic is to the east. The only miracle at that clinic is when they have enough supplies. Of course, it's less crowded now because no one takes their children there. All the children go to the clinic run by the Americans." Due to the success of the clinic, according to the article, it has become a "folk symbol of promise" among black South Africans (*My Soul* 333–34). Moreover, Jessica has become a figure to be worshipped, as captured by Dawit's description of her: "She seemed to glide rather than walk, her step was so graceful, and she wore a striking white head wrap and long white dress, probably provided by a local dressmaker. . . . No wonder they worship her, he thought. He, too, wanted to drop to his knees before her" (338). The significance of South Africans "worshipping" Jessica and viewing her clinic as a "symbol of promise" is that these images position the all-American bourgeois Negro, not Africans, as Africa's savior. The fact that the Life Brothers, who are all African and incredibly knowledgeable, do not seek to help African countries solve their socioeconomic problems implies that they are not only selfish and ethnocentric but also incapable of

---

experiences of black women. They do so, however, in relation to a culture that is not simply racist but sexist as well—a challenge that implicates white *and* black America" (70–71).

9. As Grant sees it, since black women, as of 2000, represent over 50 percent of the African American community and more than 70 percent of the Black church, "the fact that Black theology does not include sexism specifically as one of those injustices . . . suggests that the theologians do not understand sexism to be one of the oppressive realities of the Black community" (428).

being symbols of promise for Africa. Moreover, the differences between the government clinic, which is in the "east" and whose only miracles are having enough supplies to treat patients, and Jessica's clinic, which is located in the west and whose goal is to give South Africa's black children a "chance to live" (340), suggest that Africans need to look to the West for how to bring hope to Africa.

Looking westward and becoming Western, according to the novel, requires Africans to do away with *superstition* and become Protestant. For instance, while the South Africans believe, as Dawit tells Jessica, that she is "magic," she sees herself as being "blessed" (*My Soul* 339–40). The difference between the terms "magic" and "blessed" is similar to Bea's distinction between a cult and a religion—"magic" represents an unreasonable and threatening belief system, while "blessed" represents the light of Christianity. Furthermore, the novel ends with Jessica departing early from the clinic's New Year's Eve party and retreating to her bedroom to do something she has not done since Kira's death: pray and read passages from the Bible. However, as Jessica thinks to herself, "if the answers weren't in the Scriptures, maybe she could find them in herself, in her heart. She was part of something. Her new baby, this remarkable first child of the Living Blood, was a part of it too" (346). While it appears that Jessica is questioning her faith in Christianity, the fact that she sees herself as blessed and not magic or cursed indicates that she sees her immortality as God's work. In this way, Jessica is like Khaldun in that both continue to remain true to their Abrahamic faiths, even though a human, not God, made them immortal. Thus, while Lawrence contends, as I noted earlier in this chapter, that "Due concentrates most of her authorial energy on the spiritual connections with West African religion," Jessica's interpretation of her immortality in *My Soul to Keep* suggests that Due's "authorial energy" is directed toward the reaffirmation of African American Christianity. Although the Life Brothers once jokingly referred to Dawit as "Ogun: Iron Spirit, warrior, lonely self-exile" (39) and he refers to himself as Egungun, "the face of death" (313), these deities are not associated with Jessica, Alex, or Bea, who would consider such deities as the products of superstition.

Given Due's depictions of Jessica, Alex, and Bea, one could argue that the all-American bourgeois Negro is a contemporary version of the nineteenth-century black nationalists who believed that Africans needed weaning from their alleged barbarity. According to Tunde Adeleke, while early nineteenth-century black nationalists, such as Paul Cuffee and Lott Cary, "acknowledged their African roots, expressed concern for Africa, and proposed schemes for the economic elevation of Africa" (516), they also made it clear that they were not African and were glad that they were not in Africa. For example, while Cary once defined himself as "an African," he also stated in his 1821 "farewell sermon," given before his trip to Africa, that he wanted to "preach to the poor Africans the way of life and salvation. I don't know what may befall me, whether I may find a grave in the ocean, or among the *savage men, or among the savage wild beasts on the coast of Africa*" (qtd. in Adeleke 516). Moreover, "golden age" black American nationalists (e.g., Martin Delany, Alexander Crummell, and Henry McNeal Turner), who emerged in the second half of the nineteenth century, "felt compelled to prove to the Europeans how distant and different they were from Africans." Some even made the disturbing argument that what distinguished African Americans from Africans is that the former became "civilized" through enslavement and, therefore, African Americans were ready for the "task of civilizing 'primitive' Africa" (518–21). While Jessica is not nearly as extreme as the nineteenth-century black nationalists mentioned above, her view of herself as a "blessed" person who has been granted the gift of healing due to her belief in Christ's teachings and resurrection does suggest that she believes that the all-American bourgeois Negro, not Africans or even the Life Brothers, is best equipped to *save* Africa.

Considering the all-American bourgeois Negro's view of Africa, it is easy to see why Dawit does not find Christianity or any other theistic religion useful as a unifying ideology. Not only do such religions proclaim that they and only they contain absolute truths about God and the world, but they also encourage their followers to dominate, exterminate, or convert all who are not like them. Moreover, by arguing that theistic religions are ill-equipped to practice real tolerance, Dawit is also arguing that it is possible to develop a concept of black solidarity that is absent of religion. As an atheist who is not an antireligion zealot, Dawit is able to love and marry Jessica without the need to change her belief system. What allows Dawit to love Jessica as she is is the same thing that allows the Life Brothers to be brothers—the discovery of a shared goal that transcends religious differences. For example, although the group of men who would become Life Brothers represented various ages, faiths, cultures, and skills, what brought this group together, as Khaldun explains, was their hunger for knowledge, a hunger that had not been satiated by the sacred texts of their religions: "Your thirst for knowledge is the magnet that brings you to me. It is your brotherhood. You seek all knowledge, and all knowledge you shall attain" (*My Soul* 59–60). For Khaldun, the only way for there to be brotherhood among the Life Brothers was to remove religion as a basis of solidarity because their religions did not bring them to Khaldun, but their desire for knowledge. Similarly, Dawit believes that his union with Jessica is not due to a deity's plan or test; rather, it is their love for each other, a love that seems to transcend Dawit's atheism and Jessica's Christianity. As he tells Jessica before he shows her that he can return from the dead without the help of science or a deity, "our faith in each other, and our love, will be our light on this path" (186). Thus, unlike Jessica, whose religion teaches her that her love for Dawit cannot be eternal because he is an atheist, Dawit is able to love Jessica unconditionally and eternally because he has no deity to please.

By calling for a concept of black solidarity that is absent of religion, Dawit can be read as attempting to shift the debates about religion in the African American community from questions focused on the differences between the religious and the secular or between *right* and *wrong* religions to questions that ask how a religion or the term "religion" has been and continues to be used in American culture to shape social relations and practices (Jakobsen 204). As Dawit sees it, focusing on the ways in which a religion shapes social relations and practices, the all-American bourgeois Negro would realize that humans, not gods, are responsible for what happens in our lives and in the lives of others: "I've seen too much to believe God has any hand in what goes on in this world" (*My Soul* 34). It is this line of reasoning that convinces Dawit that theistic religions are lies of disempowerment.

## Why Cower to Imaginary Guardians or Tormentors?

When Alex discovers that Dawit's blood contains "Supercells" that can heal people of any deadly virus or bacterium, she tells Jessica that Dawit's blood is an example of "God's work," not the "work of man"; therefore, her advice to Jessica is to "keep God close to him." By keeping God close to Dawit, according to Alex, Dawit will one day do "the work he was born to do," work that involves using his blood to heal the sick (*My Soul* 248). Similarly, when Jessica witnesses Dawit's resurrection from what the Life Brothers refer to as "The Cleansing," a variation of hara-kiri, she tells him that his resurrection is God's work: "You have to say thank you to God, David. You told me we'd both see a miracle, and we did. You can't see a miracle without saying thank you. That's all He asks. That's all" (196). In contrast to Alex, Jessica, and even Khaldun, Dawit views the Living Blood as a gift not from God, but from nature. As he sees it, the Life Brothers could "devise a half-dozen explanations for the Living Blood's regenerative properties" (95). The difference between Dawit's and the all-American bourgeois

Negro's responses to the Living Blood, as Due explains in an interview, is interpretation:

> Jessica and Dawit have so much more actual evidence of God's miraculous nature than we do. If I were Jessica, I would be that much more convinced of Christ's divinity, and certainly that much more convinced that there is much more to this world than we understand. Dawit has the same information—perhaps more—but he has chosen to file it in a place in his consciousness that separates the so-called "miracle" from true evidence of God, much in the way a scientist might assume that there is a scientific explanation, not a divine explanation, for any visible manifestation. (Glave 702)

According to Due, Dawit's resurrection and the Living Blood are "actual evidence" of God's existence and power, but Dawit has "chosen" to question the divine origins of that evidence. While Due states in the interview that Dawit's scientific outlook is the reason he questions the divinity of his resurrection and the Living Blood, her depiction of Dawit's atheism in the novel offers a more complex explanation.

One of the reasons Dawit finds it difficult to believe that a deity exists is that Khaldun, not God, Allah, Yahweh, or Satan, made him immortal. It is, therefore, noteworthy that Dawit is not a Khaldunite because it explains why he questions the veracity of the story about the Living Blood's origin: "The storyteller whom Khaldun met those many centuries ago may have lied about the blood's origin from the start. Or, perhaps Khaldun had fabricated it all. Who could prove that Khaldun himself was not the only source?" Moreover, since Khaldun did not offer heaven as a goal to strive for because "[his] knowledge was only of the world," Dawit concluded that heaven is a "lie" (*My Soul* 95). Implicit in Dawit's commentary is that if Khaldun has the power to bring the dead back to life, then gods, devils, and the religions that give them life serve no purpose for humans, save for providing comforting answers to the Mortality Paradox. This is an argument that even Jessica concedes has validity: "Maybe David had a point. Religion was a crutch, a way people rationalized away their pain in life, like the slaves yearning for a better existence. A denial. When there is no fear of death, David had told her once, there is no need for religion" (43). While the all-American bourgeois Negro would argue that faith in Christ has removed the fear of death from the African American Christian mind because it guarantees a better place after death, Dawit would contend that faith in heaven does not mean that heaven exists. Even though Dawit will never know for certain if heaven is truly a lie because he cannot die, he is certain that the all-American bourgeois Negro and even Khaldun cannot provide creditable evidence to prove otherwise. Thus, it is the uncertainty of God's existence that explains Dawit's disgust with the thought of "cower[ing] before an invisible God like a primitive who expects lightning bolts to be flung from the skies by rain spirits." Indeed, Dawit insists that he will never be a "prisoner" to "humankind's imaginary guardians or tormentors" (95–96). By claiming that theistic religions are "primitive" belief systems that require one to be a prisoner to "imaginary" deities, Dawit is also proposing that such religions disempower their followers by claiming that gods, not humans, are responsible for the good and evil in the world.

During one of the very few times Dawit agrees to sit through a church service with Jessica and Kira, Jessica notices David staring at the church's painting of The Last Supper with "nothing short of contempt," which prompts her to ask him if he "hated God." After a slight pause, Dawit tells her that "if there is truly one God, then it's God who's displeased with me" (*My Soul* 42). On the one hand, since Dawit believes that God is imaginary, his answer is simply stating that he cannot hate what does not exist. To hate God, in other words, is to acknowledge that God exists. On the other hand, his answer also implies that if God is real in the way that Jessica believes it is, then it is God who is doing the hating. According to Harari, unlike their dualistic predecessors, in which good and evil are viewed as two independent and opposing forces, monotheistic religions believe that the evil forces in the world were created by and are subordinate to a good God. However, why would a God who is omnipotent, omniscient, and "perfectly good" allow so much evil and suffering in the world? For the monotheists, free will is God's way of allowing humans to "choose" between good and evil because if there was no evil, then there would be no need for free will. That explanation, according to Harari, is "non-intuitive" and problematized by the following example: "If God knew in advance that a particular person would use her free will to choose evil, and that as a result she would be punished for this by eternal tortures in hell, why did God create her?" (220–21). As suggested by Harari's example, if the monotheist claim that a good God is the creator of both good and evil is true, then we are forced to question God's goodness. For Dawit, as suggested by his answer, he cannot accept that a perfectly good God is ultimately responsible for the physical and emotional pain he has suffered and caused as a mortal and as an immortal. To believe that, he would have to conclude that humans lack free will and are, therefore, imprisoned by the whims of God. In other words, by requiring their followers to put their fates in a deity's hands instead of their own, monotheistic religions discourage free will, even though free will is their usual answer to why evil exists in a world created by a good God.

Dawit's experiences as an American slave suggest that the belief that a good God is responsible for the good *and* evil in the world engenders a form of passivity in those followers who are not part of the ruling classes. For example, Dawit recalls the anger he felt when Adele and other slaves did not attend his "Sunday reading lessons"; instead, they went to the "church meetings where the masters would have them pray and sing." While Adele argued that going to these church meetings "made their troubles more bearable," Dawit saw it as the slaves "trad[ing] their lives away in the hope of redemption after death" because their attendance at these meetings did not erase "the misery of their lives" (*My Soul* 96). Thus, while Glaude argues that many of the Christian slaves in America believed that their faith as one of God's "chosen" people allowed them to see themselves as self-determining agents, Dawit would ask why God allowed its chosen people to be enslaved in the first place. As Tommie Shelby contends in his discussion of why black solidarity based on the idea that God embraces the oppressed is not sustainable, "if God did not love what is good and hate what is evil, or if he could help liberate blacks from undeserved domination but did not, then they could hardly take just pride in being 'chosen' by him" (239). Moreover, Dawit's participation in the Civil War as a Union soldier tells him that it was a war among humans, not God's grace, that led to the end of slavery in America. For Dawit, when the slaves realized that humans, not gods or devils, were responsible for what happens in the world, they also realized their self-determination. While they may have believed that their participation in slave revolts, abolitionist movements, or the Civil War had divine justification, they were also inspired by the idea that they are responsible for their salvation on Earth.

Thus, it is not Dawit's scientific mind that causes him to question the divinity of his resurrection and the Living Blood, but his experiences as a mortal and an immortal. His experiences tell him that his resurrection and the Living Blood are the work of a man and that attributing unexplainable events to a God that one cannot prove exists is not only an example of blind faith, but it also makes human free will ultimately irrelevant to why things are the way they are (e.g., why there is racism, sexism, homophobia, xenophobia, war, and poverty?). While the theists, such as the all-American bourgeois Negro, believe that a good God created evil to allow humans to exercise their free will, they also believe, as expressed by Alex during her conversation about Dawit's blood and her sister's marriage, that "nothing is an accident.... Not a thing in this world" (*My Soul* 248). If what Alex says is true, then Adele and the slaves who attended their master's church meetings believed on some level that their enslavement was part of God's plan and that heaven would be the reward for those who did not stray from that plan. The problem with that plan is that it not only evokes the Curse of Ham legend to justify black enslavement, but it also associates black freedom with death, since the slaves can only attain their reward in the afterlife. Thus, as suggested by Dawit's anger at Adele and the slaves for choosing to attend their masters' church meetings instead of his reading lessons, Christianity's versions of the Resurrection Narrative and Soul Narrative are problematic pathways to black freedom because they can discourage black people from seeking heaven on earth by locating black freedom in the afterlife and by claiming that there are no accidents in the world, just God's will.

## Antizealot Atheism and Black Solidarity

According to Margaret Carter, the vampire in the "vampire-as-alien novels," which emerged after 1970, is "admirable" and "attractive" because it is, ironically, portrayed "as a rebellious outsider, as a persecuted minority, as an endangered species, and as a member of a different 'race' that legend portrays as sexually omnicompetent." What makes the post-1970 vampire's attractiveness ironic is that it possesses the very traits that the nineteenth-century vampire was vilified for having (29–30). Veronica Hollinger suggests that the shift from the old vampire to the post-1970 vampire, or what she calls the "postmodern vampire," reflects our "loss in faith in totalizing stories such as capital-H History, capital-S Science, or capital-R Religion." This loss, as Hollinger notes, has been termed the postmodern condition, a condition that has caused a "legitimation crisis" that "puts into question the grounds on which so many human behaviors and beliefs have previously been secured." The insecurity generated by this crisis has resulted in one of the positive outcomes of the postmodern paradigm: the movement of "decentering," a movement in which the voices of those who have been historically relegated to the margins of society are put in the foreground and given validation. The postmodern paradigm, therefore, is not about explaining or excluding the "abnormal"; rather, it is concerned with incorporating the abnormal "as is" (199–200).

It has been said that Booker T. Washington once noted that "if a black man is anything but a Baptist or Methodist, someone has been tampering with his religion" (Hine, Hine, and Harrold 378). Like Washington, the all-American bourgeois Negro represents that part of the African American community who have *not* lost faith in Christianity's totalizing stories and who believe that religious diversity and black solidarity are incompatible. "Working from Protestantism as the model of religion," the all-American bourgeois Negro insists that "other practices must either conform to this model or suffer by the comparison" (Jakobsen 202). Such thinking is not only reminiscent of the ethnocentrism espoused by nineteenth-century black nationalists in which the all-American bourgeois Negro must *save* Africa and Africans from themselves, but it also assumes that religious conformity will lead to an appreciation of a common heritage that will result in advancing the social, political, and economic interests of African diasporic communities. This view of African assimilation into the African American community is supported by some of the African American interviewees in Zain Abdullah's work on West African immigrants in Harlem. For instance, Lenny and Rob, African American residents of Harlem, state that Africans are not only "different," but they are also "nasty people" and "ruuude." "They're not like us," they claim, due to "cultural differences" (Abdullah 50). In the same vein as Lenny and Rob, Dean, a twenty-five-year-old Harlem resident, states that the Africans whom he likes best are the "Americanized Africans, the ones you see at the [night] club" (51–52). Like Lenny, Rob, and Dean, the all-American bourgeois Negro insists that non-protestant Africans cannot be incorporated into the African American community until they become Americanized, and being Americanized, in part, has historically meant conceptualizing difference as a threat. As Zora Neale Hurston noted in 1950, "difference to the average man [in America] means something bad" because "if people were made right, they would be just like him" (56). Similarly, the all-American bourgeois Negro believes that if Dawit was "made right," he would be a Protestant, not an atheist.

While the all-American bourgeois Negro, like Stoker's *Dracula*, equates "Christian religion [. . .] with modernity in its struggle against atavistic prereligious influences" (Herbert 102), Dawit equates his atheism with postmodernity in its struggle against "capital-R Religion." Like the postmodern vampire, Dawit is a foreigner who rebels against religion; he was enslaved as a child and as an immortal due to his religious and racial identities; and unlike his African American male counterparts, he has sexually satisfied Jessica in ways she never imagined. Moreover, Dawit's vampirism embodies a "positive vision" of the us-and-them relationships found in the vampire-as-alien novels, a vision that does not require distorting *them* into copies of *us* (Carter 44). Indeed, when Dawit marries Jessica, he does not ask her to become an atheist precisely because he accepts her as she is. Even Jessica admits that Dawit's unconditional acceptance is partly why she found him attractive. As the narrator informs us, Jessica believed that "many blacks were so quick to judge her based on nothing; but David never made hurtful assumptions about her, and that had been such a relief" (*My Soul* 50). Dawit's willingness to accept Jessica as is has been nurtured by his nomadic life, a life that has allowed him to develop a blackness that represents the diversity of Africa and the African diaspora. Since the nomad, whose home is nowhere and everywhere, lacks a clearly defined destination and nostalgia for its origins, it resists the "sense of fixed territory" and is, therefore, "never at home." At the same time, because the nomad is an "emblem of hybridity, an expression of 'polyglot practices' and aesthetics," this traveler has lived and can live anywhere (Paes De Barros 7). For example, when the South African cab driver asks Dawit if he is from Soweto because his Zulu sounds native, Dawit tells the driver that he is from Ethiopia. Dawit's response is a lie, according to the narrator, because "he could have chosen any nationality. He had as much right to North America as to Ethiopia, and belonged to Nigeria as well as Senegal and Egypt" (*My Soul* 333). Because Dawit, like most resurrection vampires since Dracula, has been a citizen of the world for centuries, he can now immerse himself into any African or Black Atlantic community without feeling or acting like a stranger.[10]

While the all-American bourgeois Negro believes that she is charged with bringing Christianity's light to all nonprotestant black people, Dawit's antizealot atheism contends, borrowing from Shelby, that "blacks clearly need a nonsectarian basis for their political solidarity" (239–40). Since the-

---

10. According to Melton, the special powers attributed to native soil is an idea that is unique to Stoker's "imagination" (487). Indeed, one of the major differences between the folkloric vampire and the nineteenth-century European literary vampire are the spaces that they terrorize. While the folkloric vampire is "restricted" to terrorizing its home village, where it lived its mortal life, Dracula and his contemporaries are "citizens of the world" (751). For example, while searching for a way out of Dracula's castle, Harker stumbles upon a room that is empty, save for a few "odd things." What stands out most in this collection of "odd things," according to Harker, is a "great heap of gold": "gold of all kinds, Roman, and British, and Austrian, and Hungarian, and Greek and Turkish money, covered with a film of dust. . . . None of it that I noticed was less than three hundred years old" (Stoker 55). Implicit in Harker's descriptions of Dracula's gold is that as long as Dracula travels with his native soil, he can live anywhere because of his ability to look and sound like the natives of the communities that he is planning to feed from. For instance, speaking of how he wants to be viewed in London, Dracula tells Harker that he does not want to be identified as a "stranger in a strange land" because that means he is visible. Instead, as Dracula puts it, "I am content if I am like the rest, so that no man stops if he see me, or pause in his speaking if he hear my words, to say, 'Ha, ha! a stranger!'" (27). Being invisible, as Dracula suggests, is a crucial part of being both a citizen of a nation and a citizen of the world.

istic religions are inherently ethnocentric, a religious-based blackness is ultimately a call for the suppression of black difference. In this view, black solidarity can only be achieved when black people share the same faith, an idea that evokes Marcus Garvey's famous "One God, One Aim, One Destiny" declaration. What makes that line of thought problematic is that it not only insists on developing a monocultural blackness, a blackness that is considered by many contemporary African Americans as outdated (D. White, Bay, and Martin 783–84), but it also wrongly assumes that differences cannot exist in a unified black community. As Abdullah argues, "differences . . . do not automatically construct a boundary forcing people to see themselves as separate and distinct. What creates and maintains the divide is the social importance or cultural meanings people attach to these differences" (51). By giving religion social importance, the all-American bourgeois Negro also creates a boundary between Africans and African Americans that precludes any real solidarity between the groups because the former are required to become a copy of the latter. As Shelby explains, "if there is group pressure to conform to some prototype of blackness, which collective identity theory would seem to require, this would likely create 'core' and 'fringe' subgroups, thus alienating those on the fringe and providing them with an incentive to defect from the collective effort" (229). Thus, while the all-American bourgeois Negro's Christian-based blackness may solve the Mortality Paradox by promising life after death, it is not equipped for black solidarity because it assumes that there is only one way to be black.

In place of the blackness offered by the all-American bourgeois Negro, Dawit's antizealot atheism begins with the premise that the only requirement for being black is having a black body. If being black simply means having a black body, then one cannot stop being black because of one's faith or lack thereof. This is why Dawit believes that a nonreligious black identity offers a more realistic approach to black solidarity than the all-American bourgeois Negro's Christian-based blackness—it allows black people to be individuals while acknowledging that having a black body makes one susceptible to black pain and blackpain. For Dawit, to argue that being black means more than having a black body is to argue that black diversity and black solidarity are incompatible. Indeed, a religious-based blackness is unable to conceptualize an image of black solidarity that will prevent the emergence of fringe groups because it strips black people of their individuality by insisting that a deity has defined how to be black. According to Dawit's antizealot atheism, the problem with that understanding of blackness is that it assumes that black diversity must be sacrificed in the name of black solidarity, an assumption that not only devalues the role that the body plays in defining a person as black or not black but also fails to acknowledge that the origin of blackness, just like the origin of whiteness, is not divine, but human. In other words, to acknowledge that humans, not gods or devils, are the reason why races exist is to acknowledge that there is no divine or authentic way to be black.

CHAPTER 3

# AFRICAN AMERICAN MANHOOD AND THE MASCULINE AFRICA NARRATIVE IN *DARK CORNER*

IN THE PREVIOUS CHAPTER, I argued that the all-American bourgeois Negro's distinction between Africans and African Americans is reminiscent of the *civilizing* discourse espoused by nineteenth-century black nationalists in which African Americans must *save* Africa so that a unified African diaspora can emerge. That image of Africa as a continent in need of salvation and civilization can be found, ironically, in Pan-Africanism's gendered visions of Africa. According to Richard Iton, "early twentieth-century Pan-Africanism often coexisted with, and in fact thrived on, a range of approaches to the importance of maintaining masculinity, and manhood rights" because Pan-Africanism, like most transnational and postnational "configurations," was not "exempt from the masculinist and heterosexist impulses that energize modern arrangements and categories and much of our understanding of the political" (259). Indeed, twentieth-century new-world blacks, especially those in the US and the Caribbean, tended to express their diasporic hegemonies in the "languages of gender and sexuality" (260). That tendency is best represented by the two problematic narratives of Africa, what I call the feminine and masculine Africa narratives, that new-world black leaders, such as W. E. B. Du Bois and Marcus Garvey, developed to resolve what Iton refers to as an "internal debate" within the African diaspora that centered on "what kind of man should be on top" (261). The feminine Africa narrative, which is represented by the all-American bourgeois Negro in Due's *My Soul to Keep,* dominated the first half of the twentieth century and emerged when the US began its imperialist mission in the 1890s. This narrative constructs an Africa that has "fallen and [is] in need of the assistance of blacks based elsewhere" (Iton 260), an Africa that has been feminized by European colonialism, requiring black men in the West to remasculinize *her.*

In contrast to this vision of new-world blacks as Africa's saviors, the masculine Africa narrative, which emerged in the latter half of the twentieth century, presumes that distance from Africa has resulted in a short supply of "normative, natural, and desirable [black] masculinities and femininities" in the West (Iton 261). According to this vision, "'masculinity' is correlated with one's closeness to 'Africa,' and the degree to which one's blackness remains 'unadulterated'" (263). Moreover, the masculine Africa narrative identifies African American men as the most diluted among black men in the West. As Iton explains, "the discursive articulations of interactions between black males in the United States and the West Indies [in the second half of the twentieth century] can be seen as paralleling those between new world blacks in general and continental Africans." Implicit in these articulations is a hierarchy of black manhood in which "Afro-West Indian males are lacking in comparison to their counterparts from the continent, and African American manhood is limited, defined, and circumscribed by, and found wanting in relation to, the models provided by black men from the Caribbean" (263). Thus, the African American community in the masculine Africa narrative is a feminine space and, according to that logic, needs to be remasculinized by African or Afro-Caribbean men to solve its crisis of dilution and emasculation.

It appears that one of the most insightful critiques of the masculine Africa narrative's image of African American manhood and its gendered notion of blackness is Brandon Massey's *Dark Corner* (2004), a black vampire novel that focuses on the journeys of David Hunter and Kyle Coiraut, young black men from different parts of the African diaspora who are searching for their absent fathers. Richard Hunter, David's absent father, abandoned his family to pursue his literary career and other women. Since Richard rarely visited David after he divorced David's not-named mother, David had very little personal knowledge of his father. After Richard's sudden and suspicious death, which made David and his mother instantly wealthy, David decides to uproot his life in Atlanta, Georgia, and travels to Mississippi to learn more about his absent father's life and questionable death. Unlike David, Kyle, a black vampire from France, has never met his absent father, a late eighteenth-century Malinese prince and warrior who became a very powerful vampire after his enslavement in the US. Once Kyle discovers that his father is not dead, but has been in a "Deep Sleep" since the early nineteenth century, Kyle leaves the life of luxury and comfort that Lisha, his mother and the mother of the vampire race, has provided for him to see if he can awaken his father. As fate would have it, David's and Kyle's journeys lead them to Mason's Corner, Mississippi, known as "Dark Corner" by its African American residents. However, while Dark Corner becomes a way station for David, it becomes a final destination for Kyle.

The outcomes of David's and Kyle's journeys suggest that it is futile and potentially dangerous for fatherless black sons to go searching for their absent fathers. Massey emphasizes this point in the novel's "Discussion Questions" section: "In the course of the story, David matures and finally becomes confident in his manhood. What are the pivotal factors in his personal evolution? What lessons does his journey offer to men who have grown up without their fathers in their lives?" Implicit in these questions is that one of the lessons that fatherless black boys might learn from David's journey is that a boy does not need his father to develop a "confident" manhood. In fact, when Richard tells David at the end of the novel that David has become an "admirable man" and "more of a man than [he] ever was" (*Dark Corner* 447), he is also implying that one's sex does not determine one's ability to teach boys how to become admirable men. On the other hand, since Kyle develops a manhood like Diallo's, a manhood that eventually kills Diallo and puts Kyle in a Deep Sleep, what lessons does Kyle's journey offer fatherless black boys? For example, in spite of Richard's confession to being a horrible man and father, he is depicted in the novel as adhering to a notion of manhood that is less problematic than Diallo's. Even though Diallo did not choose to be absent from Kyle's life and embraces the opportunity to teach him how to be a man, he is depicted as the black man who should not be a father. What is it about Diallo that makes him unfit as a black man and father for twenty-first-century African Americans?

I argue that Diallo embodies two ideological problems found in the masculine Africa narrative as it pertains to late twentieth-century African American manhood: paternal Pan-Africanism and the "heroic slave" discourse. While paternal Pan-Africanism and the heroic slave discourse address different spheres of black life (i.e., the former addresses the manhood of the black father, while the latter addresses the manhood of the black leader), both insist that masculinization must come from African, not African American culture and that women should be excluded from the masculinization process. Paternal Pan-Africanism is partly based on Daniel Patrick Moynihan's controversial depiction of poor and working-class African American families as institutions of emasculated men and matriarchal women in his *The Negro Family: The Case for National Action* (1965). Paternal Pan-Africanism is also based on the equally problematic post–civil rights Pan-Africanism that not only agreed with Moynihan's depiction of the so-called emasculated man–matriarchal woman problem but also argued that a cultural return to Africa could solve that problem. Similarly, the heroic slave, as defined by Gregory Stephens, is "a lonely slave, fighting against the system, with no help from anybody, and often betrayed by his own black brother—especially by brown men—or by his black woman who has been sleeping with the white man" (128). As an Afro-Caribbean figure of resistance, the heroic slave would be viewed within the masculine Africa narrative as the *right* leader for the African American community because he is presumed to be *blacker* and *manlier* than his American brothers. Since it is their *Americanness* that makes African American men less black and less manly than their foreign counterparts, the goal of paternal Pan-Africanism and the heroic slave discourse is to restore the *Africanness* of African American manhood by removing its Americanness. That goal, as I intend to demonstrate in this chapter, is based on American conceptions of race in which the feminine is associated with the dominated and the impure, while the masculine is associated with domination and purity. Thus, Diallo is not a restorer or an image of a black manhood absent of whiteness and femininity; instead, he is like the African Americans he despises: a mongrel.

My analysis of Diallo begins with a discussion of his staying-alive vampirism, emphasizing the role that rituals and destiny play in the differences between Diallo and Lisha. Next, I turn my attention to paternal Pan-Africanism's ideological origins, focusing on how the myths of the emasculated black man and the black matriarch influence Diallo's decision to abandon his vampire family. I follow that discussion with an examination of Diallo's heroic slave mentality, focusing on how his purity politics prevents him from fulfilling his self-defined destiny. Finally, I conclude with a discussion of why the masculine Africa narrative is lacking as an ideological foundation for understanding blackness in the twenty-first century.

## Diallo's Staying-Alive Destiny

According to Pearl, Mason's Corner's famous soothsayer, Diallo and Kyle are "high-level vampires—purebloods, if you will—and possess extraordinary strength and talents." There are very few of these vampires because "the process for a human to become one of these creatures is dangerous, lengthy, and usually fatal." In contrast to the purebloods are the "valduwe," who are the "more common" vampires. The valduwe are physically stronger and heal from injuries faster than humans, but they lack supernatural powers and, more importantly, "are under the influence of the master vampire who created them" (*Dark Corner* 266–67). Although purebloods and valduwe are different kinds of vampires, they are different kinds of the same vampire—the staying-alive vampire. Unlike the resurrection vampires in *My Soul to Keep*, who must die to attain immortality, the staying-alive vampires in *Dark Corner* are corporeal critiques of the first part of the Mortality Paradox, the idea that death is inevitable. Like the staying-alive vampires in *The Gilda Stories*, Diallo represents the elixir version of the Staying Alive Narrative in which the path to immortality is the consumption of the magical elixir of life, a legendary death-defying substance, object, or practice that halts the processes of decline and decay in the imbiber. Moreover, as I discussed in chapter 1, one of the most important aspects of this version of the Staying Alive Narrative is the idea that immortality is only for a select few, ideally for the *wise* and *virtuous*. What makes wise and virtuous people ideal for the elixir is that they, unlike the *foolish* and *immoral*, acknowledge that to be mentally fit for eternity and, therefore, eternally happy, our post-elixir selves cannot be a mere extension of our pre-elixir selves. Although the wise and virtuous believe that one must look to the past, not the future, for guidance on how to be mentally fit and eternally happy, they also contend that one must experience an ideological transformation as well as a bodily one to achieve eternal happiness. This is where the similarities between Diallo's and Gilda's vampirisms end.

The most noteworthy difference between Diallo's and Gilda's vampirisms are their elixirs of life. While vampire blood is the elixir of life in *The Gilda Stories*, rituals function as the death-defying elixir in *Dark Corner*. In order for a human to become a master vampire or pureblood, as I noted above, he or she must successfully complete the lengthy and usually fatal transformation process, a process that Diallo refers to as Lisha's "secret rituals" (*Dark Corner* 108). Unlike the Ritual of Life in *My Soul to Keep*, a resurrection ritual that the Khaldunites believe offered them the opportunity to be one with Khaldun, the staying-alive rituals in *Dark Corner* can transform humans into immortals without the need for death or a deity. As Lisha, the mother of the vampire race, explains in her response to Kyle's question about the absence of vampires in the Bible, "Heaven, salvation, nirvana—these things are for man, not for us. Our souls are the souls of predators. Would you expect a wolf to be granted eternal life in the house of God?" (194–95). On the one hand, Lisha suggests that vampires and humans have different souls: Humans have the souls of prey and vampires have the souls of predators. Read within the context of Christian doctrine, the absence of predators in Heaven means that they go to Hell after death because they prey on humans. On the other hand, Lisha's answer also suggests that humans need heaven, salvation, and God precisely because they are prey. In this view, vampires represent the next step in human evolution, and therefore, her staying-alive rituals can be read as a kind of natural selection process in which the humans who survive the process evolve into master vampires who do not need a deity to protect them from predators or to give them life after death because they are now immortal. Although Diallo survived Lisha's secret rituals, he does not become a wise and virtuous predator like Gilda or Lisha, but a foolish and immoral monster, as suggested by the differences between Diallo's and Lisha's destinies.

Prior to becoming a vampire, as he recalls in a dream during his 168-year "Deep Sleep," Diallo was a feared prince and warrior who defeated many rival villages and was held in high esteem by his family and peers. In fact, Diallo's feats of domination resulted in his acquisition of Mariama, who would become the love of his life, from a rival village as a "peace" offering. Prior to meeting Mariama, Diallo had "several wives but loved none of them, enjoying only the feel of their bodies and their subservience to his will." After Mariama and Diallo married, however, Diallo became a different man:

> He fell in love with her, cherished her as he had never cherished a woman before. Their souls bonded, and they became one. She smoothed the edges of his hard heart and calmed his desire to dominate. Unknowingly, by coaxing him to become a gentle man, she caused the erosion of his skills in battle, too.
>
> An upstart village attacked them, and both he and Mariama were captured. They were sold to the pale men, the European slave traders. (*Dark Corner* 106)

After their capture, Diallo and Mariama are separated, and Diallo is put on a slave ship that will take him to Virginia. During his voyage to America, Diallo vows to himself that "he would not live his life as anyone's slave, and they would not kill him, either. He would kill them first. It was not his destiny to serve as a slave. It was his destiny to be served by slaves" (106).

Since Diallo believes that he is on the slave ship because he became a "gentle man," he must become the man he was when he initially met Mariama in order to fulfill his destiny. In contrast to Diallo's destiny, Lisha's is the preservation of the vampire race. Unlike Diallo, who believes that waging a war against humanity will ensure such preservation, Lisha believes that peace between the two species is the solution, as she explains to Kyle in describing why only "barbaric vampires" hunt human prey: "Such vampires do not know any better; they do not understand that we are the most civilized race on earth. We are not animals, we are a sophisticated, complex species who must learn to peacefully coexist with mankind" (178). This is why, as Pearl clarifies, Lisha assists David and his crew of twenty-first-century African Americans in their quest to destroy Diallo: "Vampires thrive in anonymity, and their numbers are few. She worries that the attention Diallo will attract by starting a war will endanger their existence" (269).

Thus, the problem with Diallo's destiny is that it seeks to make Diallo the vampire an extension of Diallo the warrior-prince. While Diallo the vampire shares Lisha's vampiric ethnocentrism, Diallo the warrior-prince does not share her diplomacy or her sense of community precisely because he has been rewarded for subjugating others to his will. As expressed in Lisha's warning to Kyle before he leaves for Mason's Corner to wake Diallo from his Deep Sleep, once Diallo the vampire became an extension of his prevampiric self, Diallo the vampire also became a "monster": "For Diallo's entire life, as both a man and a vampire, his hunger for violence has been insatiable. After he left me in New Orleans, when I was pregnant with you, he roamed the countryside and murdered hundreds—not for food, not for vengeance, but because he *enjoyed* it" (*Dark Corner* 28). Given Lisha's description of Diallo's violence, his destiny can be viewed as an example of what Stanley Crouch refers to as "anarchic individuality." Unlike "heroic individuality," which is "exemplified by the person whose individual expression actually intensifies general freedom," anarchic individuality is represented by the person whose "individuality comes at the expense of everybody else," the person who is "going to do what he wants to do regardless of what it costs others for him to be happy" (261). Although Diallo claims that fulfilling his destiny will empower vampires and African Americans, his desire to be a man served by slaves indicates that if he succeeds in fulfilling his destiny, that success will be at the expense of those he claims to be empowering. Indeed, Diallo's desire to transform the vampire family into an image of the Moynihanian family is an attempt to usurp Lisha's roles as head of the vampire family and originator of vampire manhood.

## Paternal Pan-Africanism, Role Separation, and the "Good Family"

In some ways, Massey's examination of the black absent father–fatherless son relationship in *Dark Corner* can be read as an extension of Gomez's critique of hegemonic notions of family and blackness in *The Gilda Stories*. Both novels not only problematize the notion that the heteronormative nuclear family is the *normal* family, but they also depict the vampire family as more progressive than the human family. The difference between the novels' vampire families is that Gilda's represents, as I discussed in chapter 1, a critique of the *"Essence* girl" and "the snappy baby machine," while Lisha's interrogates the widely held belief that only men teach boys how to be men, a belief that has played a crucial role in the undead life of the black matriarch stereotype, the myth that black women are "overbearing, bossy, sharp-tongued, loud-mouthed, controlling, and, of course, emasculating" (Cole and Guy-Sheftall xxxiii). For example, when Diallo becomes a vampire, he soon realizes that he is no longer the *man* of the house. Indeed, we are told very early in *Dark Corner* that Lisha is the "original mother of the vampire race" (26), but we are never told about the "original" father, which suggests that males are the "nonproductive" members of the vampire family.[1] This means that Diallo will always defer to Lisha because she is not only wiser and more powerful than him, but he is also her commodity, like Mariama was to him. When Diallo and Lisha first met in Virginia, she was extremely wealthy and "feared even by the white men," whereas Diallo was a slave who was about to be executed for killing an overseer who was whipping a young female slave (107). Although Lisha saved Diallo from death and slavery by purchasing and transforming him into a vampire, he

---

1. It is noteworthy that Diallo's human family, not his vampire one, most resembles Dracula's because it not only emphasizes his prevampire monstrosity and suggests that Diallo is closer to the old vampire than the new one, but it also alludes to the type of manhood that will define his vampirism. For example, since Dracula does not need women to reproduce his own kind because only male vampires reproduce in Stoker's novel, the female body functions as a "nonproductive" body in Dracula's world (Halberstam, *Skin Shows* 101). Thus, the three female vampires who live with Dracula are not only his daughters and lovers, but they are also "proper Victorian ladies, remaining properly at home while the master of the house goes forth to do solitary battle against the forces of virtue" (Zanger 18). Like Dracula's vampire lovers, Diallo's human wives are subservient and nonproductive members of the family whose primary purpose is to serve Diallo when he returns from battling rival villages. In Diallo's human family system, femininity is associated with those who are dominated, while masculinity is associated with those who dominate. Even Mariama, whom Diallo falls in love with, was a gift, a possession exchanged between men.

abandons Lisha and, unknowingly, their unborn son. Since he believes, as indicated by his vow on the slave ship and his family structure in Mali, that a significant difference between men and women is that the former own and the latter are owned, Diallo is unable to remain in a familial or intimate relationship in which he is not the *man* of that relationship. Like Dracula, the old vampire who is alone in the battle against his enemies because his female vampires are confined to his castle, Diallo is alone in his struggle to fulfill his destiny largely because he is unwilling to accept Lisha as his superior or even equal, despite the fact that she and she alone gave birth to the vampire race.

For Diallo, since becoming a "gentle man," he has been emasculated by his African capturers, his white slave owners, and by his vampire lover and liberator. For many black nationalists of the early post–civil rights era, Diallo's fight against emasculation is symbolic of the black man's experience in twentieth-century America. They would argue that when Mariama transformed Diallo into a "gentle man," she also engendered two figures that will haunt the African American family by the middle of the twentieth century: the so-called emasculated black man and matriarchal black woman. Immortalized by E. Franklin Frazier in the 1930s, fixed in the American imagination by the 1950s television show *Amos 'n' Andy*, and revised in the 1960s by black leaders such as Dr. Martin Luther King Jr., by black periodicals such as *Ebony*, and by Moynihan's *The Negro Family*, the myth of the black matriarch has informed the antiblack feminist discourse that emerged most vehemently in the 1970s and 1980s as well as the popular notion that black men are an "endangered species" (Cole and Guy-Sheftall xxvii–xxxv). Crucial to that myth's undead life, as Robert Staples noted in 1973, is its double meaning: "that black men have been deprived of their masculinity and that black women participated in the emasculinization process" (126). According to the myth of the black matriarch, slavery, the end of Reconstruction, Jim Crow, and black women have slowly emasculated black manhood. Moreover, as argued by Moynihan in *The Negro Family*, popularly known as the "Moynihan Report," this attack on black manhood has prevented African American men from being *men* inside and outside the home: "Unquestionably, these events worked against the emergence of a strong father figure. The very essence of the male animal, from the bantam rooster to the four-star general, is to strut. Indeed, in 19th century America, a particular type of exaggerated male boastfulness became almost a national style. Not for the Negro male. The 'sassy nigger' was lynched" (16).

Unlike the myth of the black matriarch, Moynihan does not identify black women as culprits in the de-strutting of black men. However, he does contend that female-headed households are evidence of this de-strutting, which has resulted in the African American family becoming an institution that is unable to foster upward mobility in its youth, especially its boys. As Moynihan put it, "Negro children without fathers flounder—and fail" (35). According to that logic, since the female-headed household retarded the progress of the African American community, "masculinization . . . had to come from outside African American culture" (Ferguson 122). For Moynihan, the armed forces could serve as that outside influence because he believed, in spite of its history of social and institutional racism, that the US military was not only a world where "the category 'Negro' and 'white' do not exist," but it was also an "utterly masculine world," a world "run by strong men of unquestioned authority" (Moynihan 42). Ironically, as Roderick Ferguson explains, while black nationalist groups in the early post–civil rights era contested Moynihan's argument that the state should be the "appropriate catalyst to masculine agency," they did agree with his thesis, inherited from Frazier, that black men need to resume their role as patriarchs in order to overcome the black matriarch's "emasculating effects" (123). For instance, in contrast to Moynihan's solution, many black nationalists turned to Africa in hope of finding a world absent of matriarchs and emasculated men. Indeed, Ghana's independence in the 1950s not only symbolized the emergence of a new world order for many blacks in the West, but it also resulted in Kwame Nkrumah replacing Du Bois as the Pan-African movement's father figure (M. Williams 181). Unlike Marcus Garvey's "Back-to-Africa" movement, this turn to Africa did not call for African Americans to leave the US; rather, it called for a cultural return to Africa, what Ronald Walters refers to as the "Diaspora interpretation of Pan-Africanism" (82–83). An example of this Pan-Africanism is Malcolm X's recounting of his speech to an audience at Ibadan University in Nigeria in which he called for African Americans to make such a return: "I said that physically we Afro-Americans might remain in America, fighting for our Constitutional rights, but that philosophically and culturally we Afro-Americans badly needed to 'return' to Africa—and to develop a working unity in the framework of Pan-Africanism" (Haley and Malcolm X 350).

What is noteworthy about this discourse of return, as suggested by Iton, is that the African American community, not Africa, is treated as a female space:

> As the [twentieth] century progressed, new world blacks' willingness and capacity to identify [Africa] as a female space in need of guidance, custodianship, protection, or domination diminished. While such discourses

certainly persisted at the end of this period, the propensity to think of these diasporic engagements in straightforwardly hierarchical and gendered terms, with blacks outside of Africa in the dominant position, lessened significantly after the confluence of events that preceded and followed the 1945 Pan-African Conference in Manchester. At this meeting Du Bois, as the father figure of the movement, realized that Africans did not need or seek the tutelage his cohort had assumed up to that point—a fact that had become even more pronounced by the time Ghana achieved independence in 1957. (262)

Thus, for the paternal Pan-Africanist, what gave credibility to the myth of the black matriarch and the masculine Africa narrative was African independence. Indeed, both narratives, when read together, pose the following question: How can African American men think about guiding, protecting, or liberating Africa when they are prevented from being *men* in their country and in their families? As suggested by Diallo's approach to teaching Kyle how to be a powerful male vampire, one of the problems with the paternal Pan-Africanist solution to the African American male's so-called eroded blackness and manliness is that it differs very little from Moynihan's approach to masculinizing African American men.

When Kyle awakens Diallo from his Deep Sleep, Diallo demands human prey, a demand that Kyle finds "inimical—offensive, even—to his nature." As the narrator explains, "[Kyle] considered himself a civilized vampire, a lover of culture and art, with refined tastes and habits. Yet he was thinking of regressing into the kind of vampire that he despised: the ruthless predator." Before Kyle gives in to Diallo's demand, Kyle gives his father a package of blood to drink from. Diallo throws the package to the floor after taking a few sips, protesting that "the blood tastes foul." Kyle tells his father that he "must adapt" to this way of feeding because it is a "safe" way for vampires to nourish themselves (*Dark Corner* 132). Kyle's response to Diallo's demand is due to Lisha raising him to be a "civilized" vampire. As he recalls on his flight to Mason's Corner, in addition to wealth and knowledge, the civilized vampire is defined by his or her use of blood banks, instead of human prey, to acquire food:

> There was no need to ever hunt for food again. Indeed, hunting human prey seemed primitive to him, an activity pursued only by uncivilized vampires, or those who were poor and had no alternative. The few prosperous vampires who chose to hunt did so for sport, under carefully controlled conditions—the vampire equivalent of game preserves. (25)

For Diallo, such thinking is evidence that Kyle is becoming a gentle man and explains why Diallo tells Kyle that Lisha is the reason why he is repulsed by his father's demand: "Lisha is wise. But she is female. You are male. And I am your father. Only I can show you how a powerful male vampire ought to conduct himself" (138). According to Diallo, in order for Kyle to become a powerful male vampire, he must do what Diallo supposedly did: He must distance himself, physically and ideologically, from Lisha, the woman responsible for raising Kyle and teaching Diallo how to be a powerful male vampire. However, the problem with Diallo's advice is that he and Kyle will always be Lisha's *sons*, and his notion of what it means to be a powerful male vampire is not his own but Lisha's; therefore, they can never really distance themselves from Lisha, nor can they be purely masculine men precisely because Lisha is the issuing source of their manhood.

Another problem with Diallo's advice is that it disregards the fact that women can teach boys how to be men precisely because gender roles are culturally determined and, therefore, learned. As Staples noted in his 1973 critique of the myth of the emasculated black man, "men are not the only ones who teach boys about masculinity. Sex roles can also be learned by internalizing the culturally determined expectations of these roles. Consequently, black mothers can spell out the role requirements for their fatherless sons" (131–32). Lawson Bush comes to a similar conclusion thirty years later: "Black mothers participate in every aspect of the development of manhood and masculinity and . . . there is no real evidence that supports the supposition that mothers and fathers approach the process differently based on their gender" (386). Massey seems to take the arguments by Staples and Bush a step further in his portrayal of Diallo, implying that the claim that mothers cannot teach their sons how to be men is not only invalid, but dangerous. As Lisha tells David at the end of the novel, "Diallo was a cancer upon the earth," "Kyle had too much of his father in him," and both would have brought destruction upon all vampires (445–46). Implicit in Lisha's comments is that if Kyle was more like the man whom she taught him to be and less like the man whom Diallo wanted him to be, he would still be alive, instead of buried in a grave.

Diallo's view of civilized male vampires and his approach to teaching Kyle how to be a powerful man are reminiscent of the antiblack feminism that emerged in the 1970s and had become by the dawn of the twenty-first century, when Diallo awakens from his Deep Sleep, "rampant in the popular press, including the Black media, rap music, films, sitcoms, talk shows, and self-help literature" (Cole and Guy-Sheftall xxx). This antiblack feminism, as Linda La Rue noted in 1970, was part of a Pan-Africanism that relegated black women's role in the liberation movement to the home, where they were giving birth to and taking care of the babies of the future vanguard.[2] For La Rue, that role represents "the unsatisfactory male-female role relationship which [blacks] adopted from whites as the paradigm of the good family." A "good family," according to that paradigm, is one that adheres to role separation in which men are *achievers*, women are *pleasers*, and these roles are treated as "natural and divine" (117–19).[3] Role integration, in contrast, is defined as the realization that gender roles are socially constructed and that flexibility in a people's gender roles has been a "historically proven asset" to their survival (122). According to La Rue, the black liberation movement cannot be considered revolutionary until it embraces role integration and, therefore, acknowledges that it "needs" black women in a "position of struggle, not prone" (123).[4]

Like the Pan-Africanism described by La Rue, Diallo's devotion to Mariama and his abandonment of Lisha are due to his investment in role separation. Stated differently, if we contextualize Diallo's fear of being an emasculated father in relation to his everlasting devotion to Mariama, we find that Diallo's decision to abandon the vampire family represents the paternal Pan-Africanist's rejection of role integration. Although Mariama is responsible for transforming Diallo into a "gentle man" and Lisha is responsible for freeing him from slavery and making him "greater than man,"

---

2. It is important to note that this antiblack feminism was not confined to black nationalist groups. Indeed, black women who were directly involved with the civil rights movement and had put their lives at risk were not only prohibited from speaking at the 1963 March on Washington by the male leadership of the movement, but none of them were invited to the postmarch meeting at the White House with President Kennedy (Cole and Guy-Sheftall 85). These examples represent not only the stark marginalization of black women by the movement's male leaders but also, as I will discuss below, the problems that come with thinking of race in only masculinist terms: Such thinking cannot lead to black liberation because it wrongly assumes that black men, more so than black women, are the targets of American racism because the essence and fate of any race are embodied by its men.

3. As Parrillo notes in his discussion of women as an American minority group, the prevailing values in the United States during the nineteenth and early twentieth centuries held that "the nature of women was to please and the nature of men was to achieve" (347).

4. La Rue is referring to a statement that has been attributed to Stokeley Carmichael, who is also identified as the person who coined the term "black power." As Cole and Guy-Sheftall note, Carmichael's "prone" response, according to most accounts, was made in jest to a question he himself posed regarding the role of women in SNCC (Student Nonviolent Coordinating Committee). Mary King, one of the SNCC members present when Carmichael made the statement, has stated that Carmichael's joking has been taken out of context and was not any indication that SNCC was a misogynist organization (239 n. 36).

Diallo pledges his eternal allegiance and love to Mariama, not Lisha. What makes Lisha problematic for Diallo is that she refuses to be "prone"; that is to say, she refuses to be like Mariama, who simultaneously represents the Moynihanian mother and wife as well as the Africa that allowed Diallo to be master of his home and village. Thus, one of the major problems with paternal Pan-Africanism is that it encourages black fathers to abandon non-patriarchal families. Indeed, like the American men of the 1970s who abandoned the family altogether because of their refusal to coexist with working mothers,[5] Diallo's decision to abandon the vampiric family is informed by the idea that a man who consents to be the father of a family in which he is not the sole head and breadwinner is consenting to his own emasculation. Put in slightly different terms, leaving Lisha is Diallo's way of acknowledging that he is powerless to transform the vampire family into the Moynihanian family. This feeling of powerlessness helps to explain why Diallo tells Kyle that only males can teach boys how to be powerful men: If Diallo concedes that Lisha has already taught Kyle how to be such a man, he must also concede that fathers like him are obsolete and that Lisha is the reason why he is a powerful male vampire.

Diallo's obsolescence explains not only why he abandons the vampire family but also why Lisha chooses Richard as her next companion and why she did not tell Diallo that she was pregnant. Although Richard is an extremely selfish and unlikable person, his abandonment of his family reads as less problematic than Diallo's abandonment of Lisha and their unborn son. Unlike Diallo, who abandons the vampire family because it lacks role separation, Richard leaves his family because it lacks role integration. For instance, in his explanation to David for why he faked his death and became a vampire, Richard intimates that the life of a breadwinning father is unfulfilling: "When I left behind my mortal life, I provided all of the financial benefits that you and your mother could ever wish for. And I get to enjoy everlasting life as the companion of a fabulously beautiful and wise creature. Do you think that was a difficult decision for me to make?" (*Dark Corner* 447). Implicit in Richard's comments is that he did not abandon his family because he felt that his manhood was threatened, but because he did

---

5. Due, in large part, to the decline in men's wages, the rising costs of consumer goods, and the rise of the feminist movement, many American men of the 1970s were unable to become the fathers of the 1950s precisely because they needed their spouses' earnings. Instead of adapting to this new reality, a reality in which manhood, fatherhood, and breadwinning are not inextricably linked, these men choose to abandon the family altogether. Indeed, by the end of the 1970s, many American men had "broken free" from the burdens of marriage and breadwinning by avoiding or delaying relationships that could lead them into husband-hood and fatherhood (Griswold 221–23).

not like being part of the "good family" in which manhood, fatherhood, and breadwinning are inextricably linked. As Richard notes, besides her beauty, what makes Lisha more desirable than David's mother is her wealth and wisdom, traits that David's mother presumably lacks and that Diallo despises in women. Thus, by choosing Richard as her next companion and deciding to hide her pregnancy from Diallo, Lisha functions as a critique not only of black mothers like Mariama and David's not-named mother, who are symbolically prone, but also of black fathers like Diallo who are unwilling to share power with women. That unwillingness, which is a fundamental tenet of paternal Pan-Africanism, not only perpetuates the myth of the black matriarch in which black women are pegged as the reason for fatherless black homes and wayward black sons, but it is also detrimental to black boys, as suggested by Kyle's entombment at the end of the novel.

Diallo's unwillingness to share power with women is depicted as detrimental not only to the black family but to the black community as well. While Diallo views his destiny as one in which vampires will become the dominant species on the planet and the enslavement of Africans in the US has been fully redressed, Lisha and David view it as a threat to their respective communities. As they see it, Diallo's destiny is not concerned with destroying the institutions, ideologies, or even individuals that disempower vampires and African Americans; rather, his destiny is concerned with destroying those who are preventing him from becoming a slave master. In this instance, Diallo represents a warning to African Americans about black male leaders who claim to be heroically and purely black.

## Mongrels, Purebloods, and the Heroic Slave

I noted in the introduction of this chapter that the heroic slave is an Afro-Caribbean figure of resistance who is alone in his fight against the system because the brown men and black women of his community are literally and figuratively in bed with the white man. According to Stephens, the heroic slave is the product of Jamaica's "theology of black victimization," a "black authenticity discourse" based on a black-white binary that defines black people as victims of the proverbial white man and defines "brown" men (racially mixed and light-skinned black men) as the white man's partner in crime (111–12). Like the brown man, the black woman sleeping with the white man is not only the white man's partner in crime because she will be the mother of more brown people, but she is also allowing herself to be "raped" by the white man, since it is presumed that white men and black women cannot have relationships other than those of exploitation (129–30). In the masculine Africa narrative, the heroic slave functions as an image of black purity and restoration for the African American community, a community that has become a feminine space because it is too close to America and too far from Africa. As Iton explains, whether it is images of African American women seeking or being sought by foreign black male suitors (e.g., Stella of Terry McMillan's 1996 novel *How Stella Got Her Groove Back* and Meshell NedegeOcello's 1993 song "Dred Loc") or African American men returning to Africa to find themselves (e.g., Richard Pryor's and Dave Chappelle's trips to Africa), the foreign black man and the African continent in the masculine Africa narrative represent "particularly potent catalyst[s] for those seeking a certain form of restoration." However, Iton warns that this form of restoration is typically accompanied by a "gender 'normalizing'" and "disciplinary" presence in which the feminine is associated with that or with those who have been exploited or plundered (264–65). According to the logic of the masculine African narrative, since the African American community has become a feminine space, it requires a foreign black man whose blackness and manhood are absent of anything white and feminine to reblacken and remasculinize the community.

Like the heroic slave in the masculine Africa narrative, Diallo is a foreign black male who imagines himself as a catalyst of restoration and an image of purity for vampires and the African Americans of Mason's Corner. Although Diallo claims that fulfilling his destiny involves uplifting vampires to the top of the world's hierarchy and avenging the enslavement of Africans in America, his desire to be a man served by slaves indicates that if he is victorious in his war against humanity, it will be a victory for Diallo only. As David and his crew of twenty-first-century African Americans see it, Diallo's struggle to fulfill his destiny is a struggle to be a black version of Edward Mason, the novel's nineteenth-century white slave owner whose sadistic enslavement of black people resulted in the founding of Mason's Corner. As I demonstrate in the pages below, Massey's depiction of Diallo suggests that African Americans should be wary of foreign black men or African American men who possess a heroic slave mentality because they support a politics of black purity that is not only impossible and contradictory but also oppressive.

According to Franklin Bennett, a retired history professor and Mason's Corner's unofficial historian, Edward Mason came to Mississippi from Virginia in 1841 to establish a "cotton kingdom," that is, "the grandest, most prosperous plantation in Mississippi." He owned a thousand acres of land, a mansion built on a hill, and three hundred slaves who worked his land from dawn to dusk. Moreover, Franklin continues, Mason became more "sadistic and imaginative" in his torturing of his slaves because he believed that "disobedience was inimical to his mission to maintain a plantation that functioned with machinelike efficiency" (*Dark Corner* 169). Like Mason, Diallo envisions his future empire as one partly defined by the subjugation of black people. As demonstrated by Diallo's response to his failed attempt to save Mariama from slavery, his war against the plantation owners was not a war against slavery, but a war against those who hinder him from being a slave master:

> He wanted to destroy these men who caused such pain and torment. He wanted to destroy those who submissively accepted pain. He wanted to drench the world in their blood.
> He did not join Lisha on the next night's hunt. He left her.
> He began to build his army, to help him fulfill his mission, his true destiny.
> With a horde of vampire warriors behind him, he went on a bloody rampage across the land. Plantations fell, much like the rival villages had in his days as a man. He squashed them under his heels and washed himself in their blood. (108)

Although Diallo's war was directed at the white men who "caused pain and torment" by enslaving him and his people, it was also directed at black people who "submissively accepted pain." Those who accepted such pain, according to Diallo's ahistorical mind, were the most polluted by whiteness, as alluded to by Kyle's reference to his father's African American valduwe as "low-level vampires" who are "the mongrels of their species" (352). This picture of Mason's Corner's African Americans defines them as examples of black people who have been "clearly 'dominated' and transformed by 'Western' ways" (Iton 263).[6] Although their transformation was not voluntary, this historical fact is irrelevant to Diallo because, as Mary Douglas notes, pollution rules, unlike moral rules, are unambiguous: "[Pollution rules] do not

---

6. This assumption, according to Iton, is best captured by Chuck D, lead rapper for the seminal hip-hop group Public Enemy. Chuck D claimed that it was harder for the group to become popular with African American listeners as opposed to English audiences because African Americans were "still in the slave-like mentality," while black audiences in England still had their Caribbean or African roots (qtd. in Iton 282). Using the same logic as Chuck D, but for different purposes, Diallo believes that cultural mixing has not only resulted in an African American slave-like mentality, but it has become a central reason for why African Americans are only worthy to be slaves in his new empire.

depend on intention or a nice balancing of rights and duties. The only material question is whether a forbidden contact has taken place or not" (162). Even though Diallo, like the ancestors of Mason's Corner, experienced this forbidden contact as a slave in the US, he assumes that his failed war against the plantation owners and his upcoming war against humanity are evidence that he has cleansed himself of that contact.

Diallo views African Americans not only as mongrels but also as a feminine people. By associating the feminine with the impure and the subjugated, Diallo establishes a distinction between himself and African Americans in which the former represents masculine blackness and the latter represents feminine blackness. Similar to Robert Park, the Chicago School sociologist who made the racist and sexist argument that blacks are "the *lady* among the races,"[7] Diallo views African Americans as the *ladies* of the African diaspora because they are not at *war* with white America. However, Diallo's gendered conception of blackness shares the same problems as the heroic slave's theology of black victimization in which being authentically black means being a victim of white oppression. One of the problems with that theology, besides its disturbing presumption that the "white man will always prevail," is that it classifies all relations between whites and blacks as examples of rape or sexual exploitation (Stephens 129–30). By doing so, this theology not only positions black people as forever the white man's victim and reinforces the gendered racial divide between masculine whiteness and feminine blackness, but it also allows its theologians to justify certain forms of black-on-black oppression, so long as the black oppressor claims that his or her exploitation of black people is an unfortunate necessity in the struggle to free them from their victimization. In this light, Diallo believes that transforming the African Americans of Mason's Corner into valduwe is for their own benefit because they will become a masculine people controlled by a black man instead of by a white one.

Diallo relies on this racist and sexist logic to justify his attempt to subjugate a small African American town to his will, and he also uses it to justify his exclusion of Lisha from his future empire. The link that he makes between subjugation and impurity genders the African American commu-

---

7. According to Park's gendered conception of race, a Jew is an "intellectual and idealist," an East Indian is "brooding and introspective," and an Anglo-Saxon is a "pioneer and frontiersman," but "[the Negro] is primarily an artist, loving life for its own sake. His métier is expression rather than action. He is, so to speak, the *lady* among the races" (qtd. in Ferguson 58). Although Park uses male pronouns to refer to black people, his description of the *masculine races* tells us that he believes that black men are men in body only.

nity as feminine, as well as the vampire community. For example, when Kyle tells Diallo that Lisha has forbidden the creation of valduwe because they are "abominations," Diallo tells Kyle that he will never be a powerful male vampire until he "put[s] away childish things" (*Dark Corner* 142). By referring to Lisha's teachings as "childish," Diallo not only links femininity with immaturity and *weak* men, but he also treats her leadership as detrimental to the vampire people. In Diallo's eyes, as suggested by Kyle's thoughts on Diallo's impending war with humankind, Lisha's unwillingness or inability to dominate humans has resulted in vampires deferring to a lesser species:

> For too long, vampires such as Mother had lived in secret, preying upon humans as if they were lowly parasites, like miniscule fish clinging to the belly of a great whale. The truth, as his father forced him to realize, was that vampires were the superior race, and it was time for them to assume their rightful, dominant position in the world's hierarchy of species. (315)

As suggested by the passage above, Lisha and African American males are two sides of the same coin. Like the African American male of paternal Pan-Africanism, who is unable to liberate African Americans or Africa because he is prevented from being a *man* in his family and country, Lisha is unable to elevate her species because she is female. Although Lisha is the mother of the vampire species and the most powerful vampire on the planet, her sex makes her a nonproductive leader in Diallo's mind; therefore, the only thing that Lisha can do to elevate the vampire species is to concede leadership of the species to him.

What becomes clear in Diallo's gendered view of race is that Lisha and African Americans are to Diallo as brown men and the traitorous black woman are to the heroic slave. As Diallo's brown men, African Americans are "the 'weak link,' making 'the black race' susceptible to the corrupting influence of the white world" (Stephens 128). What makes African Americans weak and a threat to other black people, according to that logic, is that they are ideologically and/or biologically part white. Thus, by forming an alliance with the so-called mongrels, Lisha becomes Diallo's traitorous black woman. Although Lisha is not sleeping with the white man, she has allied herself emotionally and politically with Richard and David, respectively, an alliance that convinces Diallo that Lisha is "polluted," one who has "developed some wrong condition or simply crossed some line which should not have been crossed and this displacement unleashes danger for someone" (Douglas 140). For Diallo, the line that Lisha crossed is the line of racial fidelity, and what makes that crossing dangerous for vampires is that it has resulted in their self-subordination to humans. In this light, Lisha is also a "weak link," a vampire who is exposing the vampire race to the corrupting influences of the human world and, therefore, sabotaging her own people.

One of the main problems with Diallo's purity politics is that he is, according to his own standards, impure. For instance, Diallo's desire to be a slave master, a desire that did not exist when he was an eighteenth-century Malinese prince and warrior, indicates that he is as *polluted* as those he refers to as mongrels. Although Diallo conquered several villages when he was a warrior-prince and the people he ruled were his subjects, he did not enslave the people of the villages he defeated. In fact, Diallo's vow to be a man served by slaves emerged during his time on a slave ship to Virginia, indicating that Diallo, like the African Americans he seeks to subjugate, was also transformed by his contact with the white world.[8] Moreover, although Diallo, Lisha, and Kyle are purebloods, Diallo was once human. This means that Lisha and Kyle are the only true purebloods of the species because they were never human or valduwe. Thus, while Diallo assumes that his pre– and post–Deep Sleep wars are evidence that he is an unadulterated black male vampire, his fight to be a man served by slaves and his transformation from human to pureblood indicate that he is a mongrel.

Another problem with Diallo's purity politics is that it evokes the "battle of the sexes" myth, the misinformed idea that heterosexuality is inherently adversarial and, therefore, conflict in heterosexual intimate relationships is inevitable (Digby 1). According to Tom Digby, the battle of the sexes myth is not only based on the false assumption of gender purity, in which men are natural warriors and women are natural breeders and nurturers, but it is also most prevalent in "war-reliant" societies—such as ancient Hebrew, Nazi Germany, the US, and ISIS-ruled societies—where a "presumption of adver-

---

8. It is important to note that slavery existed on the continent of Africa before Europeans began the Atlantic slave trade in the fifteenth century (Manning 72). However, the *slavery* practiced on the African continent was qualitatively different from the slavery practiced in the Americas due to the role that social hierarchy played in premodern Africa. In his critique of John Thornton's claim that "slavery was widespread in Africa" and that the "Atlantic slave trade was the outgrowth of this internal slavery" (qtd. in Manning 58), Patrick Manning writes the following: "Africans expanded the hierarchies in their societies and cultures [due to contact with Arab merchants in the northern part of the continent and Portuguese merchants in the western part], but with respect to other cultures around the globe, African societies of the fifteenth century remained remarkably egalitarian.... As it happened, the progressive expansion of [the] slave trade brought types of [social] hierarchy that would eventually be disastrous—it created hierarchy by separating master from slave, yet it was a leveling force in that anyone was vulnerable to capture. This expansion of slavery arose not from the inherent qualities of African society but from the nature of the interactions with outsiders" (61).

sariality" and a "faith in masculine force" to solve individual and societal problems are dominant (9–16). Such presumption and faith are an integral part of Diallo's discourses on how to become a powerful male vampire and how to uplift the vampire people, as represented by his scolding of Kyle for respecting Lisha's teachings on what it means to be a vampire. By telling Kyle that he cannot "claim [his] birthright as a vampire" until he dismisses the so-called childish teachings of his mother (*Dark Corner* 142), Diallo is also telling Kyle that he cannot be a man until he eradicates all traces of the feminine from himself and concedes that his mother has become the enemy of the very people she gave birth to. However, as suggested by Douglas's discussion of sex-pollution ideas in "primitive" societies, a society that presumes that men and women are inherently adversarial and that societal problems are solved by using violent force will always be mired in contradiction and conflict:

> The whole society is especially likely to be founded on a contradiction if the system is one in which men define their status in terms of rights over women. If there is free competition between the men, this gives scope for a discontented woman to turn to her husband's or her guardian's rivals, gain new protectors and new allegiances, and so to dissolve into nothing the structure of the rights and duties which had formerly been built around her. (184)

Like Douglas's "discontented woman," Lisha turns to Diallo's rivals to destroy him. Lisha's decision to assist David and his crew in their quest to kill Diallo and Kyle suggests that if Diallo succeeds in fulfilling his destiny, he will produce a vampire society that will always be at war with itself because that society will be founded on the rigid separation and violent antagonism of the sexes, instead of their mutual dependence and harmony (Douglas 173). Thus, as Lisha sees it, Diallo is not an avenger or revolutionary as he imagines himself to be, but "a renegade who must be squelched" (*Dark Corner* 269).

It is noteworthy that Diallo is unable to recruit purebloods and African Americans to help him fight his wars, because his failure to do so suggests that the discourse of the heroic slave fosters individual, not communal liberation projects. For instance, Diallo's army of valduwe is not a sign that he has a community of vampires that are willing to fight *with* him; rather, it is evidence that he must create slaves to fight *for* him. What that tells us is that Diallo, like the heroic slave, is a self-defined community of one. By identifying the people of Mason's Corner as mongrels and Lisha as polluted,

Diallo positions himself as the only pure black man in the African American and vampire communities and, therefore, the only black man capable of restoring the blackness and manliness lost by these communities. The problem with Diallo's vision of himself, besides the fact that it refuses to acknowledge that he is a cultural and biological mongrel, is that it serves as justification for dominating the very people he claims to be empowering. In this light, Lisha and David's quest to defeat Diallo suggests that any pursuit of racial and gender purity should always be resisted because it is always accompanied by a pursuit to oppress, as represented by Diallo's Mason-like anarchic individualism. Even though Mason and Diallo would have been enemies if they were alive at the same time, both believed that the exploitation of black bodies was crucial to establishing their respective utopias: Mason had black slaves to achieve his cotton kingdom and Diallo needed African American valduwe to fulfill his destiny. Such thinking explains why David and the African Americans of Mason's Corner do not view Diallo as an image of black purity or restoration, but as an image of white supremacy in black skin.

## If One Is Black, Can One Stop Being Black?

The critiques of the masculine Africa narrative offered by *Dark Corner* problematize that narrative's premise that distance from Africa has somehow made African American men less *black* and less *manly* than black men outside of America. One of the problems with that premise is that it ignores the role that the body plays in the American construction of race. Since the notions of race and gender in the US are grounded in the myth that "the physical body offers transparent evidence of its history, identity, and behavior" (Somerville, *Queering* 9), the notion that distance from Africa makes African American men less black and less manly seems absurd in such a world. For instance, the ethnophaulisms directed at people who do not think and behave according to the supposed dictates of their racialized bodies—such as the "oreo" (one who is black on the outside, but *white* on the inside) and the "white chocolate" (one who is white on the outside, but *black* on the inside)—identify one's outside, not one's inside, as evidence of one's race. Moreover, although American culture has a long history of conceptualizing black men in relation to the feminine, the practice of lynching and castrating black men reveals that the "[black male's] threat to white masculine power arises . . . not simply from a perceived racial difference, but from the potential for gender sameness" (Wiegman 352–53). In the eyes of lynchers and castrators, black men are a threat to white masculine power in America because of their bodies; therefore, to assume that distance from Africa affects the level of one's blackness is to ignore the fact that one's identification as a black man in America is confirmed by one's body.

Another problem with the notion that distance from Africa has made African American men less *black* and less *manly* than black men outside of America is that it assumes that there is more to being black than having a black body. Since the black body does not guarantee that one is *really* black in the masculine Africa narrative, one must think and behave in particular ways to prove one's blackness. However, who determines the criteria for how to think and act authentically black? Is it Africans, African Americans, or a combination of the two? Also, what makes that individual or group a trustworthy source; that is to say, what credentials must one have in order to be an authenticator of blackness? Furthermore, can a concept of authentic blackness exist without considering how nonblack people define blackness, since "self-definition, both of groups and individuals, does not take place in a vacuum, and thus what others think of one and what one thinks of oneself result in a dynamic that makes group authenticity an on-going process" (Japtok and Jenkins 6)? In response to this last question, Wendy Alexia Rountree, who grew up as someone who was perceived by her black peers as "faking the funk" (i.e., not really black) and by whites as "authentically" black, answers no: "As I grew older . . . , I began to think that the definition of 'authentic blackness' is, in the end, based not on self-perception but on the perception of others" (107). Since part of the reason why black people are *black* is due to nonblack people defining them as such, then blackness, like its counterpart whiteness, is what Stuart Hall refers to as a "cover story" told by the Self and the Other in which an individual or group learns who they *are* by determining who they are not (344–45).

The masculine Africa narrative's conception of blackness not only devalues the role that the body plays in being black by claiming that there is more to being black than having a black body, but it also positions Africa as the issuing source of African American blackness. This view of African American blackness runs counter to the idea that was becoming popular among many African Americans at the end of the twentieth century, the idea that "although African people have the same beginnings, they are so different culturally, socially, and intellectually that they should be considered completely separate people" (Jackson and Cothran 579). It is, therefore, noteworthy that the term "African American" is used in *Dark Corner* only within academic or official contexts—when the omniscient narrator notes that Richard's literary accomplishments are comparable to the "lions" of the "African-American literary canon" (*Dark Corner* 7) and when Franklin tells David that Mason's Corner has been "over ninety percent African-American" for generations (18)—because it suggests that for most African Americans, "African American" is just their *government name*,[9] not their *real* name. As I noted in the previous chapter, by the early 1990s, the decade before Diallo awakens from his Deep Sleep, many African Americans began to question if the term "African American" was a misnomer because the term privileges their ancestors' homeland (Africa) over their immediate homeland (the US). Despite that questioning, the idea that Africa is the issuing source of African American blackness was promoted by paternal Pan-Africanists to resolve the conflicts that exist between American-born and foreign-born blacks. For example, in "Black Versus Black: The Relationships Among African, African American, and African Caribbean Persons," Jennifer V. Jackson and Mary E. Cothran contend that the conflict among these groups, a conflict influenced by the competition for social, political, and economic resources, is largely the result of their failure to "appreciate their common heritage" and their "lack of understanding" of each other (595). While Jackson and Cothran acknowledge that until recent times, people living on the continent of Africa defined themselves solely through their ethnic affiliations, not as a racial group, they also claim that once black people in America gain "true knowledge" of themselves and their history by embracing Afrocentrism, they will "recognize that they are from the same ethnic tree, the same African origin" (597). On the one hand, Jackson and Cothran argue that "the dichotomization of people into Black and White does not allow for the idea that Black people are themselves a diverse group with differences to warrant examination" (581); on the other hand, they insist that black people must develop "one African voice" if they are to get along with each other (600).

One of the problems with Jackson and Cothran's argument is that it implies that the differences among people of African descent only came into existence with the "divide and conquer" strategies of European slavery that are now sustained by the Western media (see Jackson and Cothran 597). As highlighted in Massey's depiction of Diallo's life as a warrior-prince who defeated several rival villages in Mali, their argument not only devalues the fact that precolonial Africans did not see themselves as one people or speaking with one voice, a fact that they ironically acknowledge (581), but it also "fails to appreciate and truly respect differences within the group—

---

9. "*Government name*" is an urban slang term that refers to one's official name, the name found on one's birth certificate, tax documents, or social security card. In contrast to one's street alias, the name that represents the *real* you, one's government name is the *inauthentic* you, the you defined primarily by others.

for instance, along the lines of gender, sexuality, national origin, multiraciality, generation, region, religion, cultural affiliation, and political ideology" (Shelby 10). Moreover, Jackson and Cothran assume that internal differences cannot exist in a unified black community and, therefore, ignore the fact that differences, as I noted in chapter 2, do not automatically force people to see themselves as separate and distinct; rather, it is the social importance or cultural meanings people assign to those differences that creates the divide. Thus, given its critique of the idea that distance from Africa has made African American men less black and less manly than black men elsewhere, *Dark Corner* can be read as advocating a concept of blackness in which the only requirement for being black is having a black body. Such a concept of blackness is not concerned with who is pure or impure, masculine or feminine, African or American because what makes a person black, as evidenced by the white lynchers and castrators of black men discussed above, is his or her body, not his or her beliefs and behaviors. Moreover, this concept of blackness presumes that black heterogeneity is always already a fact, that blackness has never been and may never be monolithic precisely because the link between our bodies and our ideologies is not automatic. This may be the ultimate point of Diallo's death—in order for the African American community to progress in the twenty-first century, it must discard the idea that there is more to being black than having a black body.

CHAPTER 4

# HUMAN BLACKNESS, TRANSHUMAN BLACKNESS, AND THE BLACK BODY IN *FLEDGLING*

ONE POINT that Gomez's *The Gilda Stories*, Due's *My Soul to Keep*, and Massey's *Dark Corner* seem to agree on is that the only requirement for being black is having a black body. This means that if one has a black body, then one can never stop being black, regardless of one's sexuality, religion, culture, gender identification, political affiliation, or place of birth. By questioning the idea that there is more to being black than having a black body, these novels also question the idea that the body determines one's history, identity, and behavior. However, none of these novels devote their attention to removing the body from our understanding of blackness. Even though Gilda's "a row of cotton is a row of cotton" theory offers a conception of blackness in which all humans are nothing more than gradations of the same, this theory of blackness is still grounded in the body. Thus, what is it about the human body that makes it difficult for Americans to separate it from our conceptions of the self? Octavia Butler suggested in a 1997 interview that the answer to that question is simple: "Because the body is all we really know that we have" (Mehaffy and Keating 59). In other words, as Ian Hacking puts it, "no matter how much intellectuals, both humanists and scientists, may inveigh against it, people can hardly avoid thinking of their genetic inheritance as part of what constitutes them, as part of who they are, as their essence" (92).

Butler's belief that the body is all that we know derives from her theory of "body knowledge," a theory that distinguishes knowledge of the body from how we use that knowledge:

> Don't worry about the real biological determinism. Worry about what people make of it. Worry about the social Darwinism. After all, if sociobiology, or anything like it . . . is true, then denying it is certainly not going to help. What we have to do is learn to work with and to work against people who see it as a good reason to let the poor be poor, that kind of thing—the social Darwinism. (Mehaffy and Keating 57)

According to Butler, body knowledge represents the gap between "real biological determinism," the actual facts regarding human bodies, and how we use those facts to reinforce or change the relations of power within a social universe. On the one hand, the body-self relationship in Butler's theory of body knowledge is similar to what Claire Colebrook identifies as the "second possibility for thinking the body beyond sameness and difference" in feminist theory. Unlike the first possibility, which is "linguistic in approach" and contends that "any appeal to a body is always already discursive," the second possibility proposes that "while the body may only be *referred to* through discourse or representation, it possesses a force and being that marks the very character of representation" (76–77). In this light, Butler's theory of body knowledge can be viewed as a critique of postmodern thinking and writing in which the human body is treated primarily as a "discursive entity," a "thing" that "only language and narrative can bring to life and make known to ourselves or to others" (Mehaffy and Keating 59). Butler's conception of the body-self relationship reminds us, in the words of Charles Mills, that "relations of power are relations that obtain between bodies, and we need to recognize both how power constructs these bodies (a completely familiar theoretical imperative by now) and how bodies so shaped nonetheless continue to assert their corporeality (a far less familiar theme)" (588). Thus, for Butler, the reason why it is difficult to remove the body from our understanding of the self is that the self is "pretty much, body" (Mehaffy and Keating 59).

On the other hand, while Butler argued that there is no self without a body, her theory of body knowledge reminds us that our conceptions of ourselves are not always aligned with the biological realities of our bodies. One reason for this misalignment, according to Butler's discussion of the Oankali, the extraterrestrial aliens of her *Xenogenesis* trilogy, now titled *Lilith's Brood,* is due to what she refers to in that trilogy as the "human contradition," "the idea that human beings have two characteristics that don't work well together" (Mehaffy and Keating 53):

> I put the problem into the mouths of my alien characters, the Oankali. To them, humans have two characteristics that do not work well together. People are intelligent—no problem, the Oankali were happy to see that—but also we are hierarchical. And since our hierarchical tendencies are older, they tend to focus and drive our intelligence. So I began the books after the end of a horrible nuclear war in which we've one-upped ourselves to death. (Fry 128–29)

Implicit in Butler's explanation of the human contradiction is that the gap between real biological determinism and body knowledge is largely due to our propensity to privilege our hierarchical tendencies, which have the potential to cause the extinction of our species, over our intelligence, which we developed through evolution to extend our life spans. However, while our hierarchical tendencies will always be with us, Butler suggests that we can control those tendencies through our use of knowledge of the body. This means, as Analouise Keating puts it, that "knowledge of the body can be used to empower and not necessarily to determine" (Mehaffy and Keating 57).

Drawing upon Butler's conception of the human contradiction, I refer to knowledge of the body used to "empower" humans as *intelligent body knowledge* and that which is used to "determine" humans as *hierarchical body knowledge*. Hierarchical body knowledge describes not only the practice of using knowledge of the body that will lead to us one-upping ourselves to death, but also the idea that our social hierarchies are determined by the visible differences among human populations (e.g., the hierarchies created by racism and sexism). This is the body knowledge that underlines the belief that the body is transparent evidence of its history, identity, and behavior. Intelligent body knowledge, in contrast, begins with the premise that the significant differences among humans are not expressed by our bodies, but by our ideas about our bodies. Thus, intelligent body knowledge describes the practice of using knowledge of the body to offset our hierarchical tendencies by revealing that our social hierarchies are largely products of body knowledge, not real biological determinism, and by reminding us that human bodies are more alike than different. What makes this use of knowledge of the body empowering is that it offers the possibility that we can one day become a species whose intelligence consistently focuses and drives its hierarchical tendencies.

Given Butler's theory of body knowledge and the distinctions between intelligent and hierarchical body knowledge, she would have viewed the idea that the only requirement for being black is having a black body as a rational notion of blackness within an irrational body knowledge. Since the biological notion of race is a form of hierarchical body knowledge that treats the visible differences among human populations as signs of significant human differences, it makes sense that the only requirement for being black is having a black body. However, from the intelligent body knowledge perspective, that notion of blackness and the concept of race itself wrongly assume that there is scientific and cultural consensus on what distinguishes the black body from the nonblack body. For instance, I noted in chapter 1 that most Americans, regardless of racial identification, continue to believe in the racist and debunked "one-drop" rule, as indicated by our constant identification of mixed-raced people who are part black as only black.[1] However, if it is believed that the black body's blackness ranges from the visible to the nonvisible, as suggested by the one-drop rule, then how does one tell if a mixed or nonblack body is black? Most Americans would argue that while a person may have light or white skin, that person's hair texture, lips, nose, and/or buttocks are indicators of his or her blackness. The problem with that argument is that there are many people who have curly hair, full lips, wide noses, or round buttocks who are not identified as black; therefore, those traits are not useful for solving the question of the black body's blackness. I intend to show in this chapter that Butler's *Fledgling* (2005), her first vampire novel and the last novel by her to be published before her untimely and unfortunate death in 2006,[2] offers an answer to the question

---

1. Sharon Patricia Holland refers to the one-drop rule as part of racism's "project of belonging," a project of identification that signifies two sets of relations. "One is," according to Holland, "a 'real,' biological connection, a belonging that occurs at the level of family (blood relation). . . . The second set of relations is the result of the work of identifying with others, a belonging usually imposed by a community *or* by one's own choice" (3–4). For Holland, what we learn from these two sets of relations, quoting Robert Miles and Malcolm Brown, is that "the facts of biological difference are secondary to the meanings that are attributed to them." However, unlike Miles and Brown, Holland contends that "we don't create meaning as much as we reproduce it" (4).

2. Angela C. Allen suggests that Doro, the Nubian immortal and "vampirelike" star of Butler's Patternist series, can be considered Butler's first vampire character. Unlike the evil vampires created by nineteenth-century European authors, Doro uses "telepathic powers," instead of physical force, to empty his victims' bodies (viii). While Doro may be "vampirelike," he is not a "vampire" because "the true vampire is corporeal" (Summers, *Kith and Kin* 12). That is to say, Doro is not a vampire because he lacks his own body, a requirement that distinguishes the vampire from ghosts, demons, and spirits. Indeed, Anyanwu, the immortal shape-shifting protagonist of *Wild Seed* (1980), discovers early in her relationship with Doro that he is a "spirit" who "steals the bodies of men" (14).

of what makes a body black through her portrayal of Shori Matthews, a staying-alive vampire who is unaware that she is black, a vampire, and a genetic experiment.

Narrated in the first person, *Fledgling* is about the birth and rebirth of Shori, the first surviving black woman of the Ina people. The Ina have been living with and among humans for more than ten thousand years, and some believe that they may have "evolved" alongside humans as a "cousin species like the chimpanzee," while others argue that they "arrived" from another planet waiting to go home to "paradise" (*Fledgling* 73). Although the Ina are humanlike, they are not human; they are a different species who cannot interbreed with humans or live in sunlight. Because of these inabilities, the Ina began experiments in genetic engineering to produce human-Inas. For centuries they were unsuccessful, until the birth of Shori and her siblings, whose existence causes a "crisis of race survival" among the Ina (Smith 388). Some Ina view Shori and her siblings as signs of their people's future, while others see them as signs of the Ina's demise. The Ina who fear Shori's survival tried to kill her and her family, but they were only successful in killing her family. However, Shori was injured so badly by her attackers that she awakens in a cave with amnesia, where the novel begins: "I awoke to darkness. I was hungry—starving!—and I was in pain. There was nothing in my world but hunger and pain, no other people, no other time, no other feelings" (*Fledgling* 7).[3] What allows Shori to utter the word "I" is her body, specifically her body's feelings of hunger and pain. Because these feelings exist before she becomes aware of other people or her reflection, these are the feelings that largely define that "I," an "I" that will be constantly redefined by others and herself.

After a few nights of killing and eating animals, including one human whom she mistook for a forest animal, Shori leaves the cave to find out who and what she is. While walking on a country road, she accepts a ride from Wright Hamlin, a twenty-something white male who is a construction worker on hiatus from the University of Washington. What makes Wright important to Shori's rebirth is that he is her first "symbiont"—a human who agrees to be part of an Ina family and to be used by his or her Ina for

---

3. By beginning Shori's story in this way, according to Lauren Lacey, Butler constructs a narrative in which "the reader and the protagonist share the discoveries of her identity"; therefore, Butler "creates the conditions necessary for both an unfolding mystery and for the reader to share in the protagonist's experience of adapting to increasing knowledge about who and what she is" (381). This narrative structure suggests that Butler was asking readers to interrogate their own notions of how people attain their identities by placing themselves in Shori's situation, since they, like Shori, are in the dark about who and what she is.

food, companionship, and sex—and the first human to "name" her since she emerged from the cave. Wright not only names her "Renee," which means "reborn," but he initially identifies her as a "vampire," "jailbait," and "black" because she drinks blood, looks like a ten- or eleven-year-old girl, and has brown skin. Although Shori agrees to be named by Wright, she soon realizes that the identities that he assigns to her conflict with what her body tells her. Even when Shori is reunited with the Ina, she is confronted with the fact that she does not have the final say on the question of her Inaness. Indeed, Shori has to endure an Ina court trial to determine if she is Ina or human, even though her body tells her and the Ina community that she is definitely both.

I noted in the introduction of this book that the scholarship on *Fledgling* contends that the novel denormalizes our disdain of hybridity, our boundaries of power, and our obsession with utopias. In other words, *Fledgling* is like much of Butler's previous works, which are "thematically preoccupied with the potentiality of genetically altered bodies—hybrid multi-species and multi-ethnic subjectivities—for revising contemporary nationalist, racist, sexist, and homophobic attitudes" (Mehaffy and Keating 45). I am specifically interested in Nayar's claim that "species miscegenation" in *Fledgling* is "essentially a domestication of vampires and humans into a posthuman interracialization." According to Nayar, this "domestication," a process that allows a species to "erase their characteristic 'essences' in order to fit in better with their ecosystem," eventually results in humans and vampires evolving into an "indeterminate deracinated inter-species." I argue, however, that human-vampire miscegenation in *Fledgling* is not about erasing the "essences" of humans and vampires, nor does it lead to a "posthuman interracialization"; instead, that miscegenation, as symbolized by Shori, leads to what I call *transhuman blackness*, which begins with the premise that every human, regardless of skin color, is born black because every human, except for the rare exceptions, has melanin. To appreciate the transhuman blackness offered by Butler in *Fledgling*, it is necessary to begin with a discussion of Shori's transhuman vampirism. Unlike the staying-alive vampirisms in *The Gilda Stories* and *Dark Corner*, which represent the elixir version of the Staying Alive Narrative, Shori represents that narrative's Engineering Approach, in which transhumanism is its latest manifestation. Following my discussion of Shori's transhuman vampirism, I examine the ways in which Shori's transhumanist body problematizes the hierarchical body knowledge that informs Wright's description of Shori as a "vampire," "black," and "jailbait." Finally, I conclude this chapter with a discussion of how Butler's conception of transhuman blackness answers the question that grounds this book: Is there more to being black than having a black body?

## Transhuman Vampirism

The term "transhuman" is a condensed version of "transitional human"—the stage between human and posthuman (i.e., the moment when humans are no longer *human*)—and the term "transhumanism," at its most basic level, is defined as the belief that we should use technology to *enhance* human beings (Elliot 14). Even scientists who are not self-described transhumanists believe that transhumans will be humanity's future. For example, Michio Kaku predicts that by 2100 humans will be "like the gods we once worshipped and feared," but the tools that will be used to reach this stage of development will not come from the supernatural world; rather, they will come from the "science of computers, nanotechnology, artificial intelligence, biotechnology, and most of all, the quantum theory" (12). However, it is important to note that there are different sects of transhumanism. For example, there are the libertarian transhumanists, who are said to make up roughly 27 percent of the transhumanist community and argue that individuals should have the right to enhance or alter themselves without government interference (Sirius and Cornell 107). The Mormon Transhumanist Association contends that transhumanism is God working through humans to make them better and to prepare them for the prophesied millennium (139). The psychedelic transhumanists, who are interested in "intelligence-amplification-superintelligence rather than supersentience," believe that psychedelic drugs are "mind enhancers" that can lead us to "poetic peak experiences" and "to see the evolution of humanity and beyond as much in terms of qualia as quanta" (183–86).

As suggested by these various transhumanisms, one of the issues that lacks consensus within the transhumanist community is the goals of transhumanism. For example, Nick Bostrum defines transhumanism as the belief that "current human nature is *improvable* through the use of applied science and other rational methods, which may make it possible to increase human health-span, extend our intellectual and physical capacities, and give us increased control over our own mental states and moods" (202–3; my emphasis). Here, transhumanism is a belief system that calls for the use of science and technology to make humans *better* than they are now, that is, to make us smarter, stronger, healthier, longer-lived, and less violent than we are today. On the other hand, as David Orderberg notes, there is a "minority of transhumanists" who claim that "enhancement technologies could, through 'participant evolution,' be used to create an entirely new species. This 'posthuman' species would not consist of human beings with enhanced abilities—mere 'transhumans'—but of a new kind of being, wholly superior to humans in sufficient respects for it plausibly to be called a distinct species" (207). The positions held by Bostrum and the "minority of transhumanists" described by Orderberg represent, respectively, one of the differences between what some call "moderate" and "strong" transhumanists. Moderate transhumanists, like Bostrum, believe that the goal of transhumanism is to use technology to enhance human characteristics; therefore, they are only concerned with making us *better* humans, not with making us more than human. In contrast, strong transhumanists, like Orderberg's transhumanist minority, argue that we should use technology to overcome human nature's limitations, that is, to become posthuman (McNamee and Edwards 514). While strong and moderate transhumanists may disagree on the goals of transhumanism, both tend to agree that transhumans will be smarter, stronger, healthier, less violent, and longer-lived than today's humans.

Although most scholars locate the origin of transhumanism in the West, it seems that transhumanism, as a practice, has a history older than the West. According to Harari, "there is nothing new about biological engineering, per se. People have been using it for millennia in order to reshape themselves and other organisms" (400). For Cave, transhumanism is a contemporary example of the scientific version of the Staying Alive Narrative, humanity's first immortality narrative. Unlike the elixir version of that narrative, which relies on potions, rituals, magic, and/or a deity for immortality, that narrative's scientific version, what Cave calls the Engineering Approach, is guided by the belief that the road to immortality is called "progress," the idea that we are getting better at finding death's many modes of attack and developing better defenses against these attacks. This means that the Engineering Approach is not seeking to solve the problems of mortality (e.g., aging and incurable diseases) all at once; rather, it offers a "piecemeal problem-solving strategy" (59). This piecemeal strategy, in which the problems of mortality are broken down into manageable parts and solved one by one, is referred to by some transhumanists as "achieving 'longevity escape velocity,' or living long enough to live forever" (64). However, this is where transhumanism runs into problems, according to Cave. For example, by increasing our survival rates from the deadly infections of the past, we have created ways for people to live long enough to develop the "much more lingering diseases of modernity," such as cancer and Alzheimer's. Thus, Cave concludes that transhumanists are not really helping us live longer; rather, they are helping us die slower (68).

While transhumanists, save for the ones seeking to become posthuman, would agree that we may never achieve immortality in the literal sense, recent developments in biotechnology and related fields suggest that we will be able to live long enough to live forever.[4] As Harari puts it, while it is true that we still lack the "acumen" to achieve the goals of transhumanism or even posthumanism, "there seems to be no insurmountable technical barrier preventing us from producing superhumans" (403). In *Fledgling*, Butler does not treat transhumanist technology as science fiction, but as scientific reality. By doing so, she can address a question that tends to be overlooked by the scholarship on transhumanism—what the typical transhuman will look like in order to fit in better with our ecosystem? According to Butler, the typical transhuman will look like Shori. For example, Preston Gordon, head of the Ina Council that is debating whether Shori is human or Ina,

---

4. Robert A. Freitas, Jr., a researcher who applies nanotechnology to medicine, has recently claimed the following: "[Biological, mechanical, and nanotechnological therapies] may become commonplace a few decades from today. Using annual checkups and cleanouts, and some occasional major repairs, your biological age could be restored once a year to the more or less constant physiological age that you select. You might still eventually die of accidental causes, but you'll live at least ten times longer than you do now" (qtd. in Kaku 176). Like Freitas, Organovo, the San Diego–based company that is considered one of the pioneers in the bioprinting industry, claims that future humans will be able to replace worn or defective body organs with *printed* ones made from our own cells via 3D bioprinters, inkjet-style printers that *print* living tissue (Gilpin). Although we will have the ability to replace many of the organs in our body with printed organ tissue, transhumanists realize that our brains may be the main obstacle in making the transition from human to transhuman. Marvin Minsky, a pioneer in the field of artificial intelligence and cofounder of MIT's Artificial Intelligence Laboratory, argued a little over twenty years ago that extending human life requires changing both our bodies and our brains (1212). However, he argued that replacing the brain with a new one will not work because we would lose the knowledge, experiences, and processes that make up our identities. Furthermore, although we might be able to "replace certain worn out parts of brains by transplanting tissue-cultured fetal cells," this procedure will not restore any knowledge or memories (1215). It seems that today's scientists have started the process of overcoming the obstacles that our brains pose for the transhumanist future. For example, Kaku noted in 2011 that "scientists are, for the first time in history, tracing the specific neural pathways of the brain that control specific behaviors" (103). This knowledge could be used not only to build robots and other types of machines with humanlike brains but also to help and heal patients who are suffering from the effects of stroke, brain diseases, and brain injuries (102). Thus, instead of just focusing on replacing the worn parts of the brain, today's scientists are focusing on how to heal, preserve, and replicate the brain. In the eyes of the transhumanists, this approach to the brain makes sense because it is the only way that we can live on indefinitely as the same persons without dying.

emphasizes in his defense of Shori's Inaness that she "carries the potentially life-saving human DNA that has darkened her skin and given her something we've sought for generations: the ability to walk in sunlight, to stay awake and alert during the day" (*Fledgling* 278). The life-saving human DNA that Preston is referring to is melanin, what Nina Jablonski calls a "superb natural sunscreen" (66). The Ina realize, as Jablonski notes, "melanin helps to protect us from the DNA damage caused by UVR [ultraviolet radiation] and the free radicals it produces"; therefore, those who produce less melanin (e.g., light-skinned people, people with oculocutaneous albinism, and the Ina) are "more likely to get sunburned, are less likely to tan, and are generally more susceptible to skin cancers" than those with dark skin (72–73). Indeed, melanin will not only help the Ina to withstand the sun's UVR, but it will also give them, as Preston alludes to, the ability to better defend themselves against their human enemies, who are natural daywalkers. For Preston and others who support the creation of more Shoris, they are not attempting to change or erase Ina essence in order to become daywalkers, as those who are attempting to kill Shori believe. In fact, Shori's need for symbionts, a need that all Ina have, suggests that the lack of melanin might not be an Ina essence.

Long before Shori discovers that she is Ina, her body tells her that she *needs* symbionts. During a break in the Council, Joan Braithwaite, another Shori supporter, explains why this is so:

> We need our symbionts more than most of them know. We need not only their blood, but physical contact with them and emotional reassurance from them. Companionship. I've never known even one of us to survive without symbionts. We should be able to do it—survive through casual hunting. But the truth is that that only works for short periods. Then we sicken. We either weave ourselves a family of symbionts, or we die. Our bodies need theirs. (*Fledgling* 276)

Being Ina, ironically, means being dependent on human companionship for survival; therefore, Ina who can survive without symbionts are not Ina, but human or post-Ina. In other words, although Shori has human DNA, she is still Ina because her body, like the bodies of all Ina, requires the same basics for survival: human blood and human companionship.

Like the moderate transhumanists, the Ina who support the melanization of the Ina are not attempting to change or erase the Ina's Inaness; instead, they are attempting to direct their own evolutionary development rather than leave it in the hands of nature. They realize that to make their bodies fit in better with the planet's ecosystem, the Ina need to become trans-Ina. To be trans-Ina, however, means incorporating a human essence into the Ina gene pool. For the pro-melaninization Ina, melanin not only separates Ina from humans, but it is the primary reason why humans, as opposed to the Ina, are the planet's dominant species. Indeed, the decision by the Ina to use dark-skinned humans in their genetic experiments is not guided by the idea of a black superiority–white inferiority view of humans, but by the fact that dark-skinned humans have more melanin than light-skinned humans. As I will discuss in detail below, all humans, regardless of skin color, are black, according to the Ina, because they all have some amount of melanin in them. According to that logic, while light or white skin may have social value in the US, dark skin has survival value for both humans and Ina. Thus, American whitening practices (e.g., using skin bleaching creams, limiting brown-skinned children's time in the sun to prevent them from getting darker, or choosing lighter-skinned mates with the intention of producing light-skinned offspring) would not make sense to the Ina because the human body needs the sun's UVR to "transform molecules in the skin into the precursors of vitamin D," which is important to producing healthy skeletons, regulating cell growth, and inhibiting cancer cell growth (Jablonski 64). Since melanin helps to control the destructive powers of the sun's UVR by regulating the amount of UVR entering the skin and simultaneously absorbing its healthful benefits, what Jablonski refers to as "the skin's dark secret" (64), Butler proposes in *Fledgling* that melanin is linked not only to being human but also to living long enough to live forever.

For famed political scientist Francis Fukuyama, however, transhumanism is one of the world's most dangerous ideas because it is attempting to modify human essence, an essence based on equal rights: "the first victim of transhumanism might be equality" ("Transhumanism" 42). As Fukuyama sees it, if the transhumanists have their way, the idea that all humans are entitled to political and legal equality will be destroyed. He believes that once people begin transforming themselves into something "superior," we will not only see legal, political, and economic inequalities emerge between transhumans and humans, but we will also see the same inequalities widen between the richest and poorest countries, since the marvels of biotechnology will be out of reach for the citizens of the world's poorest countries (43). Thus, for Fukuyama, the transhumanist project will not make humans *better*; rather, it will only exacerbate the inequalities that currently exist.[5]

---

5. Fukuyama makes a similar point in his chapter on genetic engineering in *Our Posthuman Future*, where he argues, quite problematically, that one of the potential problems with genetic engineering and designer babies specifically is that the technology to

Carl Elliot points out that there are ideological strands of transhumanism that might result in making today's social problems worse because they rely on an "individualistic, libertarian ideology" and/or an "idealistic faith in the power of technology to make the world a better place." For instance, "ethnic" plastic surgery, a surgical procedure in which patients seek to add or remove an "ethnic" feature, is what Elliot would call an "enhancement technology," a medical intervention aimed at improving human traits and capacities rather than curing illnesses. Since a considerable number of enhancement technologies are used as remedies for social stigma, especially those focused on the body, these technologies will most likely lead to more people seeking enhancement, instead of seeking to fix the social structures that are at the root of poverty and that make these people unhappy about their bodies (18–20). Although Butler would agree with most of Fukuyama's and Elliot's concerns, what some have called the "'genetic divide' of classes based on genetic modification" critique (Sirius and Cornell 56), she suggests in *Fledgling* that the core idea of transhumanism, the idea of making humans *better*, is worth pursuing. Unlike Fukuyama, who assumes that equality might be transhumanism's first victim, Butler suggests in *Fledgling* that this victim might be hierarchical body knowledge, since it is at the root of most social inequalities due to its insistence that bodily differences explain social hierarchies.

## Vampire, Human, Both, or Neither?

The first identity that Wright assigns to Shori is "vampire," a word and concept that is foreign to Shori. When Wright tells Shori what he knows about vampires, she begins to question the ways in which she and vampires are identified:

> Wright told me what he remembered about vampires—that they're immortal unless someone stabs them in the heart with a wooden stake, and yet

---

produce such babies could be accessible to all. As he sees it, if that technology is only accessible to "a handful of rich people genetically modifying their children for greater height or intelligence," we would have nothing to worry about, but if that technology is available to more than a "handful of rich people," then it could possibly, among other considerations, "upend existing social hierarchies and affect the rate of intellectual, material, and political progress," as well as change "our notions of justice, morality, and the good life" (78–83). It seems that Fukuyama is more concerned with genetic engineering's ability to disrupt current hierarchies than with its ability to help alleviate some of the inequalities that exist between the "handful of rich people" and the rest of humanity.

even without being stabbed they're dead, or undead. Whatever that means. They drink blood, they have no reflections in mirrors, they can become bats or wolves, they turn other people into vampires either by drinking their blood or by making the convert drink the vampire's blood. This last detail seemed to depend on which story you were reading or which movie you were watching. That was the other thing about vampires. They were fictional beings. Folklore. There were no vampires.

So what was I? (*Fledgling* 21–22)

As suggested by Shori's question, she is not asking if people like her exist because her body tells her that they exist; rather, she is asking what her body means in Wright's culture. Indeed, Wright's answers to Shori's question, as she learns from her research on vampires and from Wright's distinction between humans and vampires, tell her more about Wright's culture than they do about humans and vampires. What Shori learns about Wright's culture is that it is shaped by hierarchical body knowledge, especially by its *what you see is what you get* approach to the body-self relationship, the belief that our bodies are visible manifestations of our *real* selves. One of the problems with the what-you-see-is-what-you-get approach, as suggested by Shori and Wright's first encounter, is that what one *sees* and who one *gets* are never obvious.

When Wright picks up Shori from the side of the road, his initial plan is to take her to a hospital or a police station because she looks like a ten- or eleven-year-old girl who has suffered serious physical injuries. After suspecting Wright's plan, Shori tries to jump out of his car because she does not want anyone to know of her existence. In his attempt to prevent her from opening the car door, Wright is bitten on the hand by Shori. Driven by instinct, Shori begins to lick the blood from the bite on Wright's hand. At that moment, Wright tells Shori that she is a "vampire" (*Fledgling* 18). However, when Wright puts Shori and himself in front of his bathroom mirror, she notes that he "seemed relieved to see that the mirror reflected two people instead of one" (24). Although Wright is convinced that Shori is a vampire because she licks the blood from his hand, he dismisses that conclusion once he sees himself and Shori in the mirror. In this instance, Wright identifies Shori not by her behavior, but by her body, implying that one's body trumps one's behavior in understanding who or what one really is. Wright's view of Shori as human assumes that the mirror can reflect *all* of the body and that there are distinct boundaries between humans and non-humans. The problem with the first assumption seems obvious: The image in the mirror cannot tell Wright that Shori is mixed. Indeed, the only thing that the mirror can tell Wright about Shori is that she is a young female human with brown skin; it cannot tell him that she is also an experiment and a fifty-three-year-old vampire. Moreover, Wright's use of Shori's reflection as confirmation of her humanity mistakenly presumes that to exist is to be seen by others. For example, although Shori is unsuccessful in finding information on vampires that confirms what her body tells her about herself, she does not reason that she is unique; rather, she concludes that "whoever or whatever I was, no one seemed to be writing about my kind. Perhaps my kind did not want to be written about" (*Fledgling* 39). What Butler might be suggesting here is that while we need the other to help define what we are or are not, we do not need the other to confirm our existence because our bodies already do that.

Like the mirror's inability to reflect all of Shori's body, Wright's distinction between human and vampire is unable to reflect Shori's mixture because that distinction is one in which bodies can be either human or nonhuman, but never both because such mixture is considered nonhuman. For example, shortly after their time in the mirror, Shori recalls that besides drinking blood to stay alive, she needs to eat raw meat to heal injuries, cure illnesses, sustain growth spurts, and help carry a child. Due to this additional information, Wright concludes that Shori is "not human" (*Fledgling* 25–26). However, the evidence that Wright uses to conclude that Shori is not human is questionable at best because humans have and continue to consume blood and eat raw meat.[6] Moreover, Shori learns through her research on vampires that people "mistaken" for vampires in the past were actual people who had diseases that either made them allergic to sunlight or that convinced them that they were vampires (36–37, 39). Butler's point seems to be that if there are clear bodily and conceptual distinctions between humans and nonhumans, then Wright would not switch between human and vampire in his reading of Shori, and we would not have a history of humans mistaken for vampires. In other words, Wright's uncertainty about how to classify Shori symbolizes not only our uncertainty about what we are but also the reality that body knowledge, not the body, is what makes one human or not human.

---

6. I noted in the introduction of this book that the history of vampirism dates back to the days of hunter-gatherer humans, who drank human and nonhuman blood because they believed that it renewed vitality. While there are some cultures and religions that have taboos against the consumption of blood, food items such as blood sausage/black pudding, pig's blood cake, pig's blood sundae, blodplatter (Nordic blood pancakes), Dinuguan (Filipino pig's blood stew), and Polish Czarnina (duck blood soup) indicate that humans are not inherently disgusted by the consumption of blood as the Western vampire myth would have us believe.

Claiming that body knowledge is what distinguishes the human from the nonhuman is not to say that the body has little influence on our humanity, since body knowledge is premised on the "certainty of the flesh," in which the body functions as the primary communicator of the self (Mehaffy and Keating 59). It is to point out, however, that our distinction between the human and the nonhuman is not axiomatic, but value laden (Graham 47).[7] Fukuyama makes a similar point in his criticism of transhumanism: "The most serious political fights in the history of the United States have been over who qualifies as fully human," and "women and blacks did not make the cut in 1776 when Thomas Jefferson penned the declaration" ("Transhumanism" 42). Thus, the problem with Wright's what-you-see-is-what-you-get distinction between the human and the nonhuman is that the what you "see" and "get" are not obvious, fixed, or universal because that distinction is never outside of discourse or the changing relations of power. Indeed, when Shori asks, "So what was I?," she is questioning not only the accuracy of Wright's readings of her body but also the hierarchies that underline his readings. The hierarchies that shape Wright's reading of Shori as either human or vampire assume that the human is nature's grand achievement, an assumption that Fukuyama defends. According to Fukuyama, by acknowledging that "being human entitles a person to political and legal equality," we have essentially "drawn a red line around the human being and said that it is sacrosanct." What underlines this equality is "the belief that we all possess a human essence that dwarfs manifest differences in skin color, beauty, and even intelligence" ("Transhumanism" 42).

One problem with Fukuyama's claim is that if we now treat the human being as sacred and inviolable, why do our everyday practices—not just those in contemporary biomedicine, as he points out—tell us otherwise? The prevalence of elective plastic surgeries, performance-enhancing drugs, workout videos, religions that view the body as the locus of sin, and immortality narratives that equate living forever with a changed body, for example, indicate that many Americans, not just the transhumanists, believe that our bodies need improvement. By acknowledging the limitations of the body, these Americans are also acknowledging, as Butler proposes in *Fledgling*, that the human body, like the Ina body, does not represent the apex of biological pos-

---

7. For example, Sherryl Vint notes in her analysis of Butler's *Clay's Ark* (1984), a novel from the *Patternist* series, that Butler's explorations of the "intersections of power and difference" posit that humanity is "something that has to be achieved, not something equally and equitably granted to all people" (283). Butler appears to be making the same point in *Fledgling* to show that the reason why our distinction between the human and the nonhuman is value laden is that our understanding of the human is value laden.

sibilities.[8] For example, Russell Silk, whose family is being charged with the death of Shori's family members, declares at the Council that the Ina should avoid melaninization, even if it means gaining the ability to function in daylight, because the "cost is too great":

> What matters most to us, to every member of the Silk family, is the welfare of the Ina people. We Ina are vastly outnumbered by the human beings of this world. And how many of us have been butchered in their wars? They destroy one another by the millions, and it makes no difference to their numbers. They breed and breed and breed, while we live long and breed slowly. Their lives are brief and, without us, riddled with disease and violence. And yet, we need them. We take them into our families, and with our help, they are able to live longer, stay free of disease, and get along with one another. (297–98)

As Russell sees it, melaninizing the Ina will not result in the Ina evolving, but devolving. Although Russell acknowledges that the Ina cannot live without human companionship, he also believes that the Ina are the human's superior because the Ina are smarter, stronger, healthier, less violent, and longer-lived than humans. In this view, instead of the Ina attempting to become human, humans should be engineering themselves to become Ina.

Like Wright, Russell offers an Ina-human distinction that is unable to account for Shori's mixture because that distinction presumes that bodies can be either Ina or human, but never both. Although Russell knows that Shori is mixed, he still sees her as only human because his one-drop rule logic assumes that the Ina represent the apex of biological possibilities, even though the Ina lack melanin, the trait that has allowed humans to become the planet's dominant species. Wright's and Russell's views of Shori seem to be driven by the desire to maintain the hierarchies implied by their human-Ina distinctions; that is to say, both believe that human and Ina bodies have reached their evolutionary ends, even though Shori is proof that they are both wrong. In Russell's case, his reference to Shori as human seeks to counter the reality that Shori's melanin automatically makes her body *better* than his or any other Ina body. Similarly, Wright's reference to Shori as human, after he calls her a vampire, can be read as his attempt to counter his subordinate role in their relationship. In other words, if Wright acknowledges that Shori is a vampire, he must also acknowledge that Shori is more powerful than him and that humankind may not be the dominant species on the

---

8. Butler makes a similar argument in her *Xenogenesis* trilogy. See E. White (1993).

planet. Thus, Shori's transhuman body, a body that is more than human but not posthuman, problematizes the what-you-see-is-what-you-get approach to the body-self relationship that informs Russell's and Wright's views of Shori in which the differences and hierarchical status between human and nonhuman bodies are presumed to be clear.

In addition to maintaining the perceived hierarchy between humans and nonhumans, Russell's and Wright's views of Shori suggest that they also want to maintain the racial hierarchies that exist in US society. For instance, while Wright embraces the goals of transhumanism, as indicated by his decision to become one of Shori's symbionts, who are themselves chemically enhanced humans, his reading of Shori as "black" points to the fact that the hierarchical body knowledge that groups humans into black and nonblack is hard to let go. Indeed, while Shori's reflection challenges Wright's view of her as a vampire and her consumption of blood challenges his view of her as human, there is nothing that Shori can do that will make Wright question his view of her as black. It is, therefore, noteworthy that Wright does not question Shori's blackness until he meets the Ina because it not only suggests that it is easier for Wright to accept Shori as a mixed-species person than as mixed-race person, but it also proposes that to move beyond the biological notion of race, we need to encounter what Butler once referred to as "truly" alien people, beings who exist "with or without our belief, with [or] without our permission." However, such an encounter will not automatically lead to the unity of humankind:

> Perhaps for a moment, only a moment, this affront will [bring] us together, all human, all much more alike than different, all much more alike than is good for our prickly pride. Humanity, *E pluribus unum* at last, a oneness focused on and fertilized by certain knowledge of alien others. What will be born of that brief, strange, and ironic union? (Butler, "The Monophobic Response" 416)

On the one hand, Butler suggests that once we become aware of beings like the Ina, who exist without our belief or permission, we will start to focus on our similarities instead of our differences because we will realize that there are no human others, save for the ones we create. On the other hand, Butler critiques that view when she concludes that the "oneness" born out of our knowledge of alien people will be "brief, strange, and ironic," words that imply that this oneness will be temporary and out of character. In *Fledgling*, Butler expands upon the paradoxical tension in the passage above by suggesting that such oneness can only be achieved if humans become transhuman or if truly alien people treat us as one race (e.g., pro-melaninization Ina) instead of as a group of races (e.g., anti-melaninization Ina).

## Why Does Brown Equal Black?

While staring in Wright's bathroom mirror, Shori describes herself as a "lean, sharp-faced, large-eyed, brown-skinned person" who has a "short fuzz of black hair on [her] head" (*Fledgling* 24). The only time that the word "black" is used in Shori's description of herself is when she is referring to the color of her hair. In fact, she does not make the link between blackness and brown skin until Wright makes that link. When Wright asks Shori if her skin burns even though she is "black," Shori states the following:

> "I'm . . ." I stopped. I had been about to protest that I was brown, not black, but before I could speak, I understood what he meant. Then his question triggered another memory. I looked at him. "I think I'm an experiment. I can withstand the sun better than . . . others of my kind. I burn, but I don't burn as fast as they do. It's like an allergy we all have to the sun. I don't know who the experimenters are, though, the ones who made me black." (37)

Shori's description of herself as a "brown-skinned person" and an "experiment" indicates that she recognizes that she has been "made" black, that her blackness is not natural. However, Butler is not simply revealing the falsity of the biological notion of race, but she is also critiquing the visualness of race in which the social value of skin color is privileged over its survival value. For example, Wright's treatment of Shori's reflection as transparent evidence of her blackness can be read as his attempt to reaffirm the privileges he receives as a straight, white male in America. As Winnubst explains, what makes the vampire "forever haunting" for the straight white male subject is that the vampire is "neither subject nor Other." Since the traditional vampire lacks a mirror reflection and since subjectivity in Western culture hinges on the "visual image, the mirror reflection," the vampire is unable to "offer up the necessary visual image to be coded by the dominant signifier of phallicized whiteness" (8). In this light, what makes Wright relieved that he sees two people in the mirror instead of one is that the mirror confirms that Shori is not a vampire, but a black girl, one who is not white, male, or an adult. Thus, it is not too surprising that even though Shori tells Wright that she was "made" black, he does not question Shori's blackness or the idea of blackness until he encounters the Ina because, as Wahneema Lubiano once wrote, "the basic character of the United States not only harbored, but depended upon, a profound violation of the spirit of democracy, and that fundamental violation is racism" (vii). In other words, if Wright believed that people are made black and white, then he would not be American.

In contrast to Wright, the Ina who support the melaninization of the Ina believe that all humans, regardless of skin color, are *black* because they all have melanin, save for the rare exceptions. This view of the human body, as I noted earlier in this chapter, informed their decision to use dark-skinned humans in their genetic experiments because dark-skinned humans have more melanin than light-skinned humans. Through their experiments on the human body, the Ina have learned that human skin is "inherently colorful" because people possess different amounts and packaging of melanin due to evolution through natural selection (Jablonski 65, 75). Moreover, since adaptation to UVR has been the most important determinant in the evolution of human skin colors, skin color is useless as a sign of one's racial identity because all that dark skin and light skin can tell us is where people's ancestors might have lived and the diseases they might be susceptible to (95). This understanding of the variations in human skin color explains why Wells, the son of Preston Gordon, cannot accept Wright's contention that the people who are trying to kill Shori are Ina racists who do not like "the idea that a good part of the answer to [their] daytime problem is melanin" (*Fledgling* 153). Indeed, Wells quickly dismisses Wright's assertion and insists that human racism is not important to the Ina because "human races mean nothing to them." According to Wells, when searching for potential symbionts, the Ina are not concerned with the skin color of these humans because the only thing that matters is finding "congenial" human beings (154). In other words, the Ina have learned that skin color can only tell them how much melanin a human has; it cannot tell them, as Wells puts it, if one is "congenial."

Shori thinks to herself, however, that the response by Wells sounds less like "logic" and more like "wounded pride" (*Fledgling* 154). What makes Wells's response illogical is that the significance of Shori's birth and survival is only known to the Ina community; therefore, the individuals who are trying to kill Shori must be Ina racists. What makes his response sound like "wounded pride" is that Wells is unwilling to deal with the possibility that there are Ina who are racists. Since the Ina believe, as Russell notes, that they are more intelligent and less violent than humans, to admit that the Ina could succumb to racist thinking is to admit that the Ina may not be as intelligent and peaceful as they believe themselves to be. Butler seems to be suggesting here that intelligence does not prevent one from succumbing to hierarchical body knowledge because this approach to using knowledge of the body is informed by a body's social value, not its survival value. This means that racism does not exist because we recognize bodily differences, as Wells assumes; instead, racism exists because of the social value we assign to those bodily differences. For example, Katharine Dahlman, one of several Ina who believe that Shori is not a real Ina, declares that Shori is both a "great error" and "nothing" because she is "neither Ina nor human." Moreover, Katharine asks the Council if they want their sons to procreate with Shori because they will produce "black, human children." She recalls that when she first arrived in the US, "such people were kept as property, as slaves" (278). Like Russell, Katharine claims that there is a "cost" to mixing Ina and black human genes, even if such mixing guarantees the continuation of the Ina people. Unlike Russell, who identifies that cost as Ina purity, Katharine defines it as economic. George Lipsitz has noted that "white Americans are encouraged to invest in whiteness" precisely because whiteness has a "cash value" (vii). Similarly, Katharine believes that the Ina's pale skin allows for more economic opportunities than Shori's brown skin because blackness in America has less cash value than whiteness. In this light, the source of Wells's wounded pride is the realization that the economic value assigned to white skin in the US has become, for Ina like Katharine, a reason to remain purely Ina, a reason to overlook the survival value of dark skin.

As suggested by Butler's depiction of Katharine's and Russell's anti-melaninization arguments, racism, particularly its antiblack version, does not belong in a transhuman world because it is incapable of helping us get along with each other. The problem with race, as the pro-melaninization Ina contend, is that it cannot tell us anything about the biological differences among people with different skin colors, only their social differences. Audrey Smedley has pointed out that unlike previous constructions of human identity in which biological differences among human populations were not given significant social meaning, race imposes "social meanings on physical variations among human groups that serve as the basis for the structuring of society" (693). Moreover, since race is an ideology that structures societal inequality, it is in direct contradiction to the ideas of "freedom, democracy, equality, and human rights" that Westerners claim to champion because it equates visible differences with social inequality and claims that a deity or nature has made this so (693–94). Thus, as Wells suggests in his explanation of what the Ina look for in humans who might become symbionts, race is not a reliable way to understand human differences, nor has it helped us, as Russell would put it, get along with one another precisely because it was created to justify conquest, colonization, and enslavement.

It is, therefore, noteworthy that Wright does not question Shori's blackness, even when she tells him that she was "made" black, until he meets the Ina because it sadly suggests that it will take an encounter with truly alien people for us to realize that there are no human races, save for the ones we create. Since race was invented to rationalize one group's exploitation of other groups, Butler suggests that we need truly alien people to help us transcend race because many people profit from the reinforcement of this mythical conception of human difference.[9] While Butler appears pessimistic about our ability to come to terms with the fact that race is a myth, her vision of the transhuman future as one of mixture and mixing suggests otherwise. Thus, when Katharine asks the Council if they want their sons to mate with Shori because they will produce "black children," Butler is not only reminding us that anti-miscegenation laws, laws that were deemed unconstitutional only in 1967, were one of the ways race was reinforced in the US, but she is also suggesting through Katharine that miscegenation is still a de facto taboo. As Sharon Patricia Holland writes, "even though every human visage and quotidian encounter bears witness to miscegenation's imprint, miscegenation remains an impossibility" in US culture (5). In this light, by portraying Shori's body as a mixed body, Butler constructs the transhuman future as one where "purity is impossible" (Brox 405). Indeed, for the pro-melaninizaton Ina, the death of Katharine by Shori and the dissolution of the Silk family by the Ina Council are necessary if the Ina plan to evolve as a species, since their evolution, like that of their human brothers

---

9. For instance, Jonathan Kimmelman's discussion of the pharmaceutical industry's "reinscription of race" suggests that race tells us very little about the biological differences among humans, but it can tell us about the differences in cash value among the *races*. Indeed, the "reinscription of race" in the pharmaceutical industry appears to be based less on conclusive scientific evidence about human differences and more on how to profit from drugs that failed general testing by marketing them to specific racial groups (e.g., BiDil for African Americans and gefitinib for Asians): "In pharmaceutical development, investigators are now prospectively designing subgroup analyses into clinical trials so that drugs that fail testing at the whole population level might be rescued from attrition." While Kimmelman acknowledges that the success rate of gefitinib among Asian immigrants may point to ancestral origin, not culture or geography, as the reason for the drug's "significant efficacy" among Asians, Kimmelman also notes that "with 12% of Asian subjects responding to gefitinib treatment (versus 7% for non-Asians), the relationship between efficacy and Asian ethnic origin appears less deterministic" (428).

and sisters, requires mixing with the other.[10] In other words, Butler suggests in *Fledgling* that the transhuman future begins with acknowledging, as Holland puts it, that "we can't have our erotic life—a desiring life—without involving ourselves in the messy terrain of racist practice" (46). However, Butler is not only proposing that miscegenation will define the transhuman future, since the typical transhuman will have brown skin, but she is also offering us, as suggested by her depiction of Shori as a site of erotic desire and power, an image of a black woman who owns her erotic life.

## Blackness and Desire

Wright's decision to have sex with Shori appears to begin when she bites him on the hand and begins licking it. Wright is initially repulsed by Shori's licking, but he soon becomes aroused by it, as indicated by his reference to her as "jailbait," a term that defines her as "way too young" for sexual intercourse (*Fledgling* 18). Although we learn later that Ina venom is an addictive aphrodisiac, Wright's decision to have sex with Shori is less about Shori's venom and more about his view of Shori. For example, in her explanation of why she does not want to see a doctor, Shori reminds Wright that he thought she was a "child" before they had sex (34). Moreover, during Shori and Wright's initial meeting with Iosif, Shori's Ina father, Wright uses the same line of thinking to explain how he deduced Shori's age: "I thought she was ten or eleven when I met her. Later, I knew she had to be older, even though she didn't look it. Maybe eighteen or nineteen?" With a humorless smile, Iosif responds, "That would make things legal at least" (70). Wright is embarrassed by Iosif's remarks because the way in which he came to know Shori's age has been exposed. In Wright's mind, Shori's performance in bed, not her body, is what defines her as a woman. However, when Iosif informs Wright that Shori is fifty-three years old, but a child in Ina culture because she is unable to bear children at her stage of development, it seems that

---

10. Smedley notes that "from the standpoint of biology, there have been 'mixed' people in North America ever since Europeans first encountered indigenous Americans and the first Africans were brought to the English colonies in the 1620s" (696). Harari argues that humans are not only *racially* mixed, but we are also a mixed species. He cites recent studies that have determined that roughly up to 6 percent of human DNA comes from other human species such as Neanderthals and Denisovans (16). In his words, "it is unsettling—and perhaps thrilling—to think that we Sapiens could at one time have sex with an animal from a different species, and produce children together" (17).

Wright's insecurities about Shori's status as girl or woman reappear, as indicated by his stunned silence.

Stephanie Smith asserts that Butler's "fictional analysis" of the sexual predation on young girls in the US might be uncomfortable for some readers because it gives the impression that Shori, not Wright, is responsible for their sexual relationship. For Smith, Butler's portrayal of Shori might make some readers "wince" because her sexuality is similar to that of the nineteenth-century stereotype of black women. According to that stereotype, black women are more "animal, exotic, or erotic" than white women. While Smith admits that Shori's behavior "makes sense for the situation Butler has created," she also contends that Shori's behavior "resurrects a racist fantasy" (390). What stands out in Smith's critique are the either-or categories that she puts Shori in—she is either the insatiable stereotype who seduces Wright or the victim of Wright's racist fantasy. However, if we examine the reasons behind Wright's and Shori's decisions to sleep with each other, we find not only that Smith's either-or categories do not apply to Shori nor Wright, but also that what is possibly making Smith and the readers she references uncomfortable with Shori and Wright's relationship is that Butler is pointing out that pedophilia is not a valence issue in the US and that the black female body is always already a site of desire.

Before Shori and Wright engage in sexual intercourse, Wright wonders how much it is going to "cost" him to keep Shori with him and, at the same time, admits that he is willing to absorb that cost because of the pleasure he receives from Shori feeding on him (*Fledgling* 24). Such thoughts may be interpreted as evidence that Wright is a pedophile, an adult who has a "conscious sexual interest in prepubertal children." According to that definition, Wright is a person who has had a "very strong sexual interest in children," but individual and/or social circumstances have prevented him from acting on his interest (Finkelhor and Araji 146–47). However, since Wright is not a "true" pedophile (a "multi-case victimizer" who has had sexual encounters with at least two children) or gynephile (a "single-case victimizer" who has had sexual encounters with only one child and prefers physically mature partners), his decision to sleep with Shori is not based on a disorder, the right circumstance, or feelings of sexual or psychological impotence (Freund, Watson, and Dickey 409–10). It seems that Wright sleeps with Shori because of what Michael Kimmel calls the "Guy Code," the rules that govern the everyday behavior of American males who are between the ages of sixteen and twenty-four (Kimmel 4–6). Like race, the Guy Code is a form of hierarchical body knowledge that equates the male body with masculinity and heterosexuality. Butler suggests in *Fledgling* that the Guy Code is evidence that even though our society treats pedophilia as a "valence issue," an issue characterized by the public's near-universal approval or disapproval (Beckett 58), the ways in which males are socialized to be men in our culture indicate that one of the reasons why pedophilia exists is due to a "masculine script" of male dominance that has strong homophobic taboos (Finkelhor and Araji 157).

The first commandment of the Guy Code is "No Sissy Stuff!"; that is to say, being a man means "not being perceived as weak, effeminate, or gay" (Kimmel 45). Since the consequences for not adhering to the Guy Code are great (e.g., loss of friendships and an increased susceptibility to violence), "young men take huge chances to prove their manhood, exposing themselves to health risks, workplace hazards, and stress-related illnesses" (51). One way for a guy to avoid being read as gay in Guyland is to engage in sexual intercourse with as many women as he can, even if it requires lying or committing rape (217–41). In Wright's case, as suggested by his initial examination of Shori's body, he is willing to risk imprisonment and the stigma of being identified as a pedophile in order to avoid being perceived as gay:

> He put his hand on my shoulder and walked me over to the table. There he sat down and drew me close so that he could open one of my filthy shirts, then the other. Having reached skin, he stroked my chest. "No breasts," he said. "Pity. I guess you really are a kid. Or maybe . . . Are you sure you're female?"
> 
> "I'm female," I said. "Of course I am." (*Fledgling* 24)

Because Wright is sexually aroused by Shori licking his hand, her lack of developed breasts signals that he might be sexually aroused by males as well. Indeed, when Wright asks Shori if she is "sure" she is female, he is also asking himself if he is sure he is straight.

Wright's question, on the one hand, underscores the "unnaturalness of heterosexuality itself—that is to say, its socially constructed nature, its dependence on the semiotic construction of gender rather than on the physical (natural) existence of two sexes" (de Lauretis 129). On the other hand, the fear embodied in Wright's question, as well as his response to that fear (i.e., sleeping with Shori), indicate that "the single cardinal rule of manhood [in the US], the one from which all the other characteristics—wealth, power, status, strength, physicality—are derived is to offer constant proof that you are not gay" (Kimmel 50). It is, therefore, noteworthy that Shori tells Wright that they can have sex "if [he] wants to," because she is also telling him that if they have sex, her venom will not be the primary reason why he chooses to do so. Even though Wright acknowledges that Shori does not have any breasts or body hair, traits that he associates with girls over the age of eleven, he decides to sleep with Shori right after she declares that she is "old enough to have sex" (*Fledgling* 27). While Butler is playing on the popular aphorism "age ain't nothing but a number" (i.e., the idea that there is a gap between one's chronological and self-perceived ages, or that one's mind, not one's age, determines when one is sexually ready), she also suggests that Wright's acceptance of Shori's offer is partly informed by a need to prove to himself and to others who might discover them that he is straight.

Since Wright's decision to sleep with Shori is partly informed by the Guy Code's masculine script of male dominance and homophobia, why is Smith more concerned with Butler's depiction of Shori than with her depiction of Wright? While Smith notes that Wright could land in jail because Shori looks like a preteen girl, she also states that "Shori's resemblance to a literal black panther is disturbing" (390). Even though Wright chooses to sleep with Shori before he discovers that she is not a preteen, why does Shori's sexuality immediately bring to mind the nineteenth-century stereotype of the black woman? Moreover, if Shori was white, would Smith still be disturbed by Butler's depiction of Shori? What stereotypes, if any, would the white Shori reinforce about white women's sexuality? My point in asking these questions is to show that reading Shori as a stereotype of black women's sexuality implies that blackness "can never possess its own erotic life" because it "not only produces 'erotic value' for whiteness, but it holds the very impossibility of its own pleasure through becoming the sexualized surrogate of another" (Holland 46). As I attempt to show in the remaining pages of this chapter, Butler uses Shori to problematize that assumption about the relationship between blackness and the erotic by portraying Shori as a black woman who is a site of erotic power and desire, a black woman who is able to enjoy her erotic life and, at the same time, avoid becoming a sexual stereotype or victim.

What prevents Shori from being a victim in her erotic life is her body. Because Shori is an Ina woman, her venom can transform her Ina mates into virtual symbionts and her symbionts into virtual addicts. According to Brook, a former symbiont of Iosif who is becoming part of Shori's family, Ina reproductive practices date back to prehistoric Ina women competing amongst themselves for mates. Although Brook informs Shori that "females find mates for their sons, and males for their daughters, and it's all civilized," she also tells her that her body means "real power" in Ina society due to that competition. Since the venom of Ina women is more potent than men's, "Ina men are sort of like . . . symbionts. They become addicted to the venom of one group of sisters. That's what it means to be mated. Once they're addicted, they aren't fertile with other females, and from time to time, they need their females. Need . . . like I need Iosif" (*Fledgling* 115). As implied by Brook, because Shori is a black Ina—a woman who possesses physical abilities that humans lack, the venom that Ina men lack, and the melanin that all Ina lack—she will always be physically and emotionally stronger than her erotic partners and is, therefore, very unlikely to be victimized in her erotic life. Even when Wright tries to "hurt" Shori during sex, after he discovers that she "swings both ways" and that he will not be her only symbiont, she tells him that she was not aware that he was trying to hurt her and, in fact, is more concerned if she hurt him, since she had to "bit[e] him more than [she] had intended" to account for his hard thrusting (91). However, Smith suggests that while Shori's Inaness prevents her from being victimized by her Ina mates and symbionts, it cannot stop her from victimizing her erotic partners: "The way in which the Ina initially attack the people with whom they will eventually bond is unsettling at best, more frequently reminiscent of rape" (389). According to Theri Pickens, "Ina–symbiont relationships and Ina history expose abled whiteness as a foundational myth upon which Ina base their identity" (42). For Pickens, Ina-symbiont relationships are inherently exploitive because ableism and whiteness are about oppressing and erasing those who are disabled and not white; therefore, regardless of the sincerity behind an Ina's moral and ethical treatment of his or her symbionts, "[that] Ina's privilege reproduces itself regardless of his [or her] intent" (44). It seems that Smith's and Pickens's readings of the Ina are supported by Martin Harrison, an African American symbiont who admits to Shori that Ina-human symbiosis initially "scared the hell out of [him]" because "it sounded more like slavery than symbiosis" (*Fledgling* 210).

It appears that what Smith and Pickens devalue in their readings of Ina-symbiont relationships and what Martin emphasizes later is that humans are not forced to become symbionts. Before Martin made the decision to become one of Hayden Gordon's symbionts, he was able to take ten months to decide if the life of symbiont was for him, since he had only been bitten three times and was, therefore, not "physically addicted." Although symbiosis initially sounded like slavery to Martin, he wanted to be with the Ina so badly that "[he] quit his job, packed [his] things, put what [he] could in [his] car, gave the rest away, and drove [to the Gordon compound]" (*Fledgling* 210). As suggested by Martin's path to becoming a symbiont, even though the Ina are stronger than humans and possess venom that turns humans into addicts, they, unlike the rapist, slave owner, or drug dealer, do not use their power advantage to coerce potential symbionts or to exploit their current ones. Thus, although Shori has the power to force potential and current symbionts to submit to her erotic whims, her Inaness prevents her from victimizing her lovers because an Ina's survival is dependent on developing consensual intimate relationships with humans. In one sense, Ina-symbiont relationships can be viewed as an example of what Lewis Call refers to as the philosophy of "erotic power exchange and consensual slavery," the idea that "the exchange of power is ethically legitimate if and only if all persons involved in that exchange have given their consent" (276). As suggested by the thinking involved in Martin's decision to become a symbiont, while it is highly questionable that one would freely consent to be a slave, even in one's erotic life, what is not in question is that consensual forms of power are better for an erotic life and a society than nonconsensual forms of power. Butler's point seems to be that even though most of our erotic relationships are partly informed by unequal power relations, one does not have to become a victimizer to avoid being victimized in one's erotic life; otherwise, one's erotic relationships will not be about pleasure, but conflict.

While Shori's Inaness makes her a site of power, her blackness makes her a site of desire. For example, during the process of courting Theodora—an elderly white woman who is a widow, mother, and poet—to be one of her symbionts, Shori only feeds on Theodora at night with the lights off. Thus, Theodora has no idea what Shori looks like and is shocked when she finally sees Shori at her front door. Although Theodora figured out from the feeding sessions that Shori is a small female vampire, she could not figure out Shori's skin color. When Shori asks if it is her skin color or apparent age that is upsetting her, Theodora can only say, "I didn't want to see you" (*Fledgling* 95). Theodora did not want to see Shori because she knew that Shori did not fit her image of a vampire or whom she considered desirable: "Although according to what I've read, you're supposed to be a tall, handsome, fully grown white man. Just my luck. But you must be a vampire. How could you do this if you weren't? How could I let you do it? How could it feel so good when it should be disgusting and painful?" (97). When Theodora uses the words "supposed" and "should," she is articulating whom she has been told to find desirable. However, when she uses the word "could," she is pointing to what her body is telling her about whom she finds desirable. In other words, while Theodora has been raised to believe that being attracted to black women is "disgusting and painful," her nights with Shori tell her that what she has been told about black women is a lie. According to Pickens, "[Theodora's] desire for an able white man is palpable but not necessary" (43), implying that Shori is somehow able to compensate for the fact that she is not a tall, handsome, fully grown white man. Theodora's explanation for how Shori compensates for that lack and why she ultimately decides to be one of Shori's symbionts is quite telling—Shori has made her "feel more" than she has since she was a girl (*Fledgling* 98). Shori not only treats Theodora as a necessary part of her life, but she is also attracted to the *real* Theodora, the one who spends most of her time writing poetry in an upstairs room filled with a "disorderly mass of stuff," not society's Theodora whose living room is filled with furniture that is somehow "exactly where it should be and exactly what it should be" (95). Thus, when Theodora commits to be Shori's symbiont, even though such a commitment is supposed to be "disgusting and painful," she is also admitting to herself that believing or continuing to believe in the racist myths about black women would not only deny her the opportunity to end her loneliness, to feel wanted, and to develop a gratifying erotic life, but it would also require suppressing parts of herself.

Shori is desired not only by white humans but by the Ina as well. Although Katharine believes that most Ina would not want their sons to mate with Shori because they would produce black children, the Gordons were negotiating with Iosif before his murder to see if their sons could mate with Shori and her sisters, and even a Silk asked if he and his brothers could be mates (*Fledgling* 86, 137). One could argue that the Gordons' and the Silks' interests in Shori were not driven by desire, but by the acquisition of melanin; however, they could get melanin from white people, since the Ina realize that all humans have melanin, though some have more than others. While Shori is a site of desire for the Ina and her white symbionts, she will not be their sexualized surrogate, producing pleasure for them but not for herself. Indeed, when Shori tells Wright that she only has sex with her symbionts "if they and [she] want it" (91), she is also telling him that she refuses to engage in pleasureless sex, which includes having sex when she does not want to. Moreover, since Shori is desired because of her blackness, not in spite of it, she does not need to change her body (e.g., bleach her skin, straighten her hair, or reconstruct her nose) or perform a certain racialized stereotype to increase her erotic value for her white and white-looking partners. At the same time, when Shori asks Wright and Theodora to be her symbionts, she does not choose them because they are white, nor does she choose Brook, Celia, and Joel (Martin's son) because they are black; instead, Shori chooses these people because they "smell good," the Ina phrase for attraction or congeniality. While some might read Shori's decision to have white symbionts as an example of color-blind eroticism, the notion that we can separate sexual desire from racist practice,[11] her choices might be best

---

11. My conception of color-blind eroticism derives from Holland's critique of scholars who have, intentionally or unintentionally, "uncoupled our desire from quotidian

understood as an example of a black woman who realizes that even though she lives in a society where bodies, ideas, and desires are racialized, it is still possible for her to have erotic relationships with white people without them being "fraught with peril"[12] or conjuring up images of "domination and subordination cemented during chattel slavery."[13] The reason why such relationships are possible, as suggested by Shori's black and white symbionts, is that one's level and packaging of melanin do not determine whom one will desire or be desired by.

## Human Blackness Versus Transhuman Blackness

I have argued throughout this chapter that Butler proposes in *Fledgling* that the biological notion of race and its notion of blackness (i.e., human blackness) are products of hierarchical body knowledge and are based on a what-you-see-is-what-you-get approach to the body-self relationship in which one's body is believed to be transparent evidence of one's identity. While that notion of blackness is able to account for the ideological diversity among people with dark skin, it does not offer any evidence that those with

---

racist practice for far too long." The problem with that uncoupling, as Holland rightly points out, is that "there is no 'raceless' course of desire" precisely because quotidian racism shapes "what we know of as 'desire'" (42–43). This not only means that our erotic preferences (whom we sexually desire) are racialized, but also our erotic practices (the sexual acts we engage in); that is to say, whom we choose to be intimate with is shaped by how our partners have been racialized and by the sexual practices attributed to the racial groups that our partners belong to. According to this view, intra- and interracial intimate relationships can reinforce as well as challenge the race myth; therefore, we should avoid treating these relationships as inherently conservative or progressive. In other words, whom we are intimate with is not an indication of our racial politics.

12. Ralph Richard Banks writes that recent studies have suggested that "black women may be less likely to divorce when they marry outside the race than when they marry within it" and, therefore, counters any assumption that interracial relationships are, for black women, "fraught with peril." In fact, Banks argues that black women in interracial relationships are empowering other black women in the African American marriage market by refusing to limit themselves to black men, whose erotic lives benefit from colorism and their willingness to cross the color line (179–81).

13. Holland makes this statement in her critique of Alice Walker's reading of an interracial lesbian couple in a television documentary who engages in mistress-slave role-play. Since the white woman played the mistress and the black woman played the slave, Walker assumed, as Holland argues, that the only way to read the couple's erotic practices was in the context of actual slavery. The problem with Walker's reading, according to Holland, is that it forces blackness to take "the burden of what should be political as personal" and, therefore, "tie[s] the black female body to the inevitability of slavery's abusive sexual terrain so that every time we think of enslaved black women and sex we think pain, not pleasure" (56).

black bodies are biologically distinct from those with nonblack bodies. As Linda Vigilant explains,

> A problem with a race concept as applied to the human species is that there are no meaningful barriers to the interbreeding of individuals of different races. A species is defined biologically as the total members of a group of populations that share a common gene pool and actually or potentially interbreed with one another under natural conditions. The term subspecies is not a synonym for race. In humans there are no geographic barriers for the formation of subspecies, and physical and genetic variation fails to consistently distinguish one population from another. Races are not subspecies and are therefore not meaningful biological terms. (49)

Since black and white people, unlike Ina and humans, can interbreed with one another under natural conditions, blackness and whiteness do not describe significant biological differences between two groups of people; rather, they describe the social differences between these groups. Thus, while the idea that being black means having a black body makes sense within a what-you-see-is-what-you-get culture, that notion of blackness is irrational in the biological world because people are not born black; rather, they are made black.

Given Butler's criticisms of human blackness, how would she have answered the question that grounds my project in *The Paradox of Blackness*: Is there more to being black than having a black body? Based on her conception of transhuman blackness in *Fledgling*, it seems that she would have argued that having a human body is the only requirement for being black. Since Butler's transhuman blackness proposes that what makes a human body black is the presence of melanin and that melanin will be key to humans living long enough to live forever, the significant differences among humans are ideological, not biological. For Butler, because all humans have melanin and since melanin can make humans dark or light (see Jablonski 68–69), variations in human skin colors are evidence of evolutionary adaptation, not biologically distinct races. In this light, the difference between human blackness and transhuman blackness, as depicted in *Fledgling*, is that the former describes the social value of a group of humans and contends that there are humans who lack blackness, whereas the latter describes the survival value of all humans and proposes that every human has at least one drop of *black* blood.

CHAPTER 5

# BLACK CHURCH CORPORATISM AND THE BLACK GAY VAMPIRE IN *IMAGE OF EMERALDS AND CHOCOLATE*

IT IS SURPRISING that the African American vampire novels that I have discussed up to this point lack a black male vampire who is gay because these novels are largely concerned with black sexual politics and problematizing the notion of authentic blackness. In fact, the black gay male vampire is virtually absent in African American vampire fiction. For example, Gomez's *The Gilda Stories*, Butler's *Fledgling*, and Donna Monday's self-published novel *The Best Black Vampire Story You've Ever Read* (2006) feature black female vampires who are queer and belong to multiracial and multicultural communities; yet, none of these novels has a black male vampire who is queer. This absence is also notable in much of the African American vampire fiction with black male protagonists such as Due's *My Soul to Keep*, Kevin Brockenbrough's "'Cause Harlem Needs Heroes" (2004), Omar Tyree's "Human Heat: The Confessions of an Addicted Vampire" (2004), Zane's "Resident Evil" (2004), and Massey's *Dark Corner* and "The Patriarch" (2008), a novella that serves as an addendum to *Dark Corner*. The exceptions to this trend are Gomez's "Chicago 1927" (2000), an addendum to *The Gilda Stories*, and Brockenbrough's "The Family Business" (2004); however, neither story would be viewed as a black gay vampire story. On the one hand, although Gomez's short story includes an African American gay couple, Benny and Morris, Benny does not become a vampire until the very end of the story, so we are unable to see him live as a vampire. On the other hand, the black queer male vampires in "The Family Business" are associated with the devil and the problems that plague black working-class urban communities, so they must die to save these communities. Given this background, one is forced to ask the following question: What keeps the black gay vampire in the coffin of African American vampire fiction?

One might answer that question by arguing that the vampire genre itself is largely responsible for the absence of black gay vampires. Melton notes that there has been a recurring presence of lesbian vampires in Western vampire fiction over the centuries—for example, Coleridge's "Christabel" (1797), Le Fanu's *Carmilla* (1872), Gomez's *The Gilda Stories* (1991), and Pam Keesey's *Daughters of Darkness: Lesbian Vampire Stories* (1993) and *Dark Angels: Lesbian Vampire Stories* (1995)—but the same cannot be said of literary gay vampires (Melton 341). Although Holmes suggests that Eric Stenbock's "A True Story of a Vampyre" (1894) can be read as the first gay vampire text (176), gay vampires do not openly reappear in vampire fiction until the 1970s,[1] beginning with Stephen King's *Salem's Lot* (1975) and Anne Rice's *Interview with the Vampire* (1976).[2] For Melton, that absence has been due to the lack of gay authors who write vampire stories.[3] However, Melton's own

---

1. Unlike the vampire film genre, where the first gay male vampires appear in the 1960s and the first film with a gay male vampire to be released to the general public appeared in 1973, we do not see gay vampire fiction until the 1990s with the works of Jeffrey N. McMahan and Gary Bowen (Melton 341–42).

2. While Sean Eads argues that George Middler, the gay hardware store owner who is revealed to be a vampire at the end of *Salem's Lot*, is an "extremely minor character" (81), his presence represents how the literary gay male vampire can simultaneously support and subvert cultural norms (94). Similarly, George Haggerty argues that the gay vampires of Anne Rice's *Vampire Chronicles* are expressions of "our culture's secret desire for and secret fear of the gay man" (6). Thus, although these novels have gay vampires, they should not be read as gay vampire fiction because, as Haggerty puts it, they tell us more about the "homophobic present" than they do about male homoerotic desire (6–8).

3. Holmes attempts to address this absence by contrasting the histories offered by Keesey's first anthology, *Daughters of Darkness*, with Michael Rowe and Thomas S. Roche's *Sons of Darkness: Tales of Men, Blood, and Immortality* (1990). Holmes asks why does Keesey's anthology begin with *Carmilla*, the anthology's only male-written text, as the origin of the Western literary lesbian vampire, but Rowe and Roche's begins with Poppy Z. Brite's 1990 story as the origin of the literary gay male vampire? For Holmes, any answer to this question begins with acknowledging that "the rendering visible of male same-sex sexual desire is performed in a different manner to that of female same-sex sexual desire." As he explains, "given patriarchy in articulation with capitalism, men could encode same-sex desire at a safe remove from self through women"; therefore, "representations of women's same-sex desire—always already a threatening Other— have been, and still might be, less mediated through the body or subjectivity of an other" (175–76). What is suggested by Holmes's analysis is that in a patriarchal, capitalist, and

observations problematize his claim about this absence. For example, he cites Jeffrey N. McMahan as the "most heralded gay writer on the vampire theme," but he writes in the following paragraph that "the most significant expression of a vampiric gay relationship came not from a gay writer, but in several novels by Anne Rice" (342). The contradiction between Melton's claim and his observations appears to be the result of the assumption that there is a "necessary equivalence between gay authors, gay fictional characters, and gay readers" (Holmes 174). The problem with such an assumption, as Holmes explains, is that it defines a vampire text as gay or straight by the sexuality of the text's author or characters: "Once we generate a listing of codes by which we know whether a vampire text is gay or not—creating a set of identity-guarantors such as the gender and sexuality of the author or the characters—we very much limit what counts as authentic or pure in terms of identity" (173). Moreover, by defining the sexual identity of a vampire text in this way, we miss the opportunity to address what Holmes identifies as one of the main reasons for why gay vampires have been in the coffin of vampire fiction until the 1970s—"the ground on which we base our understandings of gender, sexuality, and identity" (174).

What is the "ground" that American understandings of gender, sexuality, and identity tend to stand on? I have noted throughout this book that part of this ground is the deeply held cultural fiction that one's body is transparent evidence of one's history, behavior, and identity. According to that fiction, the body tells us if one is black or not black, masculine or feminine, straight or queer, normal or abnormal. In chapter 4, I call that fiction the "what-you-see-is-what-you-get" approach to identity. One of the major problems with that approach is that it ignores the fact that the "what you get" part is never obvious, fixed, or universal because the meaning of something or someone is never outside discourse or the changing relations of power. Put in simpler terms, that approach to identity ignores the fact that our ideas, not our bodies, give meaning to our bodies. In this light, to ask what keeps the black gay vampire in the coffin of African American vampire fiction is to ask what ideas tend to be attached to black gay men among African Americans. To

---

homophobic culture, male writers of vampire fiction who wanted to make male same-sex desire visible in their text and, at the same time, avoid persecution could only do so through the textual bodies of women, particularly lesbians, or other others. For Holmes, male-authored vampire texts, such as the works by Coleridge and Le Fanu, that we now read as lesbian narratives might be gay male narratives written on the bodies of women. While Holmes is not arguing that the author's sex determines the true meaning of his or her characters or texts, he is reminding us that what is now read as gay, straight, lesbian, or even vampiric may have been read as something entirely different because we now have different codes for these categories of desire (176).

address this question, we need to get a sense of black America's sexual politics at the beginning of the twenty-first century.

"Black sexual politics," according to Patricia Hill Collins, is "a set of ideas and social practices shaped by gender, race, and sexuality that frame Black men and women's treatment of one another, as well as how African Americans are perceived and treated by others" (7). In contrast to its conservative counterpart, progressive Black sexual politics acknowledges that racism and heterosexism, "the prison and the closet," respectively, are not separate systems of oppression, but "mutually construct one another" to help create America's sexually repressive culture (89). According to this view, "if racism and heterosexism affect Black LGBT people, then these systems affect *all* people, including heterosexual African Americans" (95). Indeed, both systems use regulatory and disciplinary institutions (e.g., the courts and legislative bodies), practices (e.g., marriage), and ideologies (e.g., the use of binary thinking to legitimate certain social hierarchies as normal) to stigmatize the sexual practices of black and LGBTQ people as "abnormal, unnatural, and sinful" (95–97). Unlike its progressive counterpart, conservative black sexual politics not only views racism and heterosexism as mutually independent issues, but it also constructs homosexuality as an abomination to God and as a destructive force in the cultural and political life of black America.[4] As Hutchinson explains, "anti-gay sentiment amongst African Americans is strongly tied to notions of gender and ethnic identity. Homosexuality is not only believed to be a violation of God and natural law, but is viewed as undermining black masculinity and male dominance in an already precarious black nuclear family unit. In this regard, homosexuality ranks with slavery, Jim Crow, and mass-incarceration as key factors in the destabilization of black families" (*Godless Americana* 9–10). Thus, even though African American homophobia is grounded in notions of racial uplift and authenticity, it is, as I noted in chapter 1, legitimized and reinforced by the Black Church.

---

4. For example, Dillard argues that contemporary black conservative homophobia was energized by the outreach efforts of the Christian Coalition in the early 1990s. Ralph Reed, former director of the Coalition, was not only urging social and religious conservatives to build a "multiracial, multiethnic, and ecumenical movement," but his Coalition and other groups also began outreach efforts that specifically targeted African American communities. These groups warned African Americans that "homosexuals are out to distort and denigrate the historical legacy of the civil rights movement by using its symbols to press for a host of so-called special rights" (142). These outreach efforts may have worked because Reed claimed in 1995 that African Americans composed 3 to 4 percent of the Coalition's membership (163). These efforts also help to explain why many black conservatives espouse homophobic rhetoric—it is a way to prove that they are "real" conservatives and to distinguish themselves from the left and the so-called "civil rights establishment" (142).

While a considerable number of black ministers who refer to homosexuals as "fags," "sissies," "punks," and "bulldaggers" are gay themselves (E. Ward 497), these ministers continue to preach the message that homosexuality is unnatural for black people because it is a "white disease," depicting gay African Americans who are out as being "disloyal to the race" (Collins 108). Implicit in that message is that the only ways for black queer men to be loyal to the race is to put themselves in the closet or in exile. Consequently, according to that doctrine, black queer men who are out should not be represented as images of black liberation and salvation because they are living testaments of how antiblack racism in the US has sexually, spiritually, and politically emasculated black men.[5] Such an assumption, as Roger Sneed argues, constructs gay black men as victims who are always "bound in crisis with no hope of transcendence" (259). It is important to note that "homonegativity"—"contempt for individuals expressing same-sex attractions"—is not unique to the Black Church; nevertheless, "it has dire psychosocial consequences for non-heterosexual Blacks" (Jeffries, Dodge, and Sandfort 464–65). Homonegativity can also have dire physical consequences for black gay youth. Referencing Monica Miller and J. Mason's commentary on the experiences of black LGBTQ teens, Almeda Wright notes that it is disheartening to know that some religious communities create "climates in which some youth are given fuel for their taunts and abuse and other youth see few alternatives to self-destructive behaviors given the myriad negative images of their personhood promoted in their religious communities" (279). These are some of the issues that K. Murry Johnson's debut novel *Image of Emeralds and Chocolate* (2012) addresses in its critique of Black Church homonegativity.

---

5. In his discussion of the racial dimensions to male investment in the "heterosexual presumption," the presumption that heterosexuality is the "'what is' or 'what is supposed to be' of sexuality," Devon Carbado argues that "straight black male strategies to avoid homosexual suspicion could relate to the racial aspects of male privileges: heterosexual privilege is one of the few privileges that some black men have" (198–99). Unfortunately, as E. Patrick Johnson notes, "the representation of effeminate homosexuality as disempowering is at the heart of the politics of hegemonic blackness. For to be ineffectual is the most damaging thing one can be in the fight against oppression" ("The Specter" 220). In this light, the need for some black men to avoid homosexual suspicion is "less a function of what heterosexuality signifies in a positive sense and more a function of what it signifies in the negative—*not* being homosexual" (Carbado 199). However, since black people have been constructed as nonheteronormative in the US, a construction that has "impacted the psyche of African Americans" (Ferguson 105), investment in the heterosexual presumption, as I hope to show in the remainder of this chapter, does not give the returns that straight or straight-acting black men who are trying to avoid homosexual suspicion are seeking.

Set in contemporary Louisiana, *Image of Emeralds and Chocolate*—the first novel, as stated on its back cover, to combine "two never before paired genres: black gay and vampire fiction"—focuses on the romantic relationship that develops between Eric Peterson, a high school senior who is in the closet because he has been raised in a church built on heteronormative conceptions of blackness and salvation, and Emanuel Marquis LeBlanc, a black gay vampire who was born a slave in 1800. Eric attends a "prestigious, gifted high school" where he has finished all of his graduation requirements, except for one, and he is completing that requirement at Loyola University in New Orleans, "a small, private, Jesuit liberal arts university" (*Image* 3–4). Eric enrolls in one of Loyola's elective writing classes, classes in which Eric is usually the only male. While Eric appreciates the attention that he gets from being the only male in these classes, he also wishes that "he wasn't the only guy who enjoyed putting a pen to paper" (7). In some ways, Eric is like Delmar, the black queer teenager in Langston Hughes's "Blessed Assurance" (1963), who is, as Marlon Rachquel Moore puts it, a "brilliant queer" because "he is well rounded and excels in high school. He is on the honor roll, is ranked highly in his class and has avoided the allure of street life" (495). The difference between Eric and Delmar is that Eric is not a "sissy," whom Moore refers to as "the most controversial representation of black male sexuality" (495), and he will not act out "his queerness in a particularly Christian spotlight" as Delmar does (498). However, when Marquis enrolls in Eric's writing class and they become writing partners, the process begins for him to act on his queer desires in the spotlight of black manhood. While Eric writes poetry, which is his "outlet to voice his forbidden desires" (*Image* 8), Marquis writes "A Slave's Tale," a six-part novella that tells the story of how Marquis, who is referred to as Emanuel until the novella's last installment, went from being a slave to becoming the most powerful vampire on the planet.

According to the novella, Marquis was born on a plantation owned by whom he calls the "old Frenchman" in Destrehan, Louisiana. His mother, Angelique, was promised her freedom when she turned eighteen; instead, she was sold and separated from Marquis when he was eight years old and she was twenty-five. Based on Marquis's reference to the slave master's "funny colored eyes," it appears that the slave master was Marquis's father, since Marquis has emerald-colored eyes (*Image* 64). After his mother was sold, Marquis was raised by his grandparents, Momma Josette and Papa Honoré, who tried to make his childhood on the plantation as pleasant as possible. One night, while Marquis and Papa Honoré were playing on the porch of their slave cabin, the Voodoo priestess Véréne Fontenot and her three-member entourage stopped in their tracks as they passed by the cabin. Véréne turned to look at the young Marquis and went into a ten- to fifteen-second trance in which her irises disappeared. After coming out of the trance, Véréne delivers the following message to Papa Honoré: "Familiar eyes this boy has. He'll possess great power that will one day bring freedom to many" (68). While Papa Honoré and Momma Josette debated the meaning of Véréne's prophecy, it appears that the old Frenchman took the prophecy to be true because that same night he sent Marquis to work for David and Sharon Devereux, a white middle-class couple who lived in New Orleans's French Quarter. It was during this time with the Devereuxs that Marquis learned to read and, more importantly, learned why slaves were prevented from receiving an education. When David walked in on Sharon teaching Marquis to read, he immediately prohibited her from continuing the lessons, offering the following explanation: "If you teach that nigger to read, he'll start to question everything and would be no good to his master" (71). After hearing David's explanation, Marquis began to link education with freedom. Ironically, Marquis will not be able to resume his education until he is sent to the Newton farm, a place that slaves feared because many who were sent there "ended up missing or never heard of again" (72). The Newton farm is also the place where Marquis falls in love for the first time and where he becomes a vampire.

Since K. Murry Johnson credits E. Lynn Harris, along with Stephanie Meyer and L. A. Banks, for opening him up to "the world of writing, the black gay experience, and vampires" (x), one might expect that the novel will offer what Sneed would call a "conservative" approach to the Black Church–black gay relationship. In his examination of religion and spirituality in black gay literature, Sneed identifies three approaches that black gay writers have used to address the relationship between the Black Church and black gay men's spirituality: the liberal, moderate, and conservative approaches. The liberal approach, commonly found in the works of protest writers like Essex Hemphill, rejects the Black Church altogether and calls for a conception of God who is open to multiple expressions of sexuality. The moderate approach, as expressed by G. Winston James's short story "Church" (2009), identifies with traditional black churches and is focused on changing the Black Church's views on homosexuality. By showing how the Black Church and, by extension, the African American community benefit from the presence of gay black men, the moderate approach exposes how the denial and marginalization of these men hurts the community. Sneed identifies the writings of E. Lynn Harris as representative of the conservative approach in which religion and spirituality serve as a "civilizing force" for black gay men who want a life in the church. According to this approach, while the Black Church needs to change its homophobic ways, it also offers a way for black queer men to achieve the "same goods" as straight black people (256–57). Although Johnson thanks "God for giving [him] the strength, guidance, and creativity to make [his] dream of writing a meaningful black gay vampire love story a reality" (*Image* ix), which suggests that the novel will show how gay blacks can get the same goods as their straight counterparts by remaining in the Black Church, I argue that Johnson's depiction of Marquis and his partners (i.e., Jeremiah and Eric) can be read as a critique of not only the conservative approach's black gay man but also of *Black Church corporatism*.

According to Shelby, "black corporatism" is a form of Black Power nationalism which claims that instead of relying on political party elites, "spontaneous" collective action, or "free-floating" race leaders, "the black population should be organized into a single corporate person [e.g., a new political party, a national organization, the strengthening of an existing party or organization, or a federation of such associations] with recognized authority to speak for all blacks" (121). Thus, Black Church corporatism is the idea that the Black Church should be that single corporate person who has the authority to speak for all African Americans. While Black Church corporatism might make sense because most African Americans identify with some type of Christian philosophy and because the Black Church has been able to "drown out" non-Christian black voices due to the tremendous influence it has in US politics and in defining the political agenda of the African American community (Shelby 123), one of the main problems with Black Church corporatism, as suggested by *Image of Emeralds and Chocolate*, is that it is informed by the idea that there is more to being a black man than having a black body. To be more specific, Johnson's depiction of Marquis can be read as a critique of that idea, an idea that functions as a roadblock to the solidarity and progress sought by Black Church corporatism because it presumes that only straight black men are *real* men and, therefore, capable of speaking for all African Americans.[6]

I begin my discussion of the novel with an overview of Marquis's staying-alive vampirism. Like Gilda and Diallo, Marquis represents the elixir version of the Staying Alive Narrative in which it is believed that immortality can be achieved without the need for death. However, instead of a

---

6. See chapter 1 for a brief explanation of why black women came to be excluded from the pulpit of the Black Church and, therefore, why preaching remains an overwhelmingly male thing in the Black Church.

ritual-based transformation like the one Diallo goes through, Marquis's transformation from human to vampire is very similar to Gilda's in that it reads more as a blood transfusion than as a supernatural act. Indeed, due to his transformation, Marquis, like Dawit, does not view his vampiric powers as emanating from a deity; rather, they are viewed as the gifts of his new species. Next, I discuss Johnson's distinction between what I call the *education for liberation* and *education for salvation* approaches to the Bible, in which the former treats the Bible as a literary text and the latter treats its as "book knowledge." In contrast to the education for liberation approach, whose goal is to free African Americans in the here and now, the education for salvation approach locates freedom in death. I conclude this chapter with a discussion of what the novel proposes for ending the "unnatural fight" between straight and queer African American men, a fight that is perpetuated by the idea that being a black man means more than having a black body.

## Marquis's Elixir of Life

I noted in chapter 1 that the elixir version of the Staying Alive Narrative offers a path to immortality in which one can stop the processes of decline and decay that come with aging and death by simply consuming the magical elixir of life. Since the elixir is anything that helps to hold off aging and death for a little bit longer, the form it takes can shed light on the nature of immortality within an ideology, culture, or identity. Thus, it is important that the elixir of life in *Image of Emeralds and Chocolate*, like that in *The Gilda Stories*, is vampire blood because it suggests that immortality is not the work of a deity or science. Indeed, to become a vampire and, therefore, immortal in *Image*, one does not have to survive a life-threatening ritual as Diallo did, nor does one have to become a genetic experiment, as in the case of Shori. Instead, to become immortal, all one needs is to be bitten by a vampire who is willing to inject his or her blood into one's body. For example, at the beginning of Marquis's description of his transformation from human to vampire, he gives the impression that he dies before becoming a vampire. He describes a "spectacular brilliant light" that felt "good" against his skin. Standing in the light were Jeremiah, Momma Josette, and Papa Honoré, loved ones who have died, and they were chanting, "Come into the light." Hearing their chant, Marquis felt "ready to go home" and be "finally free." What comes next in his description of his transformation confirms that he did not die, but was dreaming:

> All of a sudden a pain different from the beatings I felt earlier *hit* me. I was sucked out of my hallucination and brought back to reality.
>
> It felt like acid was running through my veins. My heart started to race and thump violently in my chest, until it came to an abrupt stop. Did I have a heart attack? If I did, then why were my eyes wide open? I was lying on the floor shirtless and staring at the white plastered ceiling. Why am I still alive? What happened to Jeremiah, Momma Josette, and Papa Honoré? (*Image* 149)

What becomes clear in Marquis's transformation is that the pain caused by the vampire's acid-like blood does not bring Marquis back from the dead, but back to reality. The brilliant light Marquis saw was nothing more than a coma-induced hallucination, and his nonbeating heart was not a sign of death, but evidence that Marquis now belongs to a new species and is a "God walking amongst men" (150). Although vampires are not human in *Image*, they are humanlike; that is, vampires, like their human counterparts, can still die. For example, when Marquis asks Isildur, the slave owner who transformed him into a vampire, if vampires are immortal, Isildur states the following: "In a way. As long as you limit your exposure to sunlight, keep your head attached to your body and don't let an inexperienced vampire over drain you during the nachtruhinization process" (187). Moreover, while Isildur claims that "primitive human tools" are unable to kill vampires (187–88), he does warn Marquis that "anonymity" is of the "highest importance" to a vampire because even though a handful of humans know that vampires are real, vampires can only "coexist with [humans] as though they do not exist" (178). In other words, if it became common knowledge among humans that vampires exist, vampires might become extinct because humans have the numbers to make that extinction happen and because they have a history of causing the extinction of other human species.[7] Thus, immortality in *Image*, like that in *Gilda*, *Dark Corner*, and *Fledgling*, is not defined as living forever, but as living long enough to live forever. This means that while vampire blood allows one to delay the processes of death, it is unable to stop death.

---

7. In one of his explanations for why Homo sapiens outlived its human brothers and sisters (e.g., the Neanderthals and the Denisovans), Harari proposes the following: "Another possibility is that competition for resources flared up into violence and genocide. Tolerance is not a Sapiens trademark. In modern times, a small difference in skin colour, dialect, or religion has been enough to prompt one group of Sapiens to set out to exterminating another group. . . . It may well be that when Sapiens encountered Neanderthals, the result was the first and most significant ethnic-cleansing campaign in history" (17–18).

Since vampire blood is what gives a vampire his or her superhuman powers, what is the origin of the vampire's powers? In an exchange with a Voodoo priestess named Blanche, Marquis discovers that the origin is unknown. According to Blanche, "[Marquis's] vampire powers and [her] ability to foretell the future are one [and] the same. It comes from the same source." When Marquis inquires about that source, Blanche could only tell him that "there are all sorts of stories, but no one knows for sure" (*Image* 199). Similarly, Isildur is unsure of how vampires develop their unique "special abilities," which are in addition to their superhuman strength, speed, and health. While Isildur can fly, he is unable to turn animate and inanimate objects into gold like Sophia, the woman who became a vampire at the same time Isildur became one in 1506, nor does he have the power to control earth, wind, fire, and water as the legendary "great vampire" is claimed to do. According to Isildur, the legend of the great vampire says that this vampire will "possess multiple special abilities," a gift no other vampire has ever had (183). However, the source of this legend is as unknown as the origin of vampires and humans; therefore, no one is sure if such a vampire will ever exist. What is noteworthy about the lack of certainty on the vampire's origin is the lack of concern among vampires about their origin. As depicted in *Image*, the issue of origins is only a human concern. Even though the vampires in the novel are not literally immortal, none of them contemplate life-after-death questions or questions about the origin of their species; instead, their concerns are with the present. What this lack of concern about origins suggests is that vampire blood in *Image* makes one not only physically fit for immortality, but also mentally fit. In this instance, part of being mentally fit for immortality is adopting an agnostic approach to questions regarding origins and the future, an approach that requires one to accept that we may never know the truth about our beginning or end.

Unlike Dawit, who is convinced that an eternal guardian or tormentor does not exist, Marquis is not sure either way. On the one hand, when Marquis comes to the realization that he is a vampire, he states that he has lost his "soul" (*Image* 175), implying that he believes in the Soul Narrative. As I noted in this book's introduction, the Soul Narrative is the belief that the *real* you is immaterial or spiritual and that it is separate from and can outlive your body. Moreover, I discussed in chapter 2 that to believe in the soul, one must be convinced that there is a place where souls come from before they reach our bodies and a place where souls go after they leave our bodies. Since heaven and hell, according to the Abrahamic religions, are the places ruled by good and evil deities, respectively, places where our souls supposedly go after they leave our bodies, then it appears that Marquis believes in a deity. On the other hand, since Marquis never declares faith in a deity as a human and never speaks of his soul after the initial moments of his transformation, his statement about losing his soul sounds more like a figure of speech instead of a statement of belief. It seems that Marquis either believes that a god exists, but it is a noninterventionist god, a god that does not involve itself in quotidian human or vampire affairs, or that this god is a myth and, therefore, vampires are not one of God's or Satan's creations; rather, they are just another human species like Homo rudolfensis, Homo erectus, Homo soloenis, Homo denisova, Homo floresiensis, Homo neanderthalensis, or Homo sapiens. In either case, what Marquis learns as a staying-alive vampire whose blood functions as the elixir of life is that since God's existence or nonexistence can only be confirmed after death, something that vampires and humans attempt to hold off for as long as possible, God should not be the sole or primary focus of one's life because it has no influence on the here and now. It is this line of thought that inspires Marquis's decision to become a vampire abolitionist.

The first place Marquis visits after he becomes a vampire is the Magnolia plantation, where he comes across a white overseer evicting an elderly slave from the plantation because she is too old and, therefore, no longer able to do slave work. Marquis is so hungry for blood and incensed by this scene that he snatches the overseer without the elderly woman noticing him and drains him of his blood. While he feels "horrible" for killing the overseer and calls himself a "murderer," Marquis immediately comes to the following conclusion about his actions:

> "What would Jeremiah do in a bad situation? When given lemons, then make lemonade is what he would do," I whispered.
>
> That [night] I promised myself that I would never kill an innocent person, but instead I would become an abolitionist in my own vampirish way. (180)

What is noteworthy about Marquis's reference to Jeremiah, his first love, is that he omits the second part of Jeremiah's advice for dealing with bad situations, the part that relies on praying to a god. Jeremiah's advice, which came from his "ole grandma" who told him to make lemonade *and* "pray" when life gives you lemons (99), relies on a deity to intervene on one's behalf to sweeten a sour situation, while Marquis's deletion of the second part of Jeremiah's advice suggests that for black people to sweeten their lives in the US, they need to live as though God is a myth or a noninterventionist god. Indeed, when Marquis decides to become a vampire abolitionist, he does not ask a deity for support or approval; instead, he looks to himself. In this light, Jeremiah's lemonade advice can be viewed as a product of what I call the education for salvation approach, which is represented by Johnson's depictions of Pastors Williams and Lewis. In contrast, Marquis's agnosticism can be viewed as the product of the education for liberation approach, which informs Marquis's vampire abolitionism as well as Jeremiah's and Eric's interpretations of the Bible.

## Book Knowledge, Scapegoating, and Education for Salvation

Although advocates of black corporatism have tended to support an "authoritarian collectivism" in which the corporate unit is led by one powerful man or group of men whose leadership authority is due to "superior knowledge or divine authority," Shelby notes that black corporatism "need not be elitist, patriarchal, autocratic, messianic, or sectarian" (121). Nevertheless, Shelby argues, drawing on the work of Cathy Cohen, that black corporatism should be rejected due to its "cross-cutting political issues." In contrast to "consensus issues," which are political concerns that "constrain or oppress with equal probability (although through different manifestations) all identifiable marginal group members," cross-cutting issues are "those concerns which *disproportionally and directly* affect only certain segments of a marginal group" (122). The cross-cutting issue that seems to inform the other four (i.e., "sexism," homophobia, "strong norms of racial endogamy," and local and regional differences) is "the political role of black churches and Christian leaders, which continue to have tremendous influence in US politics, often defining the black agenda of some local communities." The Black Church not only "drown[s] out" black non-Christian voices, but it also has a "strong male bias, if not an outright patriarchal stance on gender roles and women rights," and it marginalizes the black LGBTQ community with its "proscriptions against 'homosexual acts'" (123). Thus, to problematize Black Church corporatism, one must not only question the certainty of God's existence, as Johnson does in his depiction of Marquis as an agnostic staying-alive vampire, but also the church's reading of the Bible, as represented by Johnson's portrayal of Pastors Williams and Lewis. Although Pastor Williams is a white Catholic preaching to African American slaves during the nineteenth century and Pastor Lewis is a black Protestant preaching to a middle-class African American congregation at the beginning of the twenty-first century, both teach their African American audiences to treat the Bible as book knowledge, as a text that is never to be questioned, only memorized.

The first time Marquis mentions attending church is when he is recalling his stay at the Newton plantation. However, Marquis attended church, which was held in the plantation's barn, not because he was looking for salvation, but because he wanted to have time away from Jessie, the plantation's monstrous overseer, and to get a book to resume his education. Since slaves could be whipped or killed for possessing the ability to read,[8] Marquis had to let Pastor Williams, a local clergyman who led the worship service for the slaves on the Newton plantation, believe that "he was the only literate person in the barn." However, when the pastor declared before the beginning of a prayer that "Lord, it's a shame these boys ain't allowed to read your Word," Marquis decided that the next time he attended church he would be "rebellious" because he was "tired of pretending that [he] was a stupid nigger" (100–01). Thus, when Marquis started to read the Bible in church, Pastor Williams was thrilled and excited, but for reasons that differed from Marquis's:

> Pastor Williams confessed that he always thought it was God's will for everyone to read His Word. He said my boldness was God's way of speaking to him through me.
>
> "Is there anyone else here that would like to learn to read?" Pastor Williams inquired. Jeremiah was the only person to raise his hand.
>
> I tried to encourage them. "Brothers, don't be afraid. Education is the key—."
>
> "The key to salvation," Pastor Williams interrupted!
>
> I was going to say "the key to freedom," but I didn't care what his motivation was, as long as the same end was achieved. Hands slowly rose one by one, until every hand in the room was in the air. (102–3)

As indicated by the passage above, the goal of educating black men for Pastor Williams is to bring them closer to the Christian God, a goal that is, as Marquis notes, absent of any concept of freedom without death. It is, therefore, noteworthy that unlike the Voodoo priestess, who is able to tell Mar-

---

8. One of the main reasons why slave owners did not want their slaves to be literate was the fear of black citizenship. As James Fraser explains, "slave owners were worried about losing their 'property rights' if the slaves took on more of the attributes of free citizens." In response to this fear, laws were passed throughout the US during the early eighteenth century that allowed slaves to be educated, but "they would still be slaves no matter what level of education or piety they achieved" (5).

quis that he and his people *will* be free, Pastor Williams cannot make such a guarantee because it suggests that the pastor's religion is preventing him from believing in the eventuality of black freedom. Katie Geneva Cannon's discussion of the three ideological myths used by white Christian slave apologists (i.e., Christians who were slave owners or who supported slavery) to justify slavery helps to explain the pastor's hesitance on the issue of black freedom.

According to Cannon, white Christian slave apologists argued that black people were not members of humanity; that God sent slave traders to Africa in order to free Africans of ignorance, superstition, and corruption; and that slavery was not considered a violation of God's law (414–17). What encouraged such arguments, Cannon concludes, was the following reality:

> [Wealthy slaveholders] used revenue from slave labor to pay pastors, maintain church properties, support seminaries, and sustain overseas missionaries. Seduced by privilege and profit, white Christians of all economic strata were made, in effect, coconspirators in the victimization of Black people. In other words, slave apologists were successful in convincing at least five generations of white citizens that slavery, an essential and constitutionally protected institution, was consistent with the impulse of Christian charity. (419)

Given this historical context, it is in Pastor Williams's best interest to make sure that black men view education only as a path to salvation because black freedom means a loss of revenue for the church. One could argue, however, that since the Pastor gave Marquis a math book to teach him how to calculate 10 percent because he "might pay tithes" in the future (104), the pastor is letting Marquis know that he imagines a future in which black people are free. The problem with that reading of the pastor's actions is that the reason why the pastor gave Marquis a math book was not for Marquis to calculate the price of goods or his labor, but to calculate how much of his future earnings he will give to the church if ever becomes a free man. In this scenario, black freedom is only important to Pastor Williams because it represents a new revenue stream for the church, a revenue stream that could make up for the loss that would come with the end of slavery. Moreover, the pastor's use of the term "might" suggests that he is not too convinced that such a future will ever happen, since slavery is a large reason why the Christian church thrived during antebellum America. Thus, education for salvation is not a strategy for black freedom; rather, it is a strategy for securing revenue and increasing membership for the church.

In addition to its goals of conversion and revenue accumulation, the education for salvation approach is also designed to make black people forever dependent on white men. For example, Marquis's ability to read, according to the pastor, is not a sign that God is speaking to Marquis or to the other black men in the barn; rather, it is a sign that God is speaking to the pastor "through" Marquis, implying that black men will always need white men to lead them, even when they are free, because God does not speak directly to black men. Moreover, while Pastor Williams occasionally used poetry as an "aid to help [slaves] learn to read," he did this because he believed that "scripture was like poetry" (103). For the pastor, the similarities between the two genres is that both are forms of "book knowledge," what Jonathan Culler refers to as "instances of a larger category of exemplary practices of writing and thinking, which include[s] speeches, sermons, history, and philosophy." More important, Culler notes that prior to 1850, "students were not asked to interpret [these writings], as we now interpret literary works, seeking to explain what they are 'really about.' On the contrary, students memorized them, studied their grammar, identified their rhetorical figures and their structures or procedures of argument" (21). Thus, when Pastor Williams is teaching slaves how to read poetry and the Bible, he is not teaching them to read these texts in order to discover what they are "really about," but to read them as professing absolute truths about the world that need to be memorized instead of questioned. As the pastor sees it, since literate black men should only be concerned with how to read the Bible as book knowledge, there is no need to teach them how to read it as a literary text, to read it as imaginative writing with an ideological agenda. Unfortunately, Pastor Williams's approach to the Bible is still used in many of today's African American churches, as represented by Pastor Lewis and Eric's parents.

Besides attending a prestigious high school and private university, Eric lives with his parents in "a nice middle-class neighborhood," a short distance from Sean Jenkins, Eric's best friend and fellow high school classmate who is straight. Sean lives on St. Charles Avenue, "where New Orleans' aristocratic families resided," with Roland, his openly gay brother, and Dr. Jenkins, an oncologist and single mother. Dr. Jenkins raised Roland and Sean by herself because her husband died in a car accident, not because he left the family for another woman or decided to be a deadbeat dad (*Image* 18–19). Eric's family and community are examples of what Eugene Robinson refers to as the "Mainstream middle-class majority," one of Robinson's four black Americas (i.e., the Mainstream, the Abandoned minority, the Transcendent elite, and the Emergent groups)⁹ in which three of every ten black families earn at least $50,000 a year and nearly one of ten black households earn $100,000 or more annually. Moreover, the Mainstream makes and spends most of the estimated $800 billion in purchasing power controlled by the four black Americas, which is roughly the GDP of the world's thirteenth-richest nation (Robinson 7). In addition to controlling a major share of black purchasing power in the US., another trait of the Mainstream, according to the novel, is its religious-based homophobia. Indeed, Nero once noted that some black churches have adopted heterosexist policies and practices (e.g., the practice of exorcism) that oppress black gays to "prove" the Black Church's worth to the African American middle classes ("Toward" 408–10).

While Dr. Jenkins and Sean are not ashamed of Roland being gay, Fred and Stella, Eric's parents, are devout Christians who taught Eric that homosexuality is evil; therefore, having a gay son would be their worst nightmare. For example, when Eric was in grade school, he heard the older kids refer to AIDS as a "fag disease." Since he did not know what a fag was, he asked his father to explain. Fred, who is now a retired high school music teacher who taught Eric how to play the clarinet and compose music at a young age, said that "fag" is a derogatory term and that the "proper" term for homosexual men is "gay." However, he also told the young Eric that "a gay male is a boy that likes another boy the way he should like a girl once they become adults. Those boys catch a disease called AIDS, when they do wicked and ungodly things" (*Image* 89). Fred's comments, unfortunately, are representative of one of the reasons for the increased prevalence of HIV/AIDS among blacks in the US—"the lack of an immediate response by important Black institutions, most notably the Black Church" (Harris 305). While the stigmas associated with HIV/AIDS, such as intravenous drug use and premarital sex, were some of the reasons for the Black Church's slow response, it seems that the stigma of homosexuality was the primary reason. Angelique Harris notes that addressing HIV/AIDS means, among other things, admitting that nonheteronormative modes of sexuality exist in the Black community,

---

9. Robinson describes the Transcendent elite as the smallest of the four black Americas, but that group has "such enormous wealth, power, and influence that even white folks have to genuflect." In contrast, the Abandoned minority, who represent roughly 25 percent of the African American population, are those who tend to live in urban neighborhoods or in the rural South and have "less hope of escaping poverty and dysfunction than any time since Reconstruction's crushing end." Finally, the Emergent groups, "individuals of mixed-race heritage and communities of recent black immigrants," call into question monolithic notions of blackness by problematizing the notion of racial purity and the idea that one's racial identity is their sole or primary identity (5–10).

"something the Church has tried to disassociate itself from for decades" (310). Moreover, as represented by Stella, a retired stay-at-home mom and a "soldier" for domestic cleanliness (*Image* 81), Black Church homonegativity is also about gender and the state of the race. Stella once told Eric, after the church's pastor gave a sermon on the evils of homosexuality, that she feels "sorry" for one of the women in the church because her son Leonard is gay. According to Stella, Leonard is not only "more woman" than she, but he is an example of "what happens when there's no man in the house. Homosexuality is an abomination. Praise Jesus, I don't have to deal with that type of stuff." When Eric tried to push back by asking Stella if she believes that Roland is an abomination, she responded with words that "stung" him and have kept him in the closet ever since: "I love both Sean and Roland, but you can love the sinner and not the sin. If Roland doesn't get his act together, then he'll burn in hell with the rest of the sinners" (41). This heterosexist conception of black manhood is taught and reinforced by Pastor Lewis.

The sermon that inspired Stella to say the words that would keep Eric in the closet was delivered by Pastor Michael Oscar Lewis III, leader of the "traditional, conservative, black, Baptist church" where Eric was baptized at the age of seven. Apparently, Pastor Lewis has delivered several antigay sermons over Eric's lifetime because Eric states that he hates "gay-bashing Sundays," and the following excerpt is an example of such sermons: "Church, I'm tired of watching the news and seeing these homosexuals asking for special rights. The Bible clearly says it is wrong! The men of Sodom and Gomorrah were punished for their homosexuality. . . . Homosexuals are one of the main reasons those two cities were destroyed, church!" (*Image* 39). However, Eric discovers that Genesis 19, the chapter that Pastor Lewis cites as biblical evidence of God's hatred of homosexuality, "didn't say homosexuality is wrong"; rather, its lesson is that "rape was wrong in the eyes of God." While Eric, like Pastor Lewis, does not mention that the chapter in question depicts a father offering his virgin daughters to the men of Sodom to prevent God's angels from being raped,[10] an exclusion that reminds us of Gomez's critique of the ways in which Black Church heteropatriarchy allows "safe spaces" for black gay men but not black lesbians, his overall criticism of the pastor's gay-bashing sermon is still true—that most scripture is subject to the interpretation and needs of "whatever preacher [is] behind the podium" (40).

---

10. In Genesis 19, Lot makes the following offer to the men of Sodom in order to prevent these men from raping the angels who came to visit him: "See now, I have two daughters who have not known a man: please, let me bring them out to you, and you may do to them as you wish; only do nothing to these men, since this is the reason they have come under the shadow of my roof" (Gen. 19:8).

What is even more fascinating and disturbing about Pastor Lewis's sermon is that it is pure guesswork, as suggested by his discussion of peacocks: "God made the beautiful female peacock for the male peacock. He gave her those exquisite, and very gorgeous feathers to stretch out to the heaven for her male partner's enjoyment. Why in the world would the male peacock turn his vision away from such beauty to lust after another male peacock? It just doesn't make sense church. I tell you it is straight CRAZY!" (40). Pastor Lewis's comparison of gays and peacocks represents how some black churches continue to miseducate African Americans with the education for salvation approach to the Bible.[11] For instance, even though current scholarship demonstrates that human sexualities are the product of our "natural 'urges' and 'drives,'" our social contexts, and our cultural assumptions about sexuality (Kimmel and The Stony Brook Sexualities Research Group ix), Pastor Lewis is still declaring that "God didn't make Adam and Steve! He made Adam and Eve" (*Image* 38), a declaration that wrongly presumes that queer sexualities are not natural because all humans have been and will be straight. Pastor Lewis does not find it necessary to read any non-biblical literature on the topics he preaches on (e.g., homosexuality and peacocks) because he treats the Bible as book knowledge. Moreover, since Pastor Lewis prioritizes the spiritual salvation of African Americans over telling them the truth about human sexuality, Eric begins to wonder if the pastor should have the authority to speak on the behalf of all African Americans or even the Bible. In fact, Eric concludes from his critique of the pastor's comparison of gays and peacocks that the pastor is a "DUMB-ASS" because, as Eric notes, "the male peacock is the one with the beautiful feathers" (40); there-

---

11. Robert Cross notes that Richard Hofstadter identified religion as one of the "four pressures" that have historically worked against the development of intellectualism in the US. According to Cross, "very early in American history, Hofstadter asserted, the traditional balance in Christianity 'between the mind and the heart, between emotion and intellect' began to tip toward a heavy emphasis on enthusiastic nonintellectual or anti-intellectual religion" (20). Religious anti-intellectualism was evident in the Great Awakening of the eighteenth century and in the nineteenth century, when US Protestantism "increasingly insisted on a dichotomy between fundamental religious truth and mundane understanding" (21). Thus, it is not too surprising that William Jennings Bryan, who was known as "The Great Commoner" and served as secretary of state in Woodrow Wilson's administration, made the following comment in 1923: "If we have to give up either religion or education, we should give up education" (qtd. in Cross 21). Unfortunately, such thinking would seep into the education of African Americans after the Civil War. As Cross puts it, "the education of African Americans was shaped by the historical prejudices, philanthropic predilections, and anti-intellectualism of American Whites" (26). In this light, Pastors Williams and Lewis represent, respectively, past and present forms of nonintellectual Christianity in America.

fore, instead of the pastor's analogy condemning homosexuality, it supports the idea that homosexuality is as natural as heterosexuality.

Johnson's depiction of Pastor Lewis insists that the education for salvation approach to the Bible is at the root of the cross-cutting issues that make Black Church corporatism an impractical and dangerous route to black solidarity. Pastor Lewis's interpretation of the Bible's position on homosexuality, as Eric points out, not only lacks creditable and corroborating evidence, discourages African Americans from discovering what the Bible is really about, and defines God as a homophobe, but it also sanctions antigay violence. For example, the pastor's "angry tone" not only represents God's supposed hatred of queer people, implying that God, not humans, is the origin of homophobia, but it is also directed at black gays who, in the pastor's opinion, can cause the African American community to suffer the same fate as Sodom and Gomorrah. In other words, one of the outcomes of Black Church corporatism is the scapegoating of black gays for all that is wrong in the African American community. As Charlie Campbell argues, even though the study of scapegoating is a study of "stupidity" (17), the relationship between the scapegoater and the scapegoat is a "complex" one because "the opposite of the prince is not the pauper, [but] the scapegoat." As Campbell explains, "the ruler *creates* the scapegoat, so he doesn't share his fate" (18; my emphasis). In this view, Pastor Lewis scapegoats black gays, so his congregation does not lose faith in him or in God to solve the social, political, and economic problems that African Americans as a community face.

In addition to deflecting blame from the Black Church or from himself for what is *wrong* in the African American community, the pastor's scapegoating of black gays might also be about escaping the reality that African American men have never been purely heterosexual. As Robert Reid-Pharr explains, since the production of black masculinity in the US has come to involve literal and symbolic anti-homosexual violence, striking "the homosexual, the scapegoat, the sign of chaos and crisis" is not only about returning "the community to normality, to create boundaries around Blackness" as well as allowing for "a reconnection to the very figure of boundarylessness that the assailant [i.e., the one who strikes the homosexual] is presumably attempting to escape," but it also gives voice to the fear that "there is no normal Blackness to which the Black subject, American, or otherwise, might refer" (603). This "fear" that the black gay stands in for, as Reid-Pharr notes in his analysis of Eldridge Cleaver's *Soul on Ice*, James Baldwin's *Giovanni's Room*, and Piri Thomas's *Down These Mean Streets*, is the realization that "the fiction of a pure heterosexuality no longer can be maintained, that the processes by which the 'Black' male subject is imagined as autonomous, virile, and invulnerable can no longer be rendered transparent" (617). In this light, Pastor Lewis scapegoats black gay men in an attempt to divert his congregation's attention away from the reality that the only requirement for being a black man is having a black body.

The critique of Black Church corporatism offered in *Image* holds that this conception of black solidarity is largely responsible for the homophobia that exists in the African American community and, therefore, for the invisibility of black gay vampires in African American vampire fiction. As Nero argues in "Why Are the Gay Ghettoes White?," "America's homophobic preoccupation with white masculinity" and the racist stereotype that "African American males are hyper-virile and cannot be gay" are the some of the reasons why black gay men are invisible in most parts of American culture. In fact, this homophobic and racist stereotyping has meant that "black gay men simply cannot exist, or, if they do, their existence is an anomaly that must be explained" (235). Since the existence of black gay men in many black churches has been largely explained through the education for salvation approach to the Bible, these men have been defined as harbingers of ill. As indicated by Eric's critique of Pastor Lewis's homophobic sermon, African Americans who are queer cannot "reasonably depend on corporatist black solidarity to secure their distinctive interests" (Shelby 125). However, how do black gay men, like Eric, who want to remain a part of the church reconcile the fact that Black Church corporatism excludes black gay men who are out from its conception of black solidarity? One of the answers to that question, as suggested by Marquis and Jeremiah's reading of the Adam and Eve story, which I will discuss below, is applying an education for liberation approach to the Bible. Like Eric's interpretation of the Sodom and Gomorrah story, Marquis and Jeremiah's reading of the Adam and Eve story offers an interpretation of a biblical story that accounts for gay black men as God's children and, simultaneously, rejects the conservative approach's image of the Black Church–black gay relationship.

## Education for Liberation and Divine Sexuality

While tending to the young cows on the Newton plantation with Jeremiah, Marquis begins to sing a self-composed tune in French titled "Freedom Song." In this song, Marquis not only asks God for freedom, but he also states that "a pen will be [his] weapon" and "a page will be [his] shield," implying that he will need more than a belief in God to attain his freedom (*Image* 75). When Jeremiah asks Marquis about "how" blacks will attain their freedom from slavery, Marquis simply tells him that "education is the key" (76). It seems that Marquis realizes that slavery exists in America largely because the laws in the country make it legal, not because a deity wishes it to be so. For Marquis, learning to read just for the purpose of reading the Bible is not a strategy for freedom, but a strategy of oppression. Thus, when Isildur decides to befriend Marquis, since he is convinced that Marquis will be the legendary "great vampire," Marquis accepts the offer. Due to their budding friendship, Isildur not only forbids Jessie and his men from harming Marquis, but he also allows Marquis to resume his education by granting him access to the mansion's library, since the barn church was shut down by Jessie after he discovered Marquis was teaching black men how to read. Isildur also offers the same perks to Jeremiah as he does to Marquis, and even gives Jeremiah a book of poetry simply because Marquis and Jeremiah are in love. Moreover, it is during this newly found free time that Marquis and Jeremiah imagine freedom on earth, as opposed to in heaven:

> "You' think we'll eva leave this farm, Eyez?" [Jeremiah] tossed rocks in the murky water as we strolled along the river in the bright sunlight.
> "Of course I do. I'll convince Isildur to grant us our freedom or we can put our heads together and concoct a better escape than ole' Sylvester and Jack." The thought of us living together as two free men was overwhelming. (144–45)

It is noteworthy that the thought of being free reemerges at the same time that Marquis, whom Jeremiah affectionately refers to as "Eyez," resumes his education because it suggests that way of thinking is due to Marquis reading more than the Bible. For example, Marquis and Jeremiah "got a lot of reading done" during their "free time" together, and this reading gave Marquis the confidence to believe that he could "convince" Isildur to go against his economic interest by granting him and Jeremiah freedom, since he can now reference the books from Isildur's library to make nonreligious arguments for why he and Jeremiah should be free, arguments that would supposedly be compelling to educated white men (144–45). At the same time, because Marquis has read more, he also realizes that such arguments will most likely be rejected, since slavery was supported by pseudo-scientific writings about black people's humanity or lack thereof, so he imagines an alternative plan for their freedom, a plan that Ole' Jack and Sylvester, who were captured by Isildur because "Jack got chicken," lacked (134). What is implied by Marquis's distinction between Sylvester and Ole' Jack's attempt at freedom and his and Jeremiah's plan is that education for salvation, unlike education for liberation, not only lacks practical solutions to contemporary injustices, but it also makes one fearful of freedom, since the Bible was used as divine justification for black enslavement.

Because Marquis links education with freedom, it is not surprising that he becomes an abolitionist once he becomes a vampire. He notes that his vampire abolitionism is responsible for freeing Harriet Tubman from slavery and starting the famous Underground Railroad (*Image* 224–26). He also fought for the Union forces during the Civil War with an ex-slave named Calvin, a vampire whose "unique ability" allowed him to engulf his entire body in flames and shoot fire from his hands at Confederate soldiers (233), and he became good friends with Frederick Douglass, saw Martin Luther King Jr. deliver his speech in Memphis, Tennessee, the day before his assassination in 1968, and met the young Barack Obama in Hawaii on the day of King's assassination (256–59). By associating Marquis's vampire abolitionism with individuals who represent two centuries of black freedom, Johnson is not only suggesting that one of the main reasons why African Americans achieved freedom from slavery and Jim Crow was due to their development of interpretations of the Bible that emphasized freedom for all followers of Christ, not just the white ones, but he is also depicting Marquis as a moderate black gay man, one whose "presence" is a "benefit" to African American communities; therefore, marginalizing him is a "detriment to the flourishing of [those] communities" (Sneed 256–57). As Marquis tells it, if he was marginalized by the slave community because he was gay, he would have been unable to teach the black men on the Newton plantation how to read, to help start the Underground Railroad, or to fight for the Union forces during the Civil War.

Due to Marquis's focus on freeing black people from slavery, one might argue that he represents the conservative black gay man found in the novels by E. Lynn Harris, which are referenced throughout *Image of Emeralds and Chocolate*. According to that reading of Marquis, his vampire abolitionism and his relationships with Jeremiah and Eric suggest that "morally praiseworthy behavior for Black queer men entails monogamous relationships and fidelity to the interests of the Black middle class" (Sneed 257). However, while Marquis's monogamous relationships with Jeremiah and Eric are like those found among conservative black gay men in which "religion and spirituality" serve as "civilizing force[s]" (257), his decision to be monogamous is not shaped by the idea that black gay men need to be *saved* or *civilized*, but by his personal preference. For example, Marquis notes in the last installment of "A Slave's Tale" that he falls in love with Eric, as opposed to Santiago, whom Marquis saves from an AIDS-related death by transforming him into a vampire, because Eric is not "whorish and shady like Santiago, but innocent and insecure" (*Image* 296). According to Marquis, Eric does not need salvation, but confidence, and that confidence will not come from God or the Black Church, but from Marquis, since Eric is "the only person in 173 years capable of kicking down the emotional walls [Marquis] built around [his] heart" (296). Johnson's point seems to be, which is reinforced by his depictions of Marquis and Jeremiah's first night of sex and Eric's letter to God, that black gay men must adopt not only the moderate black gay man's sense of value to the African American community, but also the liberal black gay man's conception of God to be happy in their erotic relationships.

On his eighteenth birthday, Marquis receives the first and only poem from Jeremiah, a poem that Marquis did not read as a love letter until Jeremiah kissed him. At first, Marquis yelled at Jeremiah and pushed him away because "his kiss reminded [him] of the unwanted advances sometimes made by Jessie" and because Marquis "would have been damned if [he] had been seen as anything other than a man." Before the kiss, Marquis was a virgin who "really thought" that he was "asexual," since he had no sexual desire for women. After a month of not speaking to each other, Marquis notices Jeremiah's naked body during the slaves' weekly washing in the Mississippi River and acknowledges that he is gay, not asexual. However, because Marquis, like Jeremiah, was raised by his grandparents to be Christian, he wonders if his desire for Jeremiah is "nasty" (*Image* 106–08). Marquis's views on the nastiness of gay sex change when Jeremiah jokingly tells him that he enjoys the Adam and Eve story in Genesis because he likes the idea of "populat[ing] the entire planet." What follows is Jeremiah's not-so-subtle invitation to Marquis to have sex with him: "The Lord made sex. If it's good 'nough for Adam and Eve, then it's good 'nough for me and—." Marquis's response to Jeremiah's incomplete sentence implies that he, like Jeremiah, believes that God made gay men: "I decided I had nothing to lose. 'It's good enough for me and you.' I finished his statement, while climbing on top of him and grinding my body deep into his. I didn't know what I was doing. But it all felt natural" (110). By equating their relationship to Adam and Eve's, Marquis and Jeremiah align themselves with the liberal black gay man, one who believes that God is "open to multiple expressions of sexuality" (Sneed 256). When Marquis and Jeremiah declare that sex is good enough for them and for Adam and Eve, they are also declaring that "sexual difference is not a threat to God's existence" (257). As Marquis and Jeremiah see it, God is open to multiple expressions of sexuality precisely because God created multiple sexualities. This is a point that Eric alludes to in his letter to God regarding the possibility of Marquis being "the one."

Like Marquis and Jeremiah's reading of the Adam and Eve story, Eric imagines God as one who views the erotic love between men as the same as that between straight people.

Eric's letter to God is an entry into a journal that he keeps on his laptop. The narrator notes that Eric always starts his entries with a greeting (e.g., Dear Journal, Dear Mother, or Dear Eric) because communicating his thoughts to imagined others makes it "easier to express himself and allow[s] him an outlet to get things off his chest." It is noteworthy that Eric finds it easier to tell God about his desire for another man than any real person, save for Sean and Roland, because it not only suggests that God created multiple sexualities, but also that God is not a homophobe, as Pastor Lewis would have his congregation believe:

> Dear God,
> It's Eric again. God, I'm very happy and nervous today. As you know, I met a really nice person. I'm not sure if he's for real, but I hope he is. Being a teenager, black, and gay is a very lonely existence.
> I want to be able to love somebody the same way the girls and guys express their love at the school dances and movies. I'm nowhere near ready to publicly display my affections, and don't think I'll ever reach that point; however, I would like to have my own secret love affair. Love seems like a wonderful experience that I would like to have if only for a minute. Therefore, I write this letter tonight to ask you to grant me one wish. I would like Marquis to be the one.
> Thank you. (*Image* 78–79)

For Eric to believe that the God he prays to will intervene in his life to help him develop a romantic relationship with Marquis, he must be convinced that this God does not take sides "in the dialectic between heterosexuality and homosexuality" (Sneed 259). As he indicates in his letter, it is not God who prevents Eric from publicly displaying his affections, but the heterosexism of his parents and church as well as his own insecurities about being gay. Unlike Delmar, whom I mentioned earlier in this chapter, Eric might keep his queerness a "secret" for his entire life because, as indicated by his parents' comments and Pastor Lewis's antigay sermons, he will bring shame upon his family, church, and community. It seems that Eric's letter is a subtle critique of his parents and Pastor Lewis, who believe that black gay men are not extensions of *proper* black manhood. What makes such thinking problematic is that straight black men who are Christian but harm or exploit African American communities (e.g., gang members, domestic abusers, and corrupt politicians and ministers) are viewed as *blacker, manlier,* and more *savable* than black gay men like Eric, who do not harm the community and want to be positive examples for the race. Due to this hypocrisy, Eric comes to realize, as implied in his letter, that in God's eyes, he is just a black male teenager who happens to be erotically attracted to men, but in the eyes of many black folks, he is not black or a man.

Since Marquis, Eric, and Jeremiah, like Sneed's black gay men, do not "adopt a theological orientation that would render God or Jesus Christ as gay or queer," Sneed would contend that these men do not "radically shift Black religious understandings of God and Black queer sexuality" (259). However, the problem with such an argument is that it implies that the only expression of a radical shift in African American religious thought is identifying God as queer. Since the God of the Black Church, as represented by Johnson's portrayals of Pastor Lewis and Eric's parents, is a straight male who has deemed consensual queer sex an abomination while normalizing certain instances of heterosexual rape and incest, Marquis's agnosticism and Jeremiah's and Eric's view of God as indifferent to human sexualities suggest that any representation of God that is not heterosexual, patriarchal, homophobic, and/or male would be a radical shift in the Black Church's conceptions of God and humanity. Moreover, as Johnson suggests in *Image,* black gay men who believe that marginalizing gay blacks is harmful to the African American community and that God is open to multiple expressions of human sexuality tend to adopt an education for liberation approach to the Bible. Because that approach calls for readers to treat the Bible as a literary text, as opposed to book knowledge, it also requires readers to consult non-biblical sources before rejecting or developing an interpretation of the Bible's position on sexuality. When one reads the Bible in the context of non-biblical sources, as Marquis, Jeremiah, and Eric do, one realizes, as the novel emphasizes, that the Bible's position on human sexuality is indeed subject to the political agendas or ideological projects of its interpreters. In this light, the homophobia that underlines Eric's parents' and Pastor Lewis's interpretations of the Bible is not about God's word, but about their views of what it means to be a black man who can properly represent the race.

## Transcending the "Unnatural Fight"

I have argued in this chapter that K. Murry Johnson's *Image of Emeralds and Chocolate* can be read as a warning about the dangers of the Black Church having the authority to speak for all African Americans. One of the main problems with Black Church corporatism, as captured by Johnson's portrayal of Pastor Lewis, is that it not only prioritizes the spiritual salvation of African Americans above telling the truth about human sexuality, but it also lacks creditable corroborating evidence, discourages African Americans from discovering what the Bible is "really about," and sanctions antigay violence by imagining God as a homophobe. Indeed, Pastor Lewis's black gay man lives in a world where God favors heterosexuals over homosexuals and is an example of the Black Church's "controlling image of black gay men," an image that not only normalizes the marginalization or invisibility of black gay men in the Black Church and in mainstream African American life, but also treats them as "frauds" or "imposters" (Nero, "Why Are Gay Ghettoes White?" 235). According to that image, since the black gay man is an imposter, he cannot be trusted to tell us anything significant about being an African American man or even a gay man in America. It is that image of black gay men that is countered by Johnson's depictions of Marquis and his lovers, which are informed by the idea that God does not take sides in the heterosexual-homosexual debate because it created both sides, and is, therefore, accepting of both. In fact, Marquis tells Eric that he believes that "everyone has a little homosexuality in them," which Eric translates as "the majority of people are some form of a bisexual" (*Image* 84). To come to that conclusion about God and queer sexuality, as the novel emphasizes, one must believe that homophobia is not only ungodly, but also antiblack. Such a belief, according to *Image,* can only emerge from an education for liberation approach to the Bible.

Since the education for liberation approach treats the Bible as a literary text, not as book knowledge, students of this approach acknowledge that the Bible, like the sacred texts of most, if not all, theistic religions, is open to multiple interpretations. This line of thinking not only informs Marquis and Jeremiah's declaration that sex between them is just as divine as that between Adam and Eve as well as Eric's belief that God will help him develop a romantic relationship with Marquis, but it also keeps Marquis from being bound in crisis with no hope of transcendence because he rejects both the idea that God favors heterosexuals over homosexuals and the notion that God is on the side of homosexuals because God is an anthropomorphic guardian of the oppressed (Sneed 259). The problem with both conceptions of the God–black gay man relationship, as suggested by Johnson's depiction of Marquis as a vampire abolitionist, is that black queer men are only relevant to God because they are either examples of eternal sin or examples of the eternally oppressed, but never examples of transcendence. In this light, Marquis represents the black gay man who is a hero to all African Americans, not just to black queer men, because he has transcended the sin and oppression of black homophobia and white racism.

Thus, by linking Marquis's vampire abolitionism to the education for liberation approach to the Bible, Johnson is not only proposing a way for queer African American men and African Americans in general to acknowledge that for them to attain heaven on earth, as well as in heaven, they need to live as though God is either a myth or a noninterventionist god who is not a homophobe, but he is also declaring that the only requirement for being a black man in America is having a black body. In this view, the de-blackening of black gay men inside and outside of the Black Church does not make sense because what one looks like, not whom one loves or sleeps with, determines if one is black in America. This means that homophobia, not homosexuality, has caused what Cleo Manago referred to as the "unnatural fight" between straight and queer African American men to "know and love" themselves (49). Thus, by depicting Marquis as a gay black vampire who embodies all the qualities of the Black Church's conception of the *good* black man, save for his agnosticism and same-sex eroticism, Johnson suggests in *Image* that squashing this unnatural fight requires a conception of black solidarity founded on real tolerance. Such solidarity not only allows black gay men to be different from straight black men, but it also acknowledges that queer and straight black men are just black men in the eyes of white supremacy.

CONCLUSION

# POST-BLACK, NEW BLACK, AND THE IMMORTALITY OF BLACKNESS

IS THERE MORE to being black than having a black body? I have argued that Jewelle Gomez's *The Gilda Stories,* Tananarive Due's *My Soul to Keep,* Brandon Massey's *Dark Corner,* Octavia Butler's *Fledgling,* and K. Murry Johnson's *Image of Emeralds and Chocolate* support the idea that the only requirement for being black is having a black body; thus, their answer to the question above is a resounding no. According to these African American vampire novels, since "blackness is not a club [one] can be expelled from" (Touré 24), it is impossible to deny anyone with a black body entry into the club due to his or her class, sexuality, religious belief, political affiliation, or national origin. In this view, the blackness club is a collection of many clubs; therefore, any conception of blackness that requires one to think and behave in a certain way to be considered authentically black is not only fraudulent and unrealistic, but it is always already a source of conflict. In fact, one trait that Gomez's Gilda, Due's Dawit, Massey's Diallo, Butler's Shori, and Johnson's Marquis share is the belief that being a vampire is just as important as being black. Because their vampirism has allowed them to survive the horrors of antiblack racism, Gilda, Dawit, Diallo, Shori, and Marquis do not treat their blackness as an "overriding affiliation," an identity that is "much more important in every circumstance to all others" (Maalouf 13). Thus, these black vampires are reminders that even though the body determines if one is black, black people are not just black, and to believe otherwise is itself racist.

Although the novels above agree that having a black body determines if one can be a member of the blackness club, they seem to disagree on what makes a body black. To be more specific, these novels seem to articulate a "post-blackness" or a "new black" understanding of the black body. As I noted in the introduction of this book, post-blackness describes an individualized notion of blackness that rejects any form of black corporatism, while the new black describes a cross-racial coalition of disenfranchised groups that are ultimately defined by their politics and class rather than by their physical characteristics. One of the main differences between post-blackness and the new black's blackness is that post-blackness is shaped by the belief that black and nonblack people exist, whereas the new black's blackness is guided by the belief that everyone is black. Given these definitions, *My Soul to Keep* and *Dark Corner* are post-black vampire novels, and *The Gilda Stories*, *Fledgling*, and *Image of Emeralds and Chocolate* are new-black vampire novels. To appreciate the difference between these novels, their black vampires, and the notions of blackness that they represent, I will conclude *The Paradox of Blackness in African American Vampire Fiction* with a brief discussion of which blackness might thrive in twenty-first-century America.

Since most Americans, as Joseph Graves puts it, "still believe in the concept of race the way they believe in the law of gravity—they believe in it without even knowing what it is they believe in" (xxv), it is noteworthy that Dawit and Diallo represent the magical versions of their respective immortality narratives because these black vampires suggest that post-blackness can only thrive in the world of racial myth, a world in which race, like immortality, is viewed as a product of forces beyond human control. Even though Dawit is an atheist and Diallo considers himself a god, they operate in fictional worlds where nature or God is responsible for the races and for immortality. What these post-black vampires and their novels show is that even though post-blackness critiques the idea that there is an authentic way to be black, it is still invested in the race myth. In other words, since the concept of race insists that one's racialized body determines how one will think and behave, the post-blackness emphasis on black individuality and diversity is suited to counter the body-determines-ideology discourse of race, but not the concept of race itself. Indeed, while the emphasis on black diversity has been useful for challenging monolithic conceptions and depictions of black people, it seems to have been unsuccessful in convincing most white Americans to let go of the race myth. For example, the increase in the number of white supremacist groups since the beginning of President

Obama's presidency, recent claims by white nationalist groups that diversity and multiculturalism are attempts at white genocide, and the election of Donald Trump as president indicate that a significant number of white Americans still believe that race is real and that America is a *white* nation.[1] Thus, what makes blackness immortal in the world of post-blackness is the belief that race will always matter in America; therefore, blackness will always matter. The main problem with that view is that it fails to realize that the race myth is the main reason why African Americans continue to remain on the margins of American society and, therefore, implies that African Americans will always be, as Sneed would put it, bound in crisis with no hope of transcendence.

In contrast to its post-black counterpart, the new-black vampire novel contends that since all human bodies are black, the visual differences among human bodies are nothing more than gradations of blackness. According to that view, since blackness and humans trace their origins to Africa, identifying humans as black is simply an acknowledgment that black and non-black people come from the same place.[2] For example, Gilda's "a row of cotton" theory of blackness treats all humans as gradations of blackness

---

1. Mark Potok, a senior fellow at the Southern Poverty Law Center, noted in 2014 that there were 194 anti-government "patriot" or "militia" groups in 2000 and that number dropped to 148 by 2008. However, after President Obama's election, that number increased to 1,000 by 2013 (Berman). The group that calls itself the White Genocide Project believes that "diversity" is a synonym for "white genocide" (see whitegenocideproject.com), a myth engendered by Bob Whitaker, the presidential candidate for the white nationalist American Freedom Party (AFP) and author of "The Mantra," a 221-word anti-multiculturalism credo that ends with the phrase "Anti-Racist is a Code Word for Anti-White" (see http://www.whitakeronline.org/blog/the-white-mantra/). While William Johnson, chairman of the AFP, considers Whitaker a strong candidate for the white nationalist movement, he noted in 2015 that if the AFP is unable to mainstream their platform, he believes that others will: "You got people like Donald Trump . . . , who is spouting a lot of the things we do" (www.splcenter.org/hatewatch/2015/08/13/white-nationalist-american-freedom-party-gears-2016). In fact, the Trump campaign announced Johnson as one of its California primary delegates during the primary race before claiming Johnson's inclusion was a mistake, and given his remarks about African Americans and black people in general, as well as Jews, Muslims, Mexicans, and Mexican Americans during his presidential campaign, it is, according to Lydia O'Connor and Daniel Marans, "not really surprising that he's won the support and praise of the country's white supremacists."

2. As Daniel Fairbanks puts it, "people emigrated out of Africa about sixty thousand to seventy thousand years ago and founded what ultimately became the rest of the world's population, carrying with them a subset of diversity in Africa" (34–35). Thus, unlike their mythical counterparts, the Bible's Adam and Eve, the "mitochondrial Eve" and the "Y chromosome Adam," humanity's common ancestors, were "real" and "African" (43).

because, as Sorel notes, all humans have some African blood in them. Similarly, Shori's transhuman blackness represents the idea that all humans are black because they have melanin. In Marquis's case, his theory of human sexuality, in which all humans and, therefore, all black people have a "little homosexuality in them," is a critique of conservative black sexual politics in which homosexuality is racialized as white. According to this critique, if one's sexuality determines one's race, as insisted by conservative black sexual politics, then black and white people must belong to the same race because they both have a little queer in them. Thus, in the new-black vampire novel, identifying humans as black is not a statement of racial pride, superiority, or color-blindness; rather, it is a statement of fact.

It is important to note that by claiming that being black means being economically marginalized, the new-black vampire does not represent an essentialist view of black people or an updated color-blind ideology in which the role that the racialized body plays in American culture is downplayed. Instead, the new-black vampire represents the idea that while the body continues to determine if one is black, it does not determine if one will be *treated* as black. For instance, Gilda's "a row of cotton" theory of blackness, as represented by her multiracial vampire family, offers a vision of blackness that includes those who are not identified as black (e.g., white gay men and Native American lesbians) but share some of the economic and political disadvantages faced by many African Americans. Similarly, Shori and her multiracial vampire family are considered black by the Ina because they are human or, in Shori's case, part human. While Marquis's vampire family is also multiracial, his vampire abolitionism is an argument for an expansion of *normal* black manhood that includes black gay men, who are emasculated and whitened by most black nationalists and black churches. What these examples suggest is that since some black people are viewed and treated as white and some white people are viewed and treated as black, blackness and whiteness are not categories of human difference, but categories of marginalization and privilege. As Graves explains, "racists design and utilize their ideology to help maintain their privilege against other social groups. They invented American racial categories to identify who was a member of the in- versus the outgroup. Even today, the prevailing bigotry of individual Americans and the operation of institutionalized racism force individuals into membership of one of America's social coalitions, whether that person wants to be or not" (193). In this view, as Pamela Perry puts it, whiteness is nothing more than "an ideology of domination that confers privilege" and "commits psychological and physical violence against people of color" as well as against those whites who are *off-white* (243).³ As I suggested in chapter 2, since pre-colonial Africans did not think of themselves as a racial group, but as clearly distinct ethnic groups, blackness is an identity that was engendered by a white Other, not by a black Self, to justify slavery and colonialism. Thus, according to the new-black vampire novel, since all Americans, like every human on the planet, are black, the material inequalities that exist among the so-called races are not natural or divine but created and reproduced by human minds and hands.

Despite the fact that the majority of Americans, black and nonblack, continue to believe in the race myth, the new-black vampire novel shares Jared Diamond's prediction that "the reality of human races is another commonsense 'truth' destined to follow the flat Earth [myth] into oblivion" (qtd. in Harrison 180). However, if race will one day become extinct, would that mean that blackness will also become extinct? While the new-black vampire novel depicts the race myth as an ideology on the edge of oblivion, it also proposes that blackness will remain after the race myth has fallen into the sea of oblivion because being human means being black. This view of the future of blackness can be seen as a by-product of Afrofuturist thought,

---

3. Perry notes that the "class, gender, and sexual hierarchies within whiteness" have objectified and sanctioned poor white Americans, who are often referred to as "white trash," for "not performing the proper class decorums of whiteness" (245). An example of the ways poor whites continue to be objectified and sanctioned for not being *real* whites is the popularity of "white trash" parties, parties that several of my former students attended while in middle school, high school, or college. At these parties, people dress and behave as stereotypical poor whites from the Midwest and the South. For instance, they drink cheap canned beer, eat white bread with canned beans with pork, and celebrate incest while brandishing the Confederate flag. Many of the men at these parties wear fake rotten teeth and "wife-beaters" sprinkled with food stains, and some of the women dress as pregnant and barefoot teenagers with blackened eyes. It is noteworthy that many of the students who attended white trash parties also attended "beaner" parties (those that parody working-class Mexican American culture) and "pimp and ho" parties (those that parody working-class African American culture) because their attendance at these parties reveals something about whiteness that African Americans have known since the nineteenth century: There is more to being white than having a white body. "From as early as the 1800s," as Perry notes, "African American writers and scholars critically debated what 'white' meant, but most (white) Europeans did not" (243). However, this study of whiteness, as Martin Japtok points out, has not been concerned with "merely denoting color or privilege"; instead, this study has been concerned with making whiteness visible by showing that whiteness is "something quite apart from skin color, though it may go hand in hand with it" (489). In this light, the new-black vampire novel's conception of blackness can also be viewed as an examination of whiteness, since whiteness only has meaning because of its dialogic relationship with blackness.

which Susana Morris defines in her analysis of *Fledgling* as "an epistemology that both examines the current problems faced by blacks and people of color in general and critiques interpretations of the past and future." Moreover, as Morris notes, "not only does Afrofuturism posit that blacks will exist in the future, as opposed to being harbingers of social chaos and collapse, but in 'recovering the histories of counter-futures' Afrofuturism insists that blacks fundamentally *are* the future and that Afrodiasporic cultural practices are vital to imagining the continuance of human society" ("Black Girls" 153). By linking humanity's fate to the fate of black people, the new-black vampire novel offers us a future in which blackness no longer defines one part of the human species, as it does in the post-black vampire novel and most of the Western world, but the entire species. Thus, while the new-black vampire novel's notion of blackness agrees with Diamond's prediction about race's future, it also suggests that that future cannot be achieved unless we, as Americans and as a species, acknowledge that we are nothing more than gradations of blackness. The road to that future, as Butler suggests in *Fledgling*, begins with accepting the fact that nonblack people are not born not black; rather, *we* make them not black.

# WORKS CITED

Abdullah, Zain. "African 'Soul Brothers' in the 'Hood: Immigration, Islam, and the Black Encounter." *Anthropological Quarterly,* vol. 82, no. 1, 2009, pp. 37–62. *JSTOR,* www.jstor.org/stable/25488256.

Adeleke, Tunde. "Black Americans and Africa: A Critique of the Pan-African and Identity Paradigms." *The International Journal of African Historical Studies,* vol. 31, no. 3, 1998, pp. 505–36. *JSTOR,* www.jstor.org/stable/221474.

Alexander, Elizabeth. "'Can You Be BLACK and Look at This?': Reading the Rodney King Video(s)." *The Black Public Sphere: A Public Culture Book,* edited by The Black Public Sphere Collective, U of Chicago P, 1995, pp. 81–98.

Allen, Angela C., ed. Introduction. *Dark Thirst,* Pocket, 2004, pp. vii–x.

Asante, Molefi. *Afrocentricity.* Africa World Press, 1988.

———. "Afrocentricity, Race, and Reason." *Race and Reason,* vol. 1, no. 1, 1994, pp. 20–22.

Auerbach, Nina. *Our Vampires, Ourselves.* U of Chicago P, 1995.

Banks, L. A. *Minion.* St. Martin's Griffin, 2003.

Banks, Ralph Richard. *Is Marriage for White People? How the African American Marriage Decline Affects Everyone.* Plume, 2012.

Bartlett, Wayne, and Flavia Idriceanu. *Legends of Blood: The Vampire in History and Myth.* Praeger, 2006.

Beckett, Katherine. "Culture and the Politics of Signification: The Case of Child Sexual Abuse." *Social Problems,* vol. 43, no. 1, 1996, pp. 57–76. *JSTOR,* www.jstor.org/stable/3096894.

Benshoff, Harry. "Blaxploitation Horror Films: Generic Reappropriation or Reinscription?" *Cinema Journal,* vol. 39, no. 2, 2000, pp. 31–50. *JSTOR,* www.jstor.org/stable/1225551.

Beresford, Matthew. *From Demons to Dracula: The Creation of the Modern Vampire Myth.* Reaktion, 2008.

Berman, Mark. "The Current State of White Supremacists Groups in the U. S." *The Washington Post,* 30 Dec. 2014, https://www.washingtonpost.com/news/post-nation/wp/2014/12/30/the-current-state-of-white-supremacist-groups-in-the-u-s/?utm_term=.3f75927bf152.

Bernal, Martin. "Race in History." Van Horne, pp. 75–92.

*Blacula.* Directed by William Crain, performances by William Marshall, Denise Nicholas, Vonetta McGee, and Thalmus Rasulala, AIP, 1972.

Bobo, Jacqueline, Cynthia Hudley, and Claudine Michel, eds. *The Black Studies Reader.* Routledge, 2004.

Bostrum, Nick. "In Defense of Posthuman Dignity." *Bioethics,* vol. 19, no. 3, 2005, pp. 202–14.

Boyd, Melba Joyce. "Afro-Centrics, Afro-Elitists, and Afro-Eccentrics: The Polarization of Black Studies Since the Student Struggles." *Race and Reason,* vol. 1, no. 1, 1994, pp. 25–27.

Brockenbrough, Kevin. "'Cause Harlem Needs Heroes." Thomas, *Reading of the Bones,* pp. 111–25.

———. "The Family Business." Allen, pp. 253–304.

Brooks, Kinitra. "Finding the Humanity in Horror: Black Women's Sexual Identity in Fighting the Supernatural." *Poroi,* vol. 7, no. 2, 2011, pp. 1–14.

Brox, Ali. "'Every Age Has the Vampire It Needs': Octavia Butler's Vampiric Vision in Fledgling." *Utopian Studies,* vol. 19, no. 3, 2008, pp. 391–409. *JSTOR,* www.jstor.org/stable/20719918.

Bryant, Cedric Gael. "'The Soul Has Bandaged Moments': Reading the African American Gothic in Wright's 'Big Boy Leaves Home,' Morrison's 'Beloved,' and Gomez's 'Gilda.'" *African American Review,* vol. 39, no. 4, Winter 2006, pp. 541–53. EBSCO*host,* http://search.ebscohost.com/login.aspx?direct=true&db=a9h&AN=20597826&site=ehost-live&scope=site.

Burgett, Bruce, and Glenn Hendler, eds. *Keywords for American Cultural Studies.* New York UP, 2007.

Bush, Lawson, V. "How Black Mothers Participate in the Development of Manhood and Masculinity: What Do We Know About Black Mothers and Their Sons?" *The Journal of Negro Education,* vol. 73, no. 4, 2004, pp. 381–91.

Butler, Octavia. "The Book of Martha." *Bloodchild and Other Stories.* Seven Stories Press, 2005, pp. 187–214.

———. *Fledgling.* Seven Stories, 2005.

———. "The Monophobic Response." Thomas, *Century of Speculative Fiction,* pp. 415–16.

———. *Wild Seed.* 1980. *Seed to Harvest.* Warner, 2007, pp. 1–253.

Call, Lewis. "Structures of Desire: Erotic Power in the Speculative Fiction of Octavia Butler and Samuel Delany." *Rethinking History,* vol. 9, no. 2/3, June 2005, pp. 275–96. EBSCO*host,* doi:10.1080/13642520500149194.

Campbell, Charlie. *Scapegoat: A History of Blaming Other People.* Duckworth Overlook, 2011.

Cannon, Katie Geneva. "Slave Ideology and Biblical Interpretation." Bobo, Hudley, and Michel, pp. 413–20.

Carbado, Devon W. "Privilege." Johnson and Henderson, pp. 190–212.

Carter, Margaret L. "The Vampire as Alien in Contemporary Fiction." Gordon and Hollinger, pp. 27–44.

Cave, Stephen. *Immortality: The Quest to Live Forever and How It Drives Civilization.* Crown, 2012.

Caywood, Cynthia L., and Carlton Floyd. "'She Make You Right with Yourself': Aunt Ester, Masculine Loss and Cultural Redemption in August Wilson's Cycle Plays." *College Literature*, vol. 36, no. 2, 2009, pp. 74–95. EBSCO*host*, login.ezproxy.palomar.edu/login?url=http://search.ebscohost.com/login.aspx?direct=true&db=a9h&AN=37383180&site=ehost-live&scope=site.

Chantrell, Glynnis, ed. *The Oxford Dictionary of Word Histories.* Oxford UP, 2002.

Chrisman, Robert, and Nathan Hare, eds. *Contemporary Black Thought: The Best from* The Black Scholar. Bobbs-Merrill, 1973.

Cohen, Cathy J. "Punks, Bulldaggers, and Welfare Queens: The Radical Potential of Queer Politics?" Johnson and Henderson, pp. 21–51.

Cohen, Mark Nathan. *Culture of Intolerance: Chauvinism, Class, and Racism in the United States.* Yale UP, 1998.

Cole, Johnnetta Betsch, and Beverly Guy-Sheftall. *Gender Talk: The Struggle for Women's Equality in African American Communities.* One World, 2003.

Colebrook, Claire. "From Radical Representations to Corporeal Becomings: The Feminist Philosophy of Lloyd, Grosz, and Gatens." *Hypatia*, vol. 15, no. 2, 2000, pp. 76–93. *JSTOR*, www.jstor.org/stable/3810656.

Collins, Donald Earl. *Fear of a "Black" America: Multiculturalism and the African American Experience.* iUniverse, 2004.

Collins, Patricia Hill. *Black Sexual Politics: African Americans, Gender, and the New Racism.* Routledge, 2009.

Cross, Robert D. "The Historical Development of Anti-Intellectualism in American Society: Implications for the Schooling of African Americans." *The Journal of Negro Education*, vol. 59, no. 1, 1990, pp. 19–28. *JSTOR*, www.jstor.org/stable/2295289.

Crouch, Stanley. "Straighten Up and Fly Right: An Improvisation on the Podium." *Black Genius: African American Solutions to African American Problems*, edited by Walter Mosley, Manthia Diawara, Clyde Taylor, and Regina Austin, W. W. Norton, 2000, pp. 245–68.

Culler, Jonathan. *Literary Theory: A Very Short Introduction.* Oxford, 2000.

David, Marlo D. "'Let It Go Black': Desire and the Erotic Subject in the Films of Bill Gunn." *Black Camera*, vol. 2, no. 2, 2011, pp. 26–46. *JSTOR*, www.jstor.org/stable/10.2979/blackcamera.2.2.26.

De Lauretis, Teresa. "Eccentric Subjects: Feminist Theory and Historical Consciousness." *Feminist Studies*, vol. 16, no. 1, 1990, pp. 115–50. *JSTOR*, www.jstor.org/stable/3177959.

*Diawara*, Manthia, and Phyllis R. Klotman. "Ganja and Hess: Vampires, Sex, and Addictions." *Black American Literature Forum*, vol. 25, no. 2, 1991, pp. 299–314. *JSTOR*, www.jstor.org/stable/3041688.

Digby, Tom. *Love and War: How Militarism Shapes Sexuality and Romance.* Columbia UP, 2014.

Dillard, Angela. *Guess Who's Coming to Dinner Now?: Multicultural Conservatism in America.* New York UP, 2001.

Douglas, Mary. *Purity and Danger: An Analysis of Concept of Pollution and Taboo.* 1966. Routledge Classics, 2006.

Dr. Dre. "Let Me Ride." *The Chronic,* Interscope, 1992. CD.

Due, Tananarive. *My Soul to Keep.* HarperPrism, 1998.

Eads, Sean. "The Vampire George Middler: Selling the Monstrous in '*Salem's Lot.*'" *The Journal of Popular Culture* vol. 43, no. 1, 2010, pp. 78–96.

Elliot, Carl. "Humanity 2.0." *The Wilson Quarterly,* vol. 27, no. 4, 2003, pp. 13–20. *JSTOR,* www.jstor.org/stable/40260800.

Fairbanks, Daniel J. *Everyone Is African: How Science Explodes the Myth of Race.* Prometheus, 2015.

Ferguson, Roderick A. *Aberrations in Black: Toward a Queer of Color Critique.* U of Minnesota P, 2004.

Fink, Marty. "AIDS Vampires: Reimagining Illness in Octavia Butler's 'Fledgling.'" *Science Fiction Studies,* vol. 37, no. 3, 2010, pp. 416–32. *JSTOR,* www.jstor.org/stable/25746442.

Finkelhor, Daniel, and Sharon Araji. "Explanations of Pedophilia: A Four Factor Model." *The Journal of Sex Research* vol. 22, no. 2, 1986, pp. 145–61. *JSTOR,* www.jstor.org/stable/3812437.

Fonza, Annalise. "Black Women, Atheist Activism, and Human Rights: Why We Just Cannot Seem to Keep It to Ourselves." *Cross Currents* vol. 63, no. 2, 2013, pp. 185–97. doi:10.1111/cros.12023.

Fraser, James, ed. *The School in the United States: A Documentary History.* 2nd edition, Routledge, 2009.

Fredrickson, George. *Racism: A Short History.* Princeton UP, 2002.

Freund, Kurt, Robin Watson, and Robert Dickey. "Sex Offenses Against Female Children Perpetrated by Men Who Are Not Pedophiles." *The Journal of Sex Research,* vol. 28, 1991, pp. 409–23.

Fry, Joan. "Congratulations! You've Just Won $295,000: An Interview with Octavia Butler." *Conversations with Octavia Butler,* edited by Consuela Francis, UP of Mississippi, 2010, pp. 123–33.

Fukuyama, Francis. *Our Posthuman Future: Consequences of the Biotechnology Revolution.* Picador, 2002.

———. "Transhumanism." *Foreign Policy,* no. 144, 2004, pp. 42–43. *JSTOR,* www.jstor.org/stable/4152980.

Gaines, Kevin. "African." Burgett and Hendler, pp. 12–16.

*Ganja and Hess.* Directed by Bill Gunn, performances by Marlene Clark, Bill Gunn, Leonard Jackson, Duane Jones, and Sam Waymon, 1973, All Day Entertainment, 2006.

Gilpin, Lyndsey. "3D 'Bioprinting': 10 Things You Should Know About How It Works." TechRepublic, 23 April 2014, https://www.techrepublic.com/article/3d-bioprinting-10-things-you-should-know-about-how-it-works/.

Gilroy, Paul. *Against Race: Imagining Political Culture Beyond the Color Line.* Belknap-Harvard UP, 2001.

———. "It's a Family Affair: Black Culture and the Trope of Kinship." *Small Acts: Thoughts on the Politics of Black Cultures,* Serpent's Tail, 1993, pp. 192–207.

Glaude, Eddie, Jr. *In a Shade of Blue: Pragmatism and the Politics of Black America.* U of Chicago P, 2007.

Glave, Dianne. "'My Characters Are Teaching Me to Be Strong': An Interview with Tananarive Due." *African American Review,* vol. 38, no. 4, 2004, pp. 695–705. *JSTOR,* www.jstor.org/stable/4134426.

Gomez, Jewelle. "But Some of Us Are Brave Lesbians: The Absence of Black Lesbian Fiction." Johnson and Henderson, pp. 289–97.

———. "Chicago 1927." Thomas, *Century of Speculative Fiction,* pp. 19–34.

———. *The Gilda Stories: A Novel.* Firebrand Books, 2004.

———. "Recasting the Mythology: Writing Vampire Fiction." Gordon and Hollinger, pp. 85–92.

———. "Speculative Fiction and Black Lesbians." *Signs,* vol. 18, no. 4, 1993, pp. 948–55. *JSTOR,* www.jstor.org/stable/3174916.

Gomez, Jewelle, and Barbara Smith. "Talking About It: Homophobia in the Black Community." *Feminist Review,* no. 34, 1990, pp. 47–55. *JSTOR,* www.jstor.org/stable/1395304.

Gordon, Joan, and Veronica Hollinger, eds. *Blood Read: The Vampire as Metaphor in Contemporary Culture.* U of Pennsylvania P, 1997.

Graham, N. Katherine. *How We Became Posthuman: Virtual Bodies in Cybernetics, Literature, and Informatics.* U of Chicago P, 1999.

Grant, Jacquelyn. "Black Theology and the Black Woman." Bobo, Hudley, and Michel, pp. 420–33.

Graves, Joseph L., Jr. *The Race Myth: Why We Pretend Race Exists in America.* Plume, 2005.

Grayson, Sandra M. *Visions of the Third Millennium: Black Science Fiction Novelists Write the Future.* Africa World Press, 2003.

Griswold, Robert L. *Fatherhood in America: A History.* Basic Books, 1993.

Guerrero, Ed. *Framing Blackness: The African American Image in Film.* Temple UP, 1993.

Guinier, Lani, and Gerald Torres. "Political Race and The New Black." *The New Black: What Has Changed—and What Has Not—with Race in America,* edited by Kenneth W. Mack and Guy-Uriel E. Charles, New Press, 2013, pp. 13–33.

Guran, Paula. "Tananarive Due: Unique Name for a New Dark Star." *darkecho.com,* July 1997, http://www.darkecho.com/darkecho/archives/due.html.

Hacking, Ian. "Genetics, Biosocial Groups and the Future of Identity." *Daedalus,* vol. 135, no. 4, 2006, pp. 81–95.

Haggerty, George E. "Anne Rice and the Queering of Culture." *NOVEL: A Forum on Fiction,* vol. 32, no. 1, 1998, pp. 5–18. *JSTOR,* www.jstor.org/stable/1346054.

Halberstam, Judith. "Gender." Burgett and Hendler, pp. 116–20.

———. *Skin Shows: Gothic Horror and the Technology of Monsters.* Duke UP, 1995.

Haley, Alex, and Malcolm X. *The Autobiography of Malcolm X.* Random House, 1964.

Hall, Lynda. "Passion(Ate) Plays 'Wherever We Found Space': Lorde and Gomez Queer(y)Ing Boundaries and Acting In." *Callaloo,* vol. 23, no. 1, 2000, pp. 394–421. *JSTOR,* www.jstor.org/stable/3299569.

Hall, Stuart. "Ethnicity: Identity and Difference." *Becoming National: A Reader,* edited by Geoff Eley and Ronald Grigor Suny, Oxford UP, 1996, pp. 339–49.

Hallab, Mary Y. *Vampire God: The Allure of the Undead in Western Culture.* State U of New York P, 2009.

Harari, Yuval Noah. *Sapiens: A Brief History of Humankind.* HarperCollins, 2015.

Harris, Angelique. "Framing AIDS Facts: An AIDS Education and Prevention Strategy." *Black Theology,* vol. 11, no. 3, 2013, pp. 305–22.

Harrison, Guy P. *50 Popular Beliefs That People Think Are True.* Prometheus, 2012.

Herbert, Christopher. "Vampire Religion." *Representations,* vol. 79, no. 1, 2002, pp. 100–21. *JSTOR,* www.jstor.org/stable/10.1525/rep.2002.79.1.100.

Hine, Darlene Clark, William C. Hine, and Stanley Harrold. *The African American Odyssey.* 6th edition, Pearson, 2014.

Holland, Sharon Patricia. *The Erotic Life of Racism.* Duke UP, 2012.

Hollinger, Veronica. "Fantasies of Absence: The Postmodern Vampire." Gordon and Hollinger, pp. 199–212.

Holmes, Trevor. "Coming Out of the Coffin: Gay Males and Queer Goths in Contemporary Vampire Fiction." Gordon and Hollinger, pp. 169–88.

Hopkinson, Nalo. "Greedy Choke Puppy." Thomas, *Century of Speculative Fiction,* pp. 103–12.

Hurston, Zora Neale. "What White Publishers Won't Print." Napier, pp. 54–57.

Hutchinson, Sikivu. *Godless Americana: Race and Religious Rebels.* Infidel, 2013.

———. *Moral Combat: Black Atheists, Gender Politics, and the Values War.* Infidel, 2011.

Ice Cube. "Tales from the Darkside." *Amerikkka's Most Wanted,* Priority, 1990. CD.

Iton, Richard. *In Search of the Black Fantastic: Politics and Popular Culture in the Post-Civil Rights Era.* Oxford UP, 2008.

Jablonski, Nina. *Skin: A Natural History.* U of California P, 2006.

Jackson, Jennifer V., and Mary E. Cothran. "Black Versus Black: The Relationships Among African, African American, and African Caribbean Persons." *Journal of Black Studies,* vol. 33, no.5, 2003, pp. 576–604. *JSTOR,* www.jstor.org/stable/3180977.

Jakobsen, Janet R. "Religion." Burgett and Hendler, pp. 201–04.

Japtok, Martin. "'The Gospel of Whiteness': Whiteness in African American Literature." *Amerikastudien,* vol. 49, no. 4, 2004, pp. 483–98.

Japtok, Martin, and Jerry Rafiki Jenkins (eds.). Introduction. *Authentic Blackness/"Real" Blackness: Essays on the Meaning of Blackness in Literature and Culture.* Peter Lang, 2011, pp. 1–6.

Jeffries, William L., IV, Brian Dodge, and Theo G. M. Sandfort. "Religion and Spirituality Among Bisexual Black Men in the USA." *Culture, Health & Sexuality*, vol. 10, no. 5, 2008, pp. 463–77.

Jenkins, Jerry Rafiki. "*Blacula* and the Question of Blackness." *Screening Noir*, vol. 1, no. 1, 2005, pp. 49–79.

Jenkins, Mark Collins. *Vampire Forensics: Uncovering the Origins of an Enduring Legend*. National Geographic, 2010.

Johnson, E. Patrick. "The Specter of the Black Fag: Parody, Blackness, and Hetero/Homosexual B(r)others." *Queer Theory and Communication: From Disciplining Queers to Queering the Discipline(s)*, edited by Gust A. Yep, Karen E. Lovaas, and John P. Elia. Harrington Park, 2004, pp. 217–34.

Johnson, E. Patrick, and Mae G. Henderson, eds. *Black Queer Studies: A Critical Anthology*. Duke UP, 2005.

Johnson, K. Murry. *Image of Emeralds and Chocolate*. Johnson & Franklin, 2012.

Jones, Miriam. "*The Gilda Stories*: Revealing the Monsters at the Margin." Gordon and Hollinger, pp. 151–67.

Kaku, Michio. *Physics of the Future: How Science Will Shape Human Destiny and Our Daily Lives by the Year 2100*. Anchor, 2011.

Kimmel, Michael. *Guyland: The Perilous World Where Boys Become Men*. Harper, 2008.

Kimmel, Michael, and The Stony Brook Sexualities Research Group, eds. "Introduction to Second Edition." *Sexualities: Identities, Behaviors, and Society*, Oxford UP, 2015, pp. ix–xv.

Kimmelman, Jonathan. "The Post-Human Genome Project Mindset: Race, Reliability, and Health Care." *Clinical Genetics*, vol. 70, 2006, pp. 427–32.

King, Debra Walker. *African Americans and the Culture of Pain*. U of Virginia P, 2008.

Lacey, Lauren J. "Octavia E. Butler on Coping with Power in *Parable of the Sower, Parable of the Talents*, and *Fledgling*." *Critique*, vol. 49, no. 4, 2008, pp. 379–94. *EBSCOhost*, login.ezproxy.palomar.edu/login?url=http://search.ebscohost.com/login.aspx?direct=true&db=a9h&AN=34217655&site=ehost-live&scope=site.

Lackey, Michael. *African American Atheists and Political Liberation: A Study of the Sociocultural Dynamics of Faith*. UP of Florida, 2007.

La Rue, Linda. "The Black Movement and Women's Liberation." Chrisman and Hare, pp. 116–25.

Lavelle, Ashley. "From *Soul on Ice* to *Soul on Fire*: The Religious Conversion of Eldridge Cleaver." *Politics, Religion & Ideology*, vol. 14, no. 1, 2013, pp. 75–93.

Lawrence, Novotny. *Blaxploitation Films of the 1970s: Blackness and Genre*. Routledge, 2008.

———. "Fear of a Blaxploitation Monster: Blackness as Generic Revision in AIP's *Blacula*." *Film International*, vol. 7, no. 3, 2009, pp. 14–26.

Lawrence, Tonja. "An Africentric Reading Protocol: The Speculative Fiction of Octavia Butler and Tananarive Due." Diss., *Wayne State University Dissertations*. 2010.

Lee, Ntanya, Don Murphy, and Lisa North. "Sexuality, Multicultural Education, and the New York City Public Schools." *The Radical Teacher*, no. 45, 1994, pp. 12–16. *JSTOR*, www.jstor.org/stable/20709800.

Le Fanu, Sheridan. *Carmilla*, 1872, Williams, pp. 86–148.

Lewis, Christopher S. "Queering Personhood in the Neo-Slave Narrative: Jewelle Gomez's *The Gilda Stories*." *African American Review*, vol. 47, no. 4, 2014, pp. 447–59.

Lipsitz, George. *The Possessive Investment in Whiteness: How White People Profit from Identity Politics*. Temple UP, 1998.

Lubiano, Wahneema, ed. Introduction. *The House That Race Built*. Vintage, 1998, pp. vii–ix.

Maalouf, Amin. *In the Name of Identity: Violence and the Need to Belong*. Translated by Barbara Bray, Penguin, 2000.

Manago, Cleo. "MANHOOD — WHO CLAIMS IT? WHO DOES IT CLAIM?" *The Black Scholar*, vol. 26, no. 1, 1996, pp. 48–49. *JSTOR*, www.jstor.org/stable/41068628.

Manning, Patrick. *The African Diaspora: A History Through Culture*. Columbia UP, 2009.

Martinez, Gerald, Diana Martinez, and Andres Chavez, eds. *What It Is . . . What It Was!: The Black Film Explosion of the '70s in Words and Pictures*. Hyperion, 1998.

Marx, Karl. *Das Kapital: A Critique of Political Economy*. 1867. Introduction by Serge L. Levitsky, Regenery Publishing, 2009.

Massey, Brandon. *Dark Corner*. Dafina, 2004.

———. "The Patriarch." *The Ancestors*. Dafina, 2008, pp. 117–201.

Mattis, Jacqueline S., Kiu Eubanks, Alix A. Zapata, Nyasha Grayman, Max Belkin, N'Jeri K. Mitchell, and Sharon Cooper. "Factors Influencing Religious Non-Attendance Among African American Men: A Multimethod Analysis." *Review of Religious Research*, vol. 45, no. 4, 2004, pp. 386–403. *JSTOR*, www.jstor.org/stable/3511993.

McNally, Raymond T., and Radu Florescu. *In Search of Dracula: The History of Dracula and Vampires*. Houghton Mifflin, 1994.

McNamee, M. J., and S. D. Edwards. "Transhumanism: Medical Technology and Slippery Slopes." *Journal of Medical Ethics*, vol. 32, no. 9, 2006, pp. 513–18. *JSTOR*, www.jstor.org/stable/27719694.

Medovoi, Leerom. "Theorizing Historicity, or the Many Meanings of *Blacula*." *Screen*, vol. 39, no. 1, 1998, pp. 1–21.

Mehaffy, Marilyn, and AnaLouise Keating. "'Radio Imagination': Octavia Butler on the Poetics of Narrative Embodiment." *MELUS*, vol. 26, no. 1, 2001, pp. 45–76. *JSTOR*, www.jstor.org/stable/3185496.

Melton, J. Gordon. *The Vampire Book: The Encyclopedia of the Undead*. Visible Ink, 1999.

Miller, Jerome G. *Search and Destroy: African American Males in the Criminal Justice System*. Cambridge UP, 1996.

Mills, Charles W. "Body Politic, Bodies Impolitic." *Social Research*, vol. 78, no. 2, 2011, pp. 583–606.

Minsky, Marvin. "Will Robots Inherit the Earth?" *Science Fiction: Stories and Context*, edited by Heather Masri, Bedford/St. Martin's, 2009, pp. 1211–21.

Monday, Donna. *The Best Black Vampire Story Ever Written*. Booklocker.com, 2006.

Moore, Marlon Rachquel. "Black Church, Black Patriarchy, and the 'Brilliant Queer': Competing Masculinities in Langston Hughes's 'Blessed Assurance.'" *African American Review*, vol. 42, no. 3–4, 2008, pp. 493–502.

Morris, Susana M. "Black Girls Are from the Future: Afrofuturist Feminism in Octavia E. Butler's *Fledgling*." *Women's Studies Quarterly*, vol. 40, no. 3/4, 2012, pp. 146–66. JSTOR, www.jstor.org/stable/23333483.

———. "More Than Human: Black Feminisms of the Future in Jewelle Gomez's *The Gilda Stories*." *The Black Scholar*, vol. 46, no. 2, pp. 33–45, 2016. http://dx.doi.org/10.1080/00064246.2016.1147991.

Moynihan, Daniel Patrick. *The Negro Family: The Case for National Action*. 1965.

Napier, Winston, ed. *African American Literary Theory: A Reader*. New York UP, 2000.

Nayar, Pramod K. "Vampirism and Posthumanism in Octavia Butler's *Fledgling*." *Notes on Contemporary Literature*, vol. 41, no. 2, 2011. Biography in Context. http://ic.galegroup.com/ic/bic1/AcademicJournalsDetailsPage/AcademicJournalsDetailsWindow?failOverType=&query=&prodId=BIC1&windowstate=normal&contentModules=&display-query=&mode=view&displayGroupName=Journals&;limiter=&currPage=&disableHighlighting=false&displayGroups=&sortBy=&search_within_results=&p=BIC1&action=e&catId=&activityType=&scanId=&documentId=GALE%7CA256070531&source=Bookmark&u=san22314&jsid=b4ef5acbded52af6d63574847ab54a84.

Nero, Charles. "Toward a Black Gay Aesthetic: Signifying in Contemporary Black Gay Literature." Napier, pp. 399–420.

———. "Why Are Gay Ghettoes White?" Johnson and Henderson, pp. 228–45.

Norrell, Robert J. *The House I Live In: Race in the American Century*. Oxford UP, 2006.

Nuzum, Eric. *The Dead Travel Fast: Stalking Vampires from Nosferatu to Count Chocula*. Thomas Dunne, 2007.

O'Connor, Lydia, and Daniel Marans. "Here are 13 Examples of Donald Trump Being a Racist." HuffPost, 2 Feb. 2016, https://www.huffingtonpost.com/entry/donald-trump-racist-examples_us_56d47177e4b03260bf777e83.

Orderberg, David. "Could There Be a Superhuman Species?" *The Southern Journal of Philosophy*, vol. 52, no. 2, 2014, pp. 206–26.

Paes De Barros, Deborah. *Fast Cars and Bad Girls: Nomadic Subjects and Women's Road Stories*. Peter Lang, 2004.

Parrillo, Vincent. *Strangers to These Shores*. 11th edition, Pearson, 2014.

Perry, Pamela. "White." Burgett and Hendler, pp. 242–46.

Pickens, Theri. "'You're Supposed to Be a Tall, Handsome, Fully Grown White Man': Theorizing Race, Gender, and Disability in Octavia Butler's *Fledgling*." *Journal of Literary & Cultural Disability Studies*, vol. 8, no. 1, 2014, pp. 33–48. EBSCOhost, doi:10.3828/jlcds.2014.3.

Pinn, Anthony B. *The End of God-Talk: An African American Humanist Theology*. Oxford UP, 2012.

Pinson, Hermine. "All-Around Vampires." *Callaloo*, no. 35, 1988, pp. 273–74. JSTOR, www.jstor.org/stable/2930961.

Reid-Pharr, Robert. "Tearing the Goat's Flesh: Homosexuality, Abjection, and the Production of a Late Twentieth-Century Black Masculinity." Napier, pp. 602–22.

Rice, Anne. *Interview with the Vampire*. Ballantine, 1976.

Robinson, Eugene. *Disintegration: The Splintering of Black America*. Doubleday, 2010.

Ross, Marlon B. "Some Glances at the Black Fag: Race, Same-Sex Desire, and Cultural Belonging." Napier, pp. 498–522.

Rountree, Wendy Alexia. "'Faking the Funk': A Journey Towards Authentic Blackness." Japtok and Jenkins, pp. 101–08.

Ruccio, David. "Capitalism." Burgett and Hendler, pp. 32–36.

Russell, Kathy, Midge Wilson, and Ronald Hall. *The Color Complex: The Politics of Skin Color Among African Americans*. Anchor, 1993.

Scarry, Elaine. *The Body in Pain: The Making and Unmaking of the World*. Oxford UP, 1985.

Sciurba, Katie. "The Wrong Things About Literature: Invisibility and African American Texts." *Curriculum Inquiry*, vol. 41, no. 1, 2011, pp. 126–29.

Shannon, Sandra G. "The Good Christian's Come and Gone: The Shifting Role of Christianity in August Wilson Plays." *MELUS*, vol. 16, no. 3, 1989, pp. 127–42. *JSTOR*, www.jstor.org/stable/467572.

Shelby, Tommie. *We Who Are Dark: The Philosophical Foundations of Black Solidarity*. Belknap-Harvard UP, 2005.

Sirius, R. U., and Jay Cornell. *Transcendence: The Disinformation Encyclopedia of Transhumanism and the Singularity*. Disinformation Books, 2015.

Smedley, Audrey. "'Race' and the Construction of Human Identity." *American Anthropologist*, vol. 100, no. 3, 1998, pp. 690–702. *EBSCOhost*, doi:10.1037/0003-066X.60.1.16.

Smith, Stephanie A. "Octavia Butler: A Retrospective." *Feminist Studies*, vol. 33, no. 2, 2007, pp. 385–93. *JSTOR*, www.jstor.org/stable/20459148.

Sneed, Roger A. "Like Fire Shut up in Our Bones: Religion and Spirituality in Black Gay Men's Literature." *Black Theology: An International Journal*, vol. 6, no. 2, 2008, pp. 241–261. *EBSCOhost*, login.ezproxy.palomar.edu/login?url=http://search.ebscohost.com/login.aspx?direct=true&db=a9h&AN=36043067&site=ehost-live&scope=site.

Somerville, Siobhan. "Queer." Burgett and Hendler, pp. 187–91.

———. *Queering the Color Line: Race and the Invention of Homosexuality in American Culture*. Duke UP, 2000.

Spencer, Jon Michael. "The Black Church and the Harlem Renaissance." *African American Review*, vol. 30, no. 3, 1996, pp. 453–60. *JSTOR*, www.jstor.org/stable/3042536.

Staples, Robert. "The Myth of the Impotent Black Male." Chrisman and Hare, pp. 126–37.

Stephens, Gregory. "Brown Boy Blues . . . inna Jamaica." Japtok and Jenkins, pp. 109–37.

Stoker, Bram. *Dracula*. 1897. Introduction by Maurice Hindle, Penguin, 2003.

Storey, John. *Cultural Studies and the Study of Popular Culture*. 2nd edition, U of Georgia P, 2003.

Strong, Melissa J. "The Limits of Newness: Hybridity in Octavia E. Butler's *Fledgling*." *Femspec*, vol. 11, no. 1, 2010, pp. 11–27.

Summers, Montague. *The Vampire, His Kith and Kin*. 1928. Forgotten Books, 2008.

———. *The Vampire in Lore and Legend*. 1929. Dover, 2001.

Terrell, Mary Church. "Please Stop Using the Word 'Negro.'" *Black Women in White America: A Documentary History*, edited by Gerda Lerner, Vintage, 1992, pp. 547–50.

Thaler, Ingrid. *Black Atlantic Speculative Fictions: Octavia E. Butler, Jewelle Gomez, and Nalo Hopkinson*. Routledge, 2010.

Thomas, Sheree, ed. *Dark Matter: A Century of Speculative Fiction from the African Diaspora*. Warner Books, 2000.

———. *Dark Matter: Reading of the Bones*. Warner Books, 2004.

Todd, Dennis. *Imagining Monsters: Miscreations of the Self in Eighteenth-Century England*. U of Chicago P, 1995.

Touré. *Who's Afraid of Post-Blackness: What It Means to Be Black Now*. Free Press, 2011.

Turner, Richard Brent. "Islam in the African American Experience." Bobo, Hudley, and Michel, pp. 445–71.

Tyree, Omar. "Human Heat: The Confessions of an Addicted Vampire." Allen, pp. 95–153.

Van Camp, Debbie, Lloyd Ren Sloan, and Amanda Elbassiouny. "Religious Bias Among Religiously Conscious Black Christians in the United States." *Journal of Social Psychology*, vol. 154, 2014, pp. 4–7.

Van Horne, Winston A., ed. *Global Convulsions: Race, Ethnicity, and Nationalism at the End of the Twentieth Century*. State U of New York P, 1997.

Vigilant, Linda. "Race and Biology." Van Horne, pp. 49–62.

Vint, Sherryl. "Becoming Other: Animals, Kinship, and Butler's *Clay's Ark*." *Science-Fiction Studies*, vol. 32, no. 2, 2005, pp. 281–300. *JSTOR*, www.jstor.org/stable/4241348.

Walters, Ronald W. *Pan-Africanism in the African Diaspora: An Analysis of Modern Afrocentric Political Movements*. Wayne State UP, 1997.

Ward, Elijah G. "Homophobia, Hypermasculinity, and the US Black Church." *Culture, Health, and Sexuality*, vol. 7, no. 5, 2005, pp. 493–504. *JSTOR*, www.jstor.org/stable/4005477.

Ward, Janie Victoria, and Jill McLean Taylor. "Sexuality Education in a Multicultural Society." *Educational Leadership*, vol. 49, no. 1, 1991, pp. 62–64.

West, Cornel. "Identity: A Matter of Life and Death." *Beyond Eurocentrism and Multiculturalism: Volume Two*, Common Courage Press, 1993, pp. 163–68.

———. "Nihilism in Black America." *Race Matters*, Vintage, 1994, pp. 16–31.

White, Deborah Gray, Mia Bay, and Waldo E. Martin, Jr., eds. *Freedom on My Mind: A History of African Americans with Documents*. Bedford/St. Martin's, 2017.

White, Eric. "The Erotics of Becoming: Xenogenesis and *The Thing*." *Science-Fiction Studies*, vol. 20, no. 3, 1993, pp. 394–408. *JSTOR*, www.jstor.org/stable/4240279.

White, Luise. *Speaking with Vampires: Rumor and History in Colonial Africa*. U of California P, 2006.

Wiegman, Robyn. "The Anatomy of Lynching." *A Question of Manhood: A Reader in U. S. Black Men's History and Masculinity*, edited by Darlene Clark Hine and Earnestine Jenkins, Indiana UP, 2001, pp. 349–69.

Williams, Anne, ed. *Three Vampire Tales*, Houghton Mifflin, 2003.

Williams, Michael. "The Pan-African Movement." *Africana Studies: A Survey of Africa and the African Diaspora*, edited by Mario Azevedo, Carolina Academic P, 2005, pp. 173–86.

Wilson, Katharina M. "The History of the Word 'Vampire.'" *Journal of the History of Ideas*, vol. 46, no. 4, 1985, pp. 577–83. *JSTOR*, www.jstor.org/stable/2709546.

Winnubst, Shannon. "Vampires, Anxieties, and Dreams: Race and Sex in the Contemporary United States." *Hypatia*, vol. 18, no. 3, 2003, pp. 1–20. *JSTOR*, www.jstor.org/stable/3810861.

Woodard, Jennifer Bailey and Teresa Mastin. "Black Womanhood: 'Essence' and Its Treatment of Stereotypical Images of Black Women." *Journal of Black Studies*, no. 36, vol. 2, 2005, pp. 264–281. *JSTOR*, JSTOR, www.jstor.org/stable/40034332.

Wright, Almeda M. "Varieties of Black Queer Religious Experiences," *Black Theology: An International Journal*, vol. 10, no. 3, 2012, pp. 275–291. EBSCO*host*, DOI: 10.1558/blth.v10i3.275.

Zane. "Resident Evil." *Dark Dreams: A Collection of Horror and Suspense by Black Writers*, edited by Brandon Massey, Dafina, 2004, pp. 1–17.

Zanger, Jules. "Metaphor into Metonymy: The Vampire Next Door." Gordon and Hollinger, pp. 17–26.

# INDEX

3D bioprinting, 125n4

Abandoned minority black America, 162, 163n9
Abdullah, Zain, 87, 89
activism, 25, 49–50, 58, 78–79
Addison, Linda, 6
Adeleke, Tunde, 80
*adze*, 2–3, 3n5
AFP. *See* American Freedom Party (AFP)
Africa, 2–3, 2n4, 7, 59, 75–82, 76n7, 87, 110n8, 112–13. *See also* feminine Africa narrative; masculine Africa narrative
African American, as term, 75–76, 113–14
African American Christianity, 16–18. *See also* Black Church; Christianity
*African Immortals* series (Due), 57–58
Afrocentrism, 18–19; African Americans who do not embrace, 32–33; blackness in, 76n7; embracing of, 33; freedom and, 25–26; in *Gilda*, 27–28, 31, 37; homophobia and, 44–53; and masculine Africa narrative, 114; multiculturalism and, 26n2; narrative turn of, 78n8; as "radical," 36
Afrofuturism, 8, 179–80
*Against Race: Imagining Political Culture Beyond the Color Line* (Gilroy), 32
AIDS. *See* HIV/AIDS

Alexander, Elizabeth, 38
"All-Around Vampires" (Pinson), 2n1, 6
Allen, Angela C., 120n2
American Book Award, 57
American Dream, 36, 41, 52
American Freedom Party (AFP), 177n1
"Americocentrism," 33
*Amos 'n' Andy* (television show), 99
anarchic individuality, 97, 112
antiblack feminism, 99, 102–3, 103n2
anti-miscegenation laws, 137
Arizona, 27n3
Asante, Molefi, 25–26, 32–33, 35, 45, 48, 53
*asasabonsam*, 2
*asema*, 3, 3n5
atheism, 58–59, 61, 65, 67, 70–72, 81–83, 86–90, 176
Auerbach, Nina, 7, 40, 44

"Back-to-Africa" movement, 100
Badham, John, 4
Baldwin, James, 77, 166
Banks, L. A., 6, 15n15, 57–58, 153
Banks, Ralph Richard, 145n12
baptism, 4, 17, 164
Barnes, Steven, 57n1
Bartlett, Wayne, 6–7

"battle of the sexes" myth, 110–11
"beaner" parties, 179n3
Beresford, Matthew, 7
Bernal, Martin, 5n12
*Between, The* (Due), 57, 57n1
Bigelow, Kathryn, 16
*Big Sea, The* (Hughes), 70
biological determinism, 118–19
biopolitics, racialized, 32–38, 46
bioprinting, 125n4
Black, as term, 76
Black Arts Movement, 25
Black Church: corporatism, 154, 159, 166–67, 172–73; gay black men and, 153; in *Gilda*, 50–52, 55; Harlem Renaissance and, 70; homophobia and, 46, 50–51, 72, 72n4, 150, 150n4, 151, 154, 166; in *Image of Emeralds and Chocolate*, 159–60, 164–67, 172; male bias of, 159; in *My Soul to Keep*, 58, 68, 79; role of, 16–17
black conservatives, 43, 45–46, 49, 51–52, 150n4. *See also* multicultural conservatism
black corporatism, 154, 159, 176
black nationalism, 19, 26, 52, 59, 80–81, 100, 103n2, 154
blackness. *See also* "new black"; post-Blackness: Africa and, 76n7; in Afrocentrism, 76n7; Americanness and, 37; in Asante, 35; body features and, 120; in Butler, 120; in Dark Corner, 112–14; desire and, 138–45, 145n11; in *Fledgling*, 122–23, 133–46; in *Gilda*, 35–36, 40–41, 117, 177–78; melanin and, 20–21, 126–27, 132, 135, 144; in *My Soul to Keep*, 56–58, 65; pain and, 37–38; skin color and, 14–15; slavery and, 179; transhuman, 122–28, 145–46
"blackpain," 38–39, 41, 89. *See also* pain
Black Power, 39, 71, 103n4, 154
*Black Rose, The* (Due and Due), 57n1
*Blacula* (film), 4–5, 4nn7–8, 6n13, 7, 15, 25
Blade (character), 5, 5n10
Blade (film series), 5
blaxploitation, 4, 4n8
"Blessed Assurance" (Hughes), 152

blood: in *Dark Corner*, 95; drinking of, 2n2; in *Gilda*, 30–36, 95; in hunter-gatherer societies, 130n6; in *Image of Emeralds and Chocolate*, 155–59; in modern diets, 130n6; in *My Soul to Keep*, 56, 59–60, 64, 82–83
*Blood Colony* (Due), 57
body: in Afrocentrism, 26; American Dream and, 41; blackness and, 10–11, 15–16, 19, 21, 26–27, 37, 53, 53n9, 54, 57–59, 89, 113, 115, 117, 120, 146, 154–55, 174–76; and construction of race, 112; in *Fledgling*, 121–22, 129–30, 132–33, 137–41; freedom and, 32; in Legacy Narrative, 14; "new black" understanding of, 176; pain and, 37–39; in post-blackness, 176; soul murder and, 41–42; in Soul Narrative, 12–14, 67–68
body knowledge, 118–20, 129–31, 136, 139, 145
Bonet, Lisa, 53n9
born-again Christians, 18
Bostrum, Nick, 123–24
Bowen, Gary, 148n2
Boyd, Melba Joyce, 48
Bram Stoker Award, 57
*Bram Stoker's Dracula* (film), 4
Brite, Poppy Z., 148n3
Brockenbrough, Kevin S., 6, 147–48
Brooks, Kinitra, 57–58, 78
*Brother from Another Planet, The* (film), 66, 66n3
Brown, Malcolm, 120n1
Brox, Ali, 9
Bryant, Cedric, 7
Bush, Lawson, 102
Butler, Octavia E., 6–9, 118–19, 131n7. *See also Fledgling* (Butler)
"But Some of Us Are Brave Lesbians: The Absence of Black Lesbian Fiction" (Gomez), 23

Campbell, Charlie, 166
Canaanites, 73
Cannon, Katie Geneva, 77, 78n8, 161
capitalism, 19, 26, 36, 38, 42–44, 52, 148n3
Carbado, Devon, 151n5
Carey, Mariah, 53n9

Caribbean, 3, 3n5, 15, 20, 91–92, 94, 105, 107, 114
Carmichael, Stokeley, 103n4
*Carmilla* (Le Fanu), 3n6, 148, 148n3
Carter, Margaret, 86
Cary, Lott, 80
"'Cause Harlem Needs Heroes" (Brockenbrough), 147
Cave, Stephen, 11–13, 30–31, 66, 68, 124–25
Caywood, Cynthia, 71
Chappelle, Dave, 77
"Chicago 1927" (Gomez), 147–48
Chicago School, 108
Chicano studies, 26, 36
"Child That Went with The Fairies, The" (Le Fanu), 4n6
"Christabel" (Coleridge), 148
Christian Coalition, 150n4
Christianity, 17–18, 51–52, 55–56, 65–71, 77, 96. *See also* African American Christianity; Black Church
Chuck D, 107n6
Church. *See* Black Church
"Church" (James), 153
civilizing discourse, 19, 28, 35, 59, 81, 91, 101
Civil War, 68, 85, 165n11, 169
*Clay's Ark* (Butler), 131n7
Cleaver, Eldridge, 71, 166
Clinton, George, 32
Clutchette, John, 39n5
Cole, Johnetta Betsch, 51
Colebrook, Claire, 118
Coleridge, Samuel Taylor, 148, 149n3
Collins, Donald E., 26n2
Collins, Patricia Hill, 150
color-blindness, 19, 26–27, 36–37, 40–41, 54, 144, 145n11, 178
colors, skin, 14–15, 53n9, 127, 134–38. *See also* blackness
comics, 5, 5n10
Cone, James, 78n8
Connerly, Ward, 45
conservatives, black, 43, 45–46, 49, 51–52, 150n4. *See also* multicultural conservatism

Coppola, Francis Ford, 4
corporatism. *See* black corporatism
Cothran, Mary E., 114
Crouch, Stanley, 97
Crummell, Alexander, 81
Cuffee, Paul, 80
Curse of Ham, 73

*Dark Angels: Lesbian Vampire Stories* (Keesey), 148
*Dark Corner* (Massey), 19–20, 147; "battle of the sexes" myth in, 110–11; blackness in, 112–14; blood in, 95; family in, 98–105, 98n1, 103–4; masculine Africa narrative and, 92–94, 113–15; pain in, 107; slavery in, 96–97, 107, 107n6, 110; Staying Alive Narrative in, 94–97
*Dark Shadows* (television series), 16
*Daughters of Darkness: Lesbian Vampire Stories* (Keesey), 148, 148n3
Davis, Angela, 39, 39n5
*Dead Travel Fast, The: Stalking Vampires from Nosferatu to Count Chocula* (Nuzum), 1–2
Delany, Martin, 81
desire: blackness and, 138–45, 145n11
Diamond, Jared, 179–80
diaspora, 2, 19, 32–33, 59, 87–88, 91
Digby, Tom, 110
Dillard, Angela, 26, 36, 45, 150n4
*Disintegration: The Splintering of Black America* (Robinson), 10
divine sexuality, 167–72
Dr. Dre, 76n7
Douglass, Frederick, 32, 169
*Down These Mean Streets* (Thomas), 166
Dracula, 12, 15, 24, 24n1, 98n1
*Dracula* (film, 1979), 4
*Dracula* (Stoker), 4, 24n1, 44, 55, 88n10
"Dred Loc" (Ndegeocello), 106
Drumgo, Fleeta, 39n5
Du Bois, W. E. B., 70, 77, 91
Due, Patricia Stephens, 57n1
Due, Tananarive, 6, 57n1. *See also My Soul to Keep* (Due)
Dumas, Alexandre, 3–4, 3n6
*Dust Tracks on a Road* (Hurston), 70

Eads, Sean, 148n2
education, 27n3, 49–50, 159–72
Egypt, 7
Elliot, Carl, 128
emasculated man-matriarchal woman problem, 94, 99, 102
Emergent black America, 163n9
*Essence* (magazine), 49, 98
ethnic cleansing, 156n7. *See also* genocide
Eurocentrism, 25–26, 27n2, 32, 35

Fairbanks, Daniel, 177n2
family: in *Dark Corner*, 98–105, 98n1, 103–4; in *Gilda*, 33–36, 51–52, 98; manhood and, 104n5; Moynihan Report and, 19–20, 93–94, 99–100
"Family Business, The" (Brockenbrough), 147–48
feminine Africa narrative, 91–92
feminism, antiblack, 99, 102–3, 103n2
Ferguson, Roderick, 100
*feu-follet*, 4
fiction: Gomez on, 23–24; speculative, 2, 24
*fifollet*, 4
film, 4–5, 16, 148n1
Fink, Marty, 9
*Fledgling* (Butler), 7–9, 20–21; blackness in, 122–28, 133–46; body knowledge in, 129–31; desire in, 138–45; Engineering Approach in, 122–23; "Guy Code" in, 139–41; melanin in, 126–27, 132, 135, 144; narrative structure in, 121n3; race in, 136–37; Staying Alive Narrative in, 122–23; transhumanism in, 125–26; transhuman vampirism in, 123–28; vampires in, 128–34; whites in, 143–45; women in, 141–44
Fleming, Robert, 6
Florescu, Radu, 2n2
Floyd, Carlton, 71
*Frankenstein* (Shelley), 12
Fraser, James, 160n8
Frayling, Christopher, 2n2
Frazier, E. Franklin, 99
freedom, black: body and, 32; in *Gilda*, 27–28, 38, 46–47, 52–53; in *Image of Emeralds and Chocolate*, 168–69; as intellectual matter, 32
*Freedom Family: A Mother-Daughter Memoir of the Fight for Civil Rights* (Due and Due), 57n1
Freitas, Robert A., Jr, 125n4
*From Demons to Dracula: The Creation of the Modern Vampire Myth* (Beresford), 7
Fukuyama, Francis, 127, 127n5, 131

Gaines, Kevin, 75
*Ganja and Hess* (film), 4–5, 7, 25
Garvey, Marcus, 89, 91, 100
gay male vampires, 147–74. *See also Image of Emeralds and Chocolate* (Johnson)
gender roles, 102–3
genocide, 156n7, 177, 177n1
Ghana, 3, 100–101
*Gilda Stories, The* (Gomez), 1–2, 6–8, 18–19, 148; Afrocentrism in, 27–28; black freedom in, 27–29, 38, 46–47, 52–53; blackness in, 35–36, 40–41, 117, 177–78; blood in, 30–36, 60, 95; Christianity in, 51–52, 55; death in, 29–30; family in, 33–36, 51–52, 98; immortality in, 27–29, 31; multicultural conservatism in, 27–28; pain in, 39; race in, 36; Resurrection Narrative and, 29–30, 41–42; slavery in, 39–40; Staying Alive Narrative in, 27–30; whites and whiteness in, 34–35, 40–41; womanhood in, 48–49
Gilroy, Paul, 32–33, 76n7
*Giovanni's Room* (Baldwin), 166
Glaude, Eddie, Jr., 17, 69, 78n8, 85
Golden, Thelma, 21
Gomez, Jewelle, 1–2, 6–8, 23–24, 147–48. *See also Gilda Stories, The* (Gomez)
goths, 1
"government name," 114, 114n9
Grant, Jacquelyn, 78n8, 79n9
Graves, Joseph, 176, 178
Grayson, Sandra, 58, 78
Great Awakening, 17–18, 165n11
Great Revivals, 17
"Greedy Choke Puppy" (Hopkinson), 3n5
Grenada, 3

Gronniosaw, Albert Ukawsaw, 17
Guinier, Lani, 21–22
Gunn, Bill, 4–5
"Guy Code," 103n4, 139–41
Guy-Sheftall, Beverly, 51

Hacking, Ian, 117
Haggerty, George, 148n2
Haiti, 3
Hall, Lynda, 7–8, 10, 34
Hall, Ronald, 76
Hall, Stuart, 113
Hallab, Mary, 6, 10
Harari, Yuval Noah, 84, 124–25, 138n10, 156n7
Harlem Renaissance, 70
Harris, Angelique, 163
Harris, E. Lynn, 153–54, 169
Hausa tribe, 2
Hemphill, Essex, 153
Herbert, Christopher, 55
heroic individuality, 97
heroic slave, 20, 93–94, 105–12
heterosexism, 72n4, 91, 150, 163–64, 171
heterosexual presumption, 151n5
hierarchical body knowledge, 119, 136, 139, 145
Higginbotham, Evelyn Brooks, 78n8
Hill, Donna, 6
HIV/AIDS, 9, 163–64, 169–70
Holland, Sharon Patricia, 120n1, 137–38, 145n11, 145n13
Hollinger, Veronica, 86
Holmes, Trevor, 148, 148n3, 149
homophobia, 32, 44–53, 72, 72n4, 140–41, 149n3, 150, 150n4, 151, 154, 159, 166
homosexuality, 70, 72–73. *See also* gay male vampires; lesbians; queering
Hopkins, Dwight, 78n8
Hopkinson, Nalo, 3n5
Horne, Tom, 27n3
Horror Writers Association, 57
*How Stella Got Her Groove Back* (McMillan), 106
Hughes, Langston, 70, 152
"Human Heat: The Confessions of an Addicted Vampire" (Tyree), 147

Hurston, Zora Neale, 70, 87
Hutchinson, Sikivu, 18

Ice Cube, 76n7
Idriceanu, Flavia, 3n6, 6–7
*Image of Emeralds and Chocolate* (Johnson), 21; Black Church corporatism in, 154, 172–73; Black Church in, 159–60, 164–67, 172; blood in, 155–59; book knowledge in, 159–67; divine sexuality in, 167–72; education in, 159–72; freedom in, 168–69; HIV/AIDS in, 163–64, 169–70; immortality in, 156; issues confronted in, 151; liberation in, 167–72; scapegoating in, 159–67; slavery in, 161, 168; Soul Narrative in, 157–58; Staying Alive Narrative in, 154–59
immortality, 11–12; in *Gilda*, 27–29, 31; in *Image of Emeralds and Chocolate*, 154–57; in *My Soul to Keep*, 59, 63, 65; race and, 177
imperialism, 92
incubus, 4
individuality, 41, 97, 112, 118, 176
intelligent body knowledge, 119–20
*Interview with the Vampire* (Rice), 16, 32, 148
Iton, Richard, 91–92, 100, 106, 107n6

Jablonski, Nina, 126–27
Jackson, George, 39, 39n5
Jackson, Jennifer V., 114
Jackson, Jesse, 75
Jackson, Jonathan, 39n5
Jackson, Monica, 6
Jakobsen, Janet, 74
Jamaica, 105
James, G. Winston, 153
Japtok, Martin, 179n3
Jefferson, Thomas, 131
Jenkins, Mark Collins, 7
Johnson, E. Patrick, 151–52, 151n5
Johnson, James Weldon, 70
Johnson, K. Murry, 6, 15, 151, 153. *See also Image of Emeralds and Chocolate* (Johnson)
Johnson, William, 177n1
Jones, Miriam, 7, 43

Kaku, Michio, 123, 125n4
Keating, Analouise, 119
Keesey, Pam, 148, 148n3
Kennedy, John F., 103n2
Kimmel, Michael, 139
Kimmelman, Jonathan, 137n9
King, Debra Walker, 37–38, 41, 63
King, Martin Luther, Jr., 69, 99, 169
King, Mary, 103n4
King, Stephen, 148, 148n2
Kravitz, Lenny, 53n9

Lacey, Lauren J., 9, 121n3
Lackey, Michael, 70
Larsen, Nella, 70
La Rue, Linda, 102–3, 103n4
Lavelle, Ashley, 71
Lawrence, Tonja, 58
Le Fanu, Sheridan, 3n6, 148, 148n3, 149n3
Legacy Narrative, 12–14
legacy vampires, 12–14
*Legends of Blood: The Vampire in History and Myth* (Idriceanu), 6–7
lesbians, 148; black, 23–25, 29, 47–48, 50, 55
"Let Me Ride" (Dr. Dre), 76n7
Lewis, Christopher, 7–8
liberation, 167–72. *See also* freedom, black
libertarian transhumanism, 123
Ligon, Glen, 21–22
*Lilith's Brood* (Butler), 118–19
Lipsitz, George, 136
literacy, 160n8, 162
*Living Blood, The* (Due), 57
Locke, Alain, 70
loneliness, 24–25, 61, 65, 73, 144
*loogaroo*, 3, 3n5
*Lost Boys, The* (film), 16

Mainstream black America, 162–63
Malcolm X, 77, 100
male dominance, 140
male privilege, 151n5

manhood, 99, 104n5, 112–13. *See also* emasculated man-matriarchal woman problem
Manning, Patrick, 110n8
March on Washington (1963), 103n2
Marx, Karl, 42
masculine Africa narrative, 91–94, 106, 113–15
masculinity, 166–67
Mason, J., 151
Massey, Brandon, 6. *See also Dark Corner* (Massey)
Mather, Cotton, 17
McMahan, Jeffrey N., 148n2, 149
McMillan, Terry, 106
McNally, Raymond, 2n2
medicine, 125n4, 131
melanin, 20–21, 126–27, 132, 135, 144
Melton, J. Gordon, 12, 14m14, 88n10, 148–49
men. *See* emasculated man-matriarchal woman problem; gay male vampires; manhood; masculine Africa narrative
Meyer, Stephanie, 153
Miles, Robert, 120n1
Miller, Jerome G., 40n6
Miller, Monica, 151
Mills, Charles, 118
*Minion* (Banks), 15n15
Minksy, Marvin, 125n4
miscegenation, 9, 20, 122, 137–38
Moore, Marlon Rachquel, 152
Mormon Transhumanist Association, 123
Morris, Susana M., 8–9, 180
Mortality Paradox, 11–12, 29, 65, 67, 83, 89, 95
Moynihan, Daniel Patrick, 19–20, 93–94, 99–100
multicultural conservatism, 25–28, 26n2, 31, 36, 47, 54
multiculturalism, 16, 26, 26n2, 50, 177
*My Soul to Keep* (Due), 19; Africa and, 75–82; atheism in, 67, 82, 88–90; blackness in, 56–58, 65; blood in, 56, 59–60, 64, 82–83; Christianity in, 55–56, 65–71; feminine Africa narrative and, 92; God in, 84–85;

homophobia in, 72n4; honors of, 57, 57n1; immortality in, 59, 63, 65; pain in, 63; Resurrection Narrative in, 59–65, 67, 85–86; ritual in, 60–62; slavery in, 58, 73–74, 85; theism in, 71–72, 74; women in, 63–65, 64n2

*My Soul to Take* (Due), 57

nanotechnology, 125n4
nationalism, black, 19, 26, 52, 59, 80–81, 100, 103n2, 154
Nayar, Pramod K., 9, 20, 122
Ndegeocello, Meshell, 106
*Near Dark* (film), 16
Negro, as term, 75n6, 76
*Negro Family, The: The Case for National Action* (Moynihan), 20, 94, 99–100
"new black," 21–22, 176–78
New Lights, 17–18
Niger, 2
Nigeria, 2
Nkrumah, Kwame, 100
Nuzum, Eric, 1–2

Obama, Barack, 53n9, 169, 177, 177n1
*obayifo*, 2
one-drop rule, 14–15, 53n9, 120, 120n1
Orderberg, David, 124
Organovo, 125n4
*Our Posthuman Future* (Fukuyama), 127n5

pain, 37–39, 41–42, 63, 89, 107
Pan-Africanism, 19–20, 91, 93–94, 98–105, 109, 114
*Parable* novels (Butler), 9
Paris, Peter, 78n8
Park, Robert, 108, 108n7
Parrillo, Vincent, 64
paternalism, 19–20, 93–94, 98–105, 109, 114
"Patriarch, The" (Massey), 147
*Patternist* series (Butler), 120n2, 131n7
pedophilia, 139–41
Perry, Pamela, 178, 179n3
pharmaceuticals, 137n9
Pickens, Theri, 142–44

"pimp and ho" parties, 179n3
Pinn, Anthony, 69
Pinson, Hermine, 2n1, 6
Plato, 68
post-Blackness, 21–22, 176–77
posthuman, 124
Potok, Mark, 177n1
power exchange, 143
privilege, male, 151n5
Pryor, Richard, 77
psychedelic transhumanism, 123
psychic vampirism, 14n14
Public Enemy, 107n6

quadroon, 40
QUASH (Queers United Against Straight-Acting Homosexuals), 48
queering, 8–10
queer studies, 26
*Quicksand* (Larsen), 70

race. *See also* blackness; skin colors; whites: in *Fledgling*, 136–37; in *Gilda*, 36; immortality and, 177; racism and biological notion of, 5n12
racialized biopolitics, 32–36, 46
racial prejudice: racism vs., 5n12
racism: in *Fledgling*, 136; homosexuality and, 150; one-drop rule and, 120n1; queer critique of, 25; racial prejudice vs., 5n12; religion and, 73–74
Reed, Juan Y., 50
Reed, Ralph, 150n4
Reid-Pharr, Robert, 166
religion. *See* atheism; Black Church; Christianity; theism; theology
"Resident Evil" (Zane), 147
Resurrection Narrative, 11–12; *Gilda* and, 29–30, 41–42; in *My Soul to Keep*, 59–65, 67, 85–86; Staying Alive Narrative vs., 62
Ricaut, Paul, 5n11
Rice, Anne, 5, 16, 32, 148, 148n2, 149
ritual, 60–62
Robinson, Eugene, 10–11, 162–63, 163n9
Roche, Thomas S., 148n3
Rogers, J. A., 70

Ross, Marlon, 44–45
Rowe, Michael, 148n3
row-of-cotton theory, 53–54, 117, 177–78
Royce, Josiah, 69
Russell, Kathy, 75

*Salem's Lot* (King), 148, 148n2
salvation, 159–67
Sayles, John, 66
scapegoating, 159–67
Scarry, Elaine, 38
Schumacher, Joel, 16
Sciurba, Katie, 27n3
*Scream, Blacula, Scream* (film), 4n8
*Search and Destroy: African American Males in the Criminal Justice System* (Miller), 40n6
sexuality, divine, 167–72
Shannon, Sandra, 71
Shelby, Tommie, 85, 88–89, 154
Shelley, Mary, 12
Simone, Nina, 77
skin colors, 14–15, 53n9, 127, 134–38. *See also* blackness
slave, heroic, 20, 93–94, 105–12
slavery, 5n12, 8, 17–18; in Africa, 110n8; blackness and, 179; Christianity and, 161; in *Dark Corner*, 96–97, 107, 107n6, 110; in *Gilda*, 39–40; in *Image of Emeralds and Chocolate*, 161, 168; literacy and, 160n8; in *My Soul to Keep*, 58, 68–69, 73–74, 85; women and, 145n13
Smedley, Audrey, 136, 138n10
Smith, Barbara, 45
Smith, Stephanie A., 8
SNCC. *See* Student Nonviolent Coordinating Committee (SNCC)
Sneed, Roger, 151, 153–54
Soledad Brothers, 39, 39n5
solidarity, 19, 33–34, 59, 71, 74, 81–82, 87–89
Somerville, Siobhan, 8
*Sons of Darkness: Tales of Men, Blood, and Immortality* (Roche), 148n3
soucouyant, 3n5
soul, 67–68
soul murder, 41

Soul Narrative, 12–13, 67–68, 157–58
*Soul on Ice* (Cleaver), 166
"soul-stealing witches," 2
soul vampires, 12–14
*Speaking with Vampires: Rumor and History in Colonial Africa* (White), 2n4
speculative fiction, 2, 24
Spencer, Jon Michael, 70
*State of the Greek and Armenian Churches* (Ricaut), 5n11
Staying Alive Narrative, 11–12, 20–21; in *Dark Corner*, 94–97; Engineering Approach of, 122–23; in *Fledgling*, 122–23; in *Gilda*, 27–30; in *Image of Emeralds and Chocolate*, 154–59; Resurrection Narrative vs., 62; transhumanism and, 124
Stenbock, Eric, 148
Stephens, Gregory, 20, 94, 105
Stoker, Bram, 4, 24n1, 44, 55, 88n10
Strong, Melissa J., 9
Student Nonviolent Coordinating Committee (SNCC), 103n4
succubus, 4
*sukuyan*, 3, 3n5
Summers, Montague, 5n11
superstition, 58–59, 80
Surinam, 3
symbolic violence, 37–38

"Tales from the Darkside" (Ice Cube), 76n7
Taylor, Jill McLean, 49n8
Terrell, Mary Church, 75, 75n6
Thaler, Ingrid, 1–2, 8, 29, 48
theism, 71–72, 74
theology, 78–79, 78n8
Thomas, Piri, 166
Togo, 3
tolerance, 69–70
Torres, Gerald, 21–22
Touré, 10–11, 21
Transcendent elite, 163n9
transhuman, as term, 123
transhumanism: in *Fledgling*, 125–26; in Fukuyama, 127–28; goal of, 123–24; libertarian, 123; moderate, 124; Mormon, 123; origin of, 124–25; psyche-

delic, 123; Staying Alive Narrative and, 124; strong, 124
transhuman vampirism, 123–28
Trinidad, 3
"True Story of a Vampyre, A" (Stenbock), 148
Trump, Donald, 177, 177n1
Tubman, Harriet, 169
Turner, Henry McNeal, 81
*Two Trains Running* (Wilson), 71
Tyree, Omar, 6, 147

Underground Railroad, 169
Underwood, Blair, 57n1

vampire: history of term, 5n11; transhuman, 123–28
*Vampire, Le* (Dumas), 3–4, 3n6
*Vampire Book, The: The Encyclopedia of the Undead* (Melton), 12
*Vampire Chronicles* (Rice), 5, 148n2
*Vampire Forensics: Uncovering the Origins of an Enduring Legend* (Jenkins), 7
*Vampire God: The Allure of the Undead in Western Culture* (Hallab), 6
*Vampire Huntress* series (Banks), 15n15, 57–58
"Van Helsing party," 1
Vigilant, Linda, 146
Vint, Sheryl, 131n7
violence, 37–38, 40, 75, 97, 111, 156n7, 166, 178

Walker, Alice, 145n13
Walker, C. J., 57n1
Ward, Elijah G., 46
Ward, Jamie Victoria, 49n8
Washington, Booker T., 86
Washington, DC, 1

*wazimamoto*, 2n4
Wheatley, Phyllis, 17
Whitaker, Bob, 177n1
White, Luise, 2n4
White Genocide Project, 177n1
whites: in *Fledgling*, 143–45; in *Gilda*, 34–35, 40–41; goth culture among, 1; homosexuality and, 151; vampires as belonging to culture of, 1–2
white supremacy, 28, 112, 174, 176, 177n1
"white trash" parties, 179n3
*Who's Afraid of Post-Blackness* (Touré), 10
Williams, Delores, 78n8
Wilson, August, 71
Wilson, Katharina, 5n11
Wilson, Midge, 75
Wilson, Woodrow, 165n11
Winnubst, Shannon, 7, 14, 24n1, 47, 134
"witch-wives," 2
womanhood: in *Gilda*, 48–49
women. *See also* feminine Africa narrative: Black Church and, 51; in *Dark Corners*, 105; in *Dracula*, 98n1; in *Fledgling*, 141–44; in Moynihan Report, 99–100; in *My Soul to Keep*, 63–65, 64n2, 78–79; slavery and, 145n13; theology and, 78–79, 79n9
women's studies, 26
Woods, Tiger, 53n9
Wright, Almeda, 151
Wright, Elizabeth, 45–46

*Xenogenesis* trilogy (Butler), 118–19, 132n8

Yoruba, 2

Zane, 6, 147
Zanger, Jules, 15–16

www.ingramcontent.com/pod-product-compliance
Lightning Source LLC
Chambersburg PA
CBHW030137240426
43672CB00005B/169